THE HOLY SPIRIT
AND THE
GOSPEL TRADITION

S.P.C.K. Large Paperbacks

THE HOLY SPIRIT
AND THE
GOSPEL TRADITION

By

C. K. BARRETT

LONDON

S·P·C·K

First published in 1947
New edition 1966
Sixth impression 1975
S.P.C.K.
Holy Trinity Church
Marylebone Road
London NW1 4DU

Printed in Great Britain by
Hollen Street Press Ltd.
Slough, Berks.

SBN 281 00579 6

CONTENTS

ABBREVIATIONS

The following abbreviations have been used, in addition to others which it is unnecessary to explain.

Ap. and Ps.—R. H. Charles, *The Apocrypha and Pseudepigrapha of the Old Testament in English*, Oxford, 1913.

BDB—Francis Brown, S. R. Driver, and Charles A. Briggs, *Hebrew and English Lexicon of the Old Testament*, Oxford, 1906.

ET—*The Expository Times*, Edinburgh, 1889 ff.

GST—R. Bultmann, *Die Geschichte der synoptischen Tradition,* 2nd ed., Göttingen, 1931.

HTR—*The Harvard Theological Review*, Cambridge, Massachusetts, 1908 ff.

JTS—*The Journal of Theological Studies*, London, 1899 ff.

LS—H. G. Liddell and R. Scott, *Greek-English Lexicon*, new ed. by H. Stuart Jones and R. McKenzie, Oxford, 1925 ff.

Moulton-Milligan—J. H. Moulton and G. Milligan, *Vocabulary of the Greek New Testament*, London, 1930.

MPG—J. Migne, *Patrologia, Series Graeca*, Paris, 1844 ff.

RE—*Realencyclopädie für protestantische Theologie und Kirche*, 3rd ed., Leipzig, 1896 ff.

SBE—*Sacred Books of the East.*

SNT—*Die Schriften des neuen Testaments*, ed. J. Weiss, 3rd ed., Göttingen, 1917 ff.

Str.-B.—H. L. Strack and P. Billerbeck, *Kommentar zum neuen Testament aus Talmud und Midrasch*, Munich, 1922 ff.

Studies—I. Abrahams, *Studies in Pharisaism and the Gospels*, Cambridge, 1st Series 1917, 2nd Series 1924.

TWNT—*Theologisches Wörterbuch zum neuen Testament*, ed. by G. Kittel, Stuttgart, 1933 ff.

Wellhausen, *Einleitung*—J. Wellhausen, *Einleitung in die drei ersten Evangelien*, Berlin, 1st ed. 1905, 2nd ed. 1911.

NOTE

The Manuscript of this book was practically complete by the summer of 1943. Since then it has been read and criticized by Dr. D. Daube, the Rev. F. N. Davey, the Rev. Professor F. S. Marsh, the Rev. N. H. Snaith, and the Rev. Dr. V. Taylor. To all these scholars I am deeply grateful, not only for their comments on this essay, but for much else, in instruction and in encouragement. It is only right to add that none of them (I think) agrees with all that I have said.

I am indebted also to my friend the Rev. G. W. Underwood, who has helped me in reading the proofs.

NOTE TO THE NEW EDITION

It was the writing of this book, more than twenty years ago, that first led me to see the central and decisive role of eschatology in the gospels and to grasp some of the historical and theological problems in the origins of Christianity. If I were writing it today I should express myself differently on a number of points, but the main contention seems to me to have gained in strength and to retain its relevance.

In this edition it has been possible to make only small corrections.

Durham,
December 1965.

C. K. BARRETT

INTRODUCTION

NO more certain statement can be made about the Christians of the first generation than this: they believed themselves to be living under the immediate government of the Spirit of God. After various necessary preliminaries, the most ancient book of Church History opens with a formal account of the inspiration of the disciples for their task, when, on the day of Pentecost, the Holy Spirit descended upon them in tongues of flame (Acts 2. 1-4). The note so impressively struck at the outset is not subsequently changed. There is hardly a chapter of the book in which the Spirit is not represented as at work. Every critical point in the Church's history, as here described, is made the scene of the Spirit's intervention. Thus, when the seven "deacons" were appointed, it was laid down that they should be men full of the Spirit (Acts 6. 3, cf. 6. 5). When Paul, in process of conversion and preparation for his mission, waited obediently at Damascus, Ananias was sent to him in order that he might receive the Holy Spirit (Acts 9. 17). When Peter first preached to the Gentiles, it was at the Spirit's command; and that he had rightly understood his instructions was indicated by a repetition of the event of Pentecost for the benefit of Cornelius and his circle (Acts 10. 19 f., 44-47; 11. 12, 15 f.). The most critical point of the whole story—the separation of Paul and Barnabas for the purpose of undertaking missionary work of far wider scope than any that the original disciples had attempted—is recorded in these words: "The Holy Ghost said, Separate me Barnabas and Saul. . . . So they, being sent forth by the Holy Ghost, went down to Seleucia" (Acts 13. 2, 4). So the decrees ascribed to the apostles and elders in council are introduced by the clause, "It seemed good to the Holy Ghost, and to us" (Acts 15. 28); and the route of Paul's journeys in Asia Minor, and his determination to make the decisive journey to Jerusalem, are attributed to the influence of the Spirit (Acts 16. 6 f.; 19. 21; 20. 22 f.). It is clear that the author of Acts thought of the history of the Church, at least in its early days, as governed, from first to last, by the Spirit of God.[1]

This picture of events cannot have been created by a late writer, of romantic inclination, who unblushingly idealized an entirely different state of affairs, since it is substantially the same as that suggested by much earlier documents. Paul's well-known account of spiritual persons and their gifts, in 1 Cor., bears it out, as also, and even more instructively, do certain other passages of his in which the Spirit is not under particular

[1] "The most immediate and striking impression regarding the origin and progress of early Christianity which we gain from the New Testament is the strong consciousness of the first believers of being under the power and direction of the Spirit of God."—Dr Vincent Taylor, in the Headingley Lectures on *The Doctrine of the Holy Spirit*, 41.

consideration. For example, in Gal. 3 he momentarily turns aside from his biblical and theological discussion of faith and works as alternative roads to salvation to use a pragmatic argument: Did you receive the Spirit, he asks, as the result of faith, or as the result of works of law? (Gal. 3. 2). The protasis of this sentence, which is taken for granted by both sides and left to be understood, is that the Galatians certainly had received the Spirit, by whatever means. The experience of the Church of Thessalonica was evidently no different (e.g., 1 Thess. 5. 19).

We have no other Christian documents so old as the Pauline epistles; but to draw from this fact the conclusion that only the churches of Paul's foundation were interested in the gift and doctrine of the Holy Spirit, and that the author of Acts, having some acquaintance with Pauline Christianity, ascribed to the whole Church a character which was proper only to a part of it, would be quite unjustifiable. For although Paul had to engage in controversy with Christians of other parties on a variety of issues, it does not appear that he ever had to defend the validity of the spiritual gifts of his followers. Again, Ephesians and 1 Peter, though they derive from the Pauline wing of the Church, are yet sufficiently independent of the apostle for us to use them as evidence of a preoccupation with the Spirit that was not simply Paul's.[1] The Pastoral Epistles preserve the same emphasis; and, much more important, so do the Johannine writings. These all belong to the latest period of the writing of the NT and cannot have been completed much, if at all, before A.D. 100; but they represent a line of tradition that was to a great extent independent, though none the less saturated with a deep and well thought out doctrine of the Spirit. As markedly as does Acts, the Fourth Gospel points to a corporate reception of the Spirit as the beginning of the apostolic ministry of the Church (Jn. 20. 22 f.).

There is then no disputing our original statement that the Church of the first century believed that the Holy Spirit had been poured out upon it in a quite exceptional manner. It would therefore be surprising, were it not a fact to which we are well accustomed, to find that the Synoptic Gospels, on which alone we can rely for knowledge of the life and teaching of Jesus, are almost silent about the Holy Spirit, and that the teaching attributed to Jesus in them contains, on that subject, very few sayings, and those of doubtful authenticity. We have to ask whether this means that there is here a gulf between Jesus and the community which later professed allegiance to him. Whence did the Church derive its notions about the Spirit, and its certainty that it was inspired? Is it possible to believe that its faith and experience were in any way connected with Jesus? Or must we assume some other source in Hellenistic religion or Oriental mysticism? If we can answer this question we shall have taken an important, and perhaps a decisive, step towards the solution of the general problem of the relation between Jesus and the primitive Church,

---

[1] There seem to be good reasons for the view that Ephesians was not written by Paul.

between his preaching of the Kingdom of God and the gospel of personal and spiritual salvation.

It is a question, however, that has not yet been satisfactorily answered, even in the two most recent monographs on the subject. These are *Pneuma Hagion*, by Dr Leisegang, and *Jesus und der Geist nach synoptischer Ueberlieferung*, by Dr Windisch.[1]

Leisegang examines in turn a number of the most important references to the Spirit; for example, Jesus' conception by the Spirit, his baptism in the Jordan and the descent of the dove, the sin against the Holy Spirit. His conclusion is revealed in the sub-title of his book—"The origin in Greek mysticism of the concept of the Spirit in the Synoptic Gospels"; and he says explicitly: "In the first place it may clearly be seen from the present investigation that the Holy Spirit as a concept bound up with the life and teaching of Jesus, and the myths and speculations attached to it, are foreign elements within the Synoptic Gospels, which crept into the narratives of the deeds and sayings of the Saviour from Hellenistic thought and belief."[2] This conclusion is reached by considering on what basis the teaching of the Gospels may be understood, whether on that of Palestinian thought or on that of Hellenistic piety. Leisegang adduces a great mass of Hellenistic material, which he argues belongs to the same cycle of thought and belief as the Gospel teaching about the Spirit.

Windisch moves by a different route to a more complicated conclusion. He first proves that the sayings of the Gospels which refer to the Spirit can be shown to be unauthentic;[3] all are insertions due to editorial activity. But he refuses to draw the conclusion that the question, *War Jesus Pneumatiker?* (Was Jesus a "pneumatic"?) must be answered in the negative. For, he says, it is not enough merely to consider passages which contain the word πνεῦμα; many other factors have to be taken into consideration, and these in fact demonstrate a very close connection between Jesus and the Spirit, and a very high degree of personal inspiration. There was, Windisch thinks, a double process in the history of the tradition. At first, many incidents and sayings which revealed Jesus as a "spiritual" person[4] were suppressed in the interests of a "higher" Christology; later the Church read back its own experience and doctrine of the Holy Spirit into the empty space which had been left in its account of Jesus. In this way are explained both the fewness of the explicit references to the Spirit which is so striking a feature of the tradition, and the late and Hellenistic character of those which do occur. As Windisch says, the positive result of his study (in which we may contrast it with that of Leisegang) is to demonstrate an important continuity between Jesus and the Community.

[1] In *Studies in Early Christianity*, edited by S. J. Case. See also *Reich Gottes und Geist Gottes*, by W. Michaelis.
[2] *Op. cit.* 140.
[3] He discusses (a) the saying of the Baptist, (b) the baptism narrative, (c) the temptation narrative, (d) the expulsion of demons through the Spirit, (e) blasphemy against the Spirit, (f) the promise of the Spirit to the disciples.
[4] It is unfortunate that there is no English equivalent of *Pneumatiker*. See below, pp. 113 f.

There remains room for a fuller discussion of the historical continuity (if such there be) between Jesus and his Church in respect of the Holy Spirit, especially in the light of the eschatological teaching of Jesus, which, as we shall see, supplies the clue to the problems that are raised. It cannot be too frequently or too strongly emphasized that the thought of Jesus was cast in an eschatological mould, and that it cannot be understood if it is considered apart from that mould. The eschatological problem is not considered by Leisegang and Windisch; apparently they think that the doctrine of the Spirit is one that can be detached and treated by itself. But this is not so.

In the investigation that follows, sayings and incidents connecting Jesus himself with the Spirit will first be examined, and then those connecting the Church with the Spirit. Finally, the question of the relation between eschatology [1] and the Spirit, and the question why the Synoptic references to the Spirit are so few, will be considered and answered in the light of the previous discussions.

---

[1] By this word we intend to denote a view of the world and of history based upon the notion of two ages, This Age and The Age to Come, the latter being thought of as close at hand rather than remote.

PART ONE

2

THE CONCEPTION OF JESUS BY THE HOLY SPIRIT

INTRODUCTION. The birth of Jesus is described only in the first and third Gospels. The narratives contained in these Gospels are entirely different; hardly contradictory so much as without a point of contact. A few names coincide—Mary, Joseph, Bethlehem—but, for the rest, the accounts diverge. According to Matthew, Mary and Joseph lived in Bethlehem, where the birth of Jesus took place; this was followed by the flight into Egypt, after which the holy family began to reside in Nazareth. According to Luke, those who were reckoned the parents of Jesus were inhabitants of Nazareth who, by reason of a census, happened to be in Bethlehem at the time of the birth of Mary's son. The former Evangelist narrates the obeisance of the Eastern Magi, the latter supplies instead the description of the shepherds, and has interwoven with his account of the birth of Jesus a very similar account of John the Baptist. In fact, between the two writers there is real agreement only in denying that Joseph (or any other human being) fathered the child, and in asserting that Mary's pregnancy was inaugurated by the Holy Spirit (Mt. 1. 18, 20; Lk. 1. 35). Moreover, there is no evidence to suggest any literary relationship between the two narratives.

In the three chapters with which we are chiefly concerned (Mt. 1 ; Lk. 1 f.) certain questions of textual criticism arise. In Mt. 1. 16 there is some evidence for a reading which presupposes a natural birth from Mary and Joseph. This reading we need not discuss, not only because it is unlikely that it represents what Matthew wrote but also because, even if it were the true reading, it would not imply more than that the Matthaean genealogy came from a quarter where it was not believed that Jesus was born of a virgin; that Matthew himself so believed is quite certain. It has been proposed that in Lk. 1. 34 we should accept the reading of the Old Latin MS *b*, which omits *v.* 38 and in place of *v.* 34 reads, "Behold the handmaid of the Lord, be it unto me according to thy word". *b* is supported by *e* in so far as *e* omits *v.* 38. The variant of *b* does in fact remove from the third Gospel the necessary implication of virgin birth; but that one Old Latin MS alone has preserved the text is so improbable as to be wellnigh incredible.[1] It is different in Lk. 2. 5 where "We should probably read τῇ γυναικὶ αὐτοῦ with lat. vt. (codd.) and syr. sin., the reading of ℵBD etc. being an early modification under the influence of 1. 26 [read 1. 27], and the reading of the majority of the MSS a conflation of the two readings".[2]

[1] Of course the error of supposing that the majority of MSS must be right is to be avoided; but in this case the variant can be satisfactorily explained as a slip.
[2] Creed, *ad loc.*

5

This variant, however, by no means outweighs, nor indeed contradicts, the plain statements which ascribe the birth of Jesus to the Holy Spirit.

We need not linger over these variant readings. Possibly they are wholly explicable as due to accidental alteration. If not, their importance is rather that they point to areas where the beliefs expressed in the Gospels were not received than that they reveal an earlier stage of the textual tradition than that represented by the old Greek codices.

It is important here to point out that we are not required by our subject to deal with the general problem which is raised by the facts alleged in the Gospels, the problem whether Jesus was or was not born of a virgin, out of the course of nature. We have to consider only the particular assertion that the conception and birth of Jesus were due to the activity of the Holy Spirit.

ALLEGED PARALLELS TO THE NT NARRATIVES. To the belief that Jesus was born of a virgin through the agency of the Holy Spirit parallels have been adduced by learned men. The process seems to have been begun on the Christian side, by the second-century apologists[1] who used the parallels to show that their doctrine ought not to appear incredible to pagans—a dangerous use of analogy. It was continued, and still continues, in use by those who allege that the Christian story too is a myth divorced from history. It is beyond doubt that not a few of the parallels have a certain relevance to the birth narrative as a whole, though just what that relevance is constitutes a difficult and vexed question. Certainly they help to place the narratives in the Hellenistic world, though not very precisely. E. Meyer[2] says of the birth narrative: "This narrative has its analogy and model in the popular belief of the Hellenistic world." But this is hardly to say more than that that Hellenistic world believed in the existence of not a few beings who were both human and divine, and that it had proved convenient and attractive to find a correspondingly mixed mythological origin for them.

A number of the alleged parallels may be dismissed as quite unimportant for our purpose.

(a) Such are most of the pagan myths; for example, the begetting of Hercules, Perseus and Alexander by Zeus; of Ion, Asclepius, Pythagoras, Plato and Augustus by Apollo. There is no need to repeat the stories in detail; a good list can be found in Meyer (*loc. cit.*); cf. Toynbee, *A Study of History*, Vol. VI. 267-275, 450 f., cf. 469. It is more important here to point out the fundamental distinctions between these stories and those of Mt. and Lk. We may notice first the frankly mythological style of most of the pagan tales. We must be careful not to press this point too far, for it would be wrong to assert that the Gospel narratives are not also mythological; but the difference is none the less real. Compare, for example, with the simplicity and (in spite of the miracle) naturalness of Lk. 1 f.,

---

[1] So, e.g., Justin, *Apol.* 1. 21 f., 54; cf. 33, 56; Tertullian, *Apol.* 21; cf. Origen, *c. Cels.* 1. 37.
[2] *Ursprung und Anfänge*, I. 54.

Suetonius' (*Augustus*, 94) account of the conception of Augustus, with its snake, and thunderbolt, and so forth. The profusion of physical portents and omens gives to the pagan document an atmosphere not only of myth but of mere magic and thaumaturgy. That there is also a difference of moral tone between the Gospels and their parallels is of course apparent, but in this connection does not matter; for we are comparing form and history, not morals.

A second and more important point is that in the pagan stories of divine births no stress is laid upon the virginity of the mother. In a few cases absence of intercourse before impregnation by the god is implied.[1] But even in these cases—and this is the point that concerns us—there is no suggestion that the woman conceived the child as a virgin. It is never implied that conception was due to anything other than the ordinary sexual act with accompanying loss of virginity, the only exceptional circumstance being that the female of the pair was a woman, the male a god.

Out of this point arises a third difference. The divine power which effects pregnancy is always a personal god, with name and individuality, who acts, in this respect, in precisely the same way as a man. That such a view of the gods was by no means incredible or repulsive to the Hellenistic world is proved by the story of Paulina and Mundus, told by Josephus in *Ant.* 18. 3. 4 (65-80). Over against this, the NT speaks in the most impersonal and abstract terms possible among men who were not given to abstract thought. It is noteworthy that the infancy narratives of both Matthew and Luke, while assigning a large part to angels, attribute the birth of Jesus, not to the Angel of the Lord, but to the Spirit, the least personal of what may be called the Jewish hypostatizations of the divine presence. It is not insignificant that the word spirit is in Greek ($\pi\nu\epsilon\hat{\upsilon}\mu\alpha$) neuter, and in Hebrew and Aramaic (רוּחַ, רוּחָא: ruah, ruha') generally feminine. The verbs used in this connection in Lk. (1. 35) are also instructive ($\dot{\epsilon}\pi\dot{\epsilon}\rho\chi\epsilon\sigma\theta\alpha\iota$ and $\dot{\epsilon}\pi\iota\sigma\kappa\iota\dot{\alpha}\zeta\epsilon\iota\nu$); the latter obviously denotes non-material action, and so, according to frequent usage in the LXX, does the former, which is never used of sexual intercourse, and is on two occasions connected with $\pi\nu\epsilon\hat{\upsilon}\mu\alpha$.[2]

A fourth difference may be noticed, subsidiary to that which has just been examined, namely, that in the pagan parallels the god often accomplishes the act of impregnation in a material, non-human, form. Apollo begot Augustus in the form of a snake; Olympias, the mother of Alexander, saw a thunderbolt fall upon her womb; Zeus came upon Danaë in a stream of gold. There is no suggestion of physical contact or action of any sort in the NT.

These alleged pagan parallels show that, in the Hellenistic world, men

---

[1] In the accounts of Plato's birth (Diogenes Laertius, *Lives of the Philosophers*, III. (Plato) 1, 2 ; Plutarch, *Quaest. Conv.* 8. 1. 2) it is said that Ariston, his mother's husband, saw Apollo in a vision ; the god forbade him to have intercourse with Perictione until she had borne a child. Danaë, the mother of Perseus, and Olympias, the mother of Alexander, were virgins until their union with Zeus.

[2] Num. 5. 14, 30, $\pi\nu\epsilon\hat{\upsilon}\mu\alpha$ $\zeta\eta\lambda\dot{\omega}\sigma\epsilon\omega s$; Is. 32.15, $\pi\nu\epsilon\hat{\upsilon}\mu\alpha$ $\dot{\alpha}\phi'$ $\dot{\upsilon}\psi\eta\lambda o\hat{\upsilon}$ ($\dot{\epsilon}\pi\dot{\epsilon}\lambda\theta\eta$ in אAQ ; B has $\ddot{\epsilon}\lambda\theta\eta$).

felt it necessary, and proper, to explain the appearance of heroes and demi-gods by a story of a miraculous birth brought about by the physical intervention of a personal god. They are therefore important for our study, inasmuch as they indicate that, if the Matthaean and Lucan birth narratives were affected, and perhaps generated, by the problem of explaining the appearance in flesh of one who was believed to be Son of God, this problem would certainly have been felt, and therefore may possibly have first been raised, in the Hellenistic world. But the cases we have so far considered, of the semi-divine begetting of individuals by a god and a woman, have no contact with the Matthaean and Lucan stories at the point where we are concerned with them, namely, the statement that the conception of Jesus was due not to an act of paternity on the part of a god, but to the supernatural and non-material action of the Holy Spirit.

(*b*) Of hardly greater importance are certain allusions to so-called miraculous births in the OT. These may be considered severally.

Gen. 17. 15-22; 18. 9-15; 21. 1-7. Abraham was 100 years old and had had no child by his wife Sarah, who was 90. A birth was now a physical impossibility. Yet a birth was promised by God, and took place. This is certainly regarded by the biblical writers as a miracle; [1] but there is no trace in any of the Genesis accounts (and they are drawn from both P and JE) of the view that Isaac was the son of Sarah and a divine being. The miracle consisted in the enabling of Abraham and Sarah to have a son in a non-miraculous manner.

Judg. 13. 2-25. This case is substantially the same as that of Abraham and Sarah. Manoah's wife is barren. The angel of the Lord announces the birth of a son, and this duly takes place. The only supernatural features of the story are the annunciations, and the cure of the woman's barrenness.

1 Sam. 1. Again the circumstances are similar; Hannah, Elkanah's favourite wife, is barren; in answer to prayer she is allowed to bear a son. Here all possibility of divine paternity is excluded by the words: "And Elkanah knew Hannah his wife; and the Lord remembered her. And it came to pass, when the time was come about, that Hannah conceived, and bare a son" (1. 19 f.).

Is. 7. 14. This is a very different passage from those which have been discussed, and a full treatment of the prophecy would run to great length. It is enough here to point out two considerations which show that it is not relevant to our study. (i) The word (עַלְמָה, 'almah) rendered παρθένος by the LXX and *virgin* in the English versions does not mean virgin, but *young woman*, whether married or not. (ii) The prophet expected the birth to take place in his own days and the child to be an ordinary child.

---

[1] It was so regarded by Paul, and no doubt by his Jewish contemporaries also. Passages quoted by Str.-B. (I. 27, 49) show that though the child was believed to have been born of the seed of Abraham and no other, God himself prepared Sarah's womb. Of the NT account of the birth of Jesus Str.- B. say (I. 49): "Thus over against Jewish thought Mt. 1. 18 means something entirely new."

He uses the language of conception and birth, as he later (7. 15 f.) speaks of the child's advancing knowledge, as a measure of time (cf. Mic. 5. 2); but there is no notion here of birth by the Spirit.

(c) Parallels in Philo to the notion of virgin birth are worthy of more consideration. First, and most important, come passages in which it appears that Philo treats some of the OT passages which we have just considered as real instances of virgin birth. If this really is Philo's view it is important, for it would mean, not, of course, that virgin births took place or were believed to have taken place by the biblical writers, but at least that it was believed in Alexandria in the first century A.D. that, in exceptional circumstances, virgin birth was possible, and even to be expected.

The most important Philonic passage is de Cher. 40-52. If we read only 45-47 we certainly meet with the notion of divine begetting, and much is said in the context about virginity. Philo mentions the wives of the four great Jewish heroes. Sarah, he says, conceived when none were present but she and God (μονωθεῖσαν, an inference from the fact that Abraham is not mentioned in Gen. 21. 1); therefore it must have been God who begot her child, though it was for Abraham's benefit. Similarly with Leah, since God "opened her womb" (Gen. 29. 31), the act of the husband. Rebecca became pregnant ἐκ τοῦ ἱκετευθέντος, i.e., God (Gen. 25. 21). Moses found Zipporah pregnant ἐξ οὐδενὸς θνητοῦ τὸ παράπαν (Exod. 2. 22). But to take these passages thus in isolation is to misunderstand them. Philo at the beginning of the section makes it clear that, as usual, he is allegorizing: φαμεν εἶναι γυναῖκα τροπικῶς αἴσθησιν (41). How far from the thought of real births he is may be seen in 50: "When God begins to consort with the soul, He makes what before was a woman into a virgin again, for He takes away the degenerate and emasculate passions which unmanned it (αἷς ἐθηλύνετο) and plants instead the native growth of unpolluted virtues." He adds (51), arguing from Jer. 3. 4, that since a virgin is always liable to change, God is said rather to be the husband of virginity than of a virgin. From all this (and much beside) it is quite clear that Dr Machen is right in saying,[1] "As soon as one attains the slightest insight into the allegorical method of using the OT, one sees clearly that when Philo speaks of a virgin-birth or a divine begetting in the passages which are now in view, he is thinking of a divine begetting of the soul of man, or a divine begetting of certain virtues in the soul of man, and not at all of a divine begetting of human beings of flesh and blood who actually lived upon this earth." Obviously, quite apart from the question of the mode of operation of God in his begetting, and the fact that nothing is said by Philo about virgin birth strictly understood,[2] there is no parallel here with the Gospels, which of course always speak of the birth of a historical person.

We may more briefly dismiss a second class of passages which really

---

[1] The Virgin Birth of Christ, 303.
[2] That a god should mate with a virgin is no more a parallel to the NT concept of virgin birth than that a man should do so.

have no bearing at all upon the virgin birth. In *de Fug. et Inv.* 108 f. it is said that the divine Word (λόγος θεῖος) has for its father God, and its mother Wisdom. In *de Ebr.* 30 God begets, by his knowledge (ἐπιστήμη) the κόσμος αἰσθητός (συνὼν ὁ θεὸς οὐχ ὡς ἄνθρωπος ἔσπειρε γένεσιν). In *Leg. Alleg.* 2. 49 νοῦς is said to have for father God, and for mother the virtue and wisdom of God (ἡ ἀρετὴ καὶ σοφία τοῦ θεοῦ). In these passages we have indeed the concept of an act of begetting on the part of God; but the two facts, that the begetting belongs wholly to the spiritual world and that nothing is said about either virginity or the Spirit of God, are sufficient to show that they have no importance for our purpose.

So far, then, the parallels to the Gospel narratives of the birth of Jesus have broken down. There is nothing truly akin to those narratives in the pagan stories of divine births, in the OT, or in the Philonic passages which have been quoted; and it is noteworthy that all the parallels break down (if nowhere else) at the point with which we are most concerned, that is, the part played by the Spirit of God.[1] The pagan parallels are personal and materialistic; instead of the influence of the Spirit we have sexual intercourse on the part of a god. In the OT also the Spirit is not named and in every case there is an ordinary begetting by a man (Is. 7. 14 falls out of consideration on other grounds); Philo too says nothing of the Spirit, and in his work the notion of virgin birth (in so far as it appears at all) contains much that is allegorical, and little or nothing that is historical and miraculous.[2] There are, however, three explanations of the Virgin Birth which take particular account of the part played by the Spirit. They are those given by Leisegang,[3] Dr Thomas Walker[4] and Norden.[5]

Leisegang has a double theory, dealing separately with Mt. and Lk. Mt., according to him, reveals a background of Semitic folk belief, while Lk. is to be understood in relation to Hellenistic religion.

In his treatment of Mt. Leisegang begins from the expression (1. 18) ἐν γαστρὶ ἔχειν ἐκ. . . . He argues that according to Greek usage the force of ἐκ is necessarily to imply the action of a *personal* spirit. He quotes in support of this statement Pausanias, *Desc. Gr.* 2. 26. 4, and Gen. 38. 25. It is true that in each of these cases the preposition introduces a person, as Leisegang says, not a mere force. But unfortunately Leisegang does not quote Gen. 38. 24, where we have ἰδοὺ ἐν γαστρὶ ἔχει ἐκ πορνείας. If the expression ἐν γαστρὶ ἔχειν ἐκ could be used with an abstract noun there is no reason to suppose that it could not have been used by a Greek writer to describe pregnancy due to any cause. The fact that it is usually applied to a person means no more than that most pregnancies are rightly ascribed to persons.

From this not very secure foundation in ancient Greek usage Leisegang

---

[1] So also the miraculous birth of Moses, if this is implied by the Passover Haggadah; see D. Daube, *The New Testament and Rabbinic Judaism* (1956), 5-9.
[2] Machen, *op. cit.* 302.
[3] *Pneuma Hagion*, 14-72.
[4] *Is not this the Son of Joseph?*
[5] *Die Geburt des Kindes.*

proceeds to modern Semitic beliefs about the powers of the *welis* believed to inhabit holy places, attested by S. I. Curtiss [1] for modern Palestine. Apparently it is believed that these local demons (Baals) are able to have intercourse with women, who bear them children. Now it is true that there is much in these modern beliefs that is akin to practices which archaeology can demonstrate in the customs of the ancient Semites, and it is certainly probable that even in the course of millennia there would be little change in the faith and cultus of an isolated nomad people. But it remains to be shown that this faith and cultus had, or could have had, any influence either in the actual environment of the childhood of Jesus, or (what is more important) in the Christian circles in which the Matthaean birth narrative was formed and told. That this was so seems in the highest degree unlikely. If the evidence of Mt. and Lk. is worth anything at all, Joseph and Mary were pious Jews, and moved in the society of pious Jews. That they believed in demons is likely enough; but whether they would share the sort of superstition that inevitably leads to immorality is quite a different question. Certainly it is impossible to mistake the general character of the material peculiar to Matthew's Gospel; much of it is plainly of Jewish origin and enjoins a righteousness exceeding that of the Scribes and Pharisees; and it is quite incompatible with the sort of belief which Leisegang posits as the background of the Matthaean birth narrative.

Leisegang compares with Mt. 1. 18, 20, Gen. 21. 1 f.; 29. 31; 30. 2, 22; and Judg. 13. 1 ff.; but these verses have nothing to do with his case. In Gen. 29. 31; 30. 22 there is the expression, God "opened her womb", and it is true that Philo says that this is the act of a husband (*de Cher.* 46). But the Hebrew means this no more than does the Greek.[2] On Gen. 21. 1 f. see above. Judg. 13. 1 ff. also has no reference to the sort of intercourse that Leisegang speaks of. He is on firmer ground in mentioning Gen. 6. 1 ff., where the sons of God have intercourse with the daughters of men. This passage itself is probably mythical, but it undoubtedly influenced later thought; e.g., in two places referred to by Leisegang, 1 *Enoch* 106. 6, 12 and *Protev. James* 14. 1. In *Enoch* (Fragment of the book of Noah, Maccabean or earlier), Lamech suspects that the strange son born to him is not his child but the child of an angel. Enoch admits that some angels are in fact transgressing, but tells Lamech that the child is his (106. 18; 107. 2). In *Protev. James*, Joseph, finding Mary pregnant, fears lest "That which is in her be the seed of an angel". But it is important to notice that in each case the possibility of such a supernatural birth is regarded with horror; and it is very difficult indeed to believe that such a thought could have been taken over and applied forthwith to the Holy Spirit.[3]

[1] *Primitive Semitic Religion Today*, 112-123.

[2] פָּתַח רֶחֶם (pathaḥ reḥem, "to open the womb") is parallel to סָגַר רֶחֶם (ṣagar reḥem, "to close the womb"), 1 Sam. 1. 5. Numerous Rabbinic passages (e.g. *Ta'an.* 2a, *Midr. Ps.* 78 § 5 (173b); Str.-B. I. 737, III. 3) show that the phrase in question was not interpreted as Leisegang interprets it.

[3] We may add also *Acts of Thomas*, 42 f. (James, *Apocryphal NT* 385 f.), where a devil has intercourse with a woman five years.

Leisegang's explanation of Matthew's account of the Virgin Birth is unacceptable: it presupposes ideas which we cannot believe to have been held by those among whom the birth story was told. Wherever it may have originated, it neither suggests the atmosphere of the Arab holy place nor yet recalls the angel legend of Gen. 6.

Leisegang finds a very different origin for the Lucan narrative. Here the Holy Spirit is not, he thinks, personal, but an impersonal force. He draws attention to the fact that in Lk. 1 f. the activity of the Spirit is twofold; the Spirit is connected with the pregnancy of Elisabeth (1. 15— this is doubtful) and of Mary (1. 35), and is also the source of prophetic speech (1. 41, 67; 2. 25-27). Leisegang brings these two works of the Spirit together and tries to explain the one by the other. He deals first with the important word ἐπισκιάσει (1. 35).[1] It recalls first of all Exod. 40. 29 (LXX; Hebrew, 40. 35), where the cloud of the glory of God overshadows the tabernacle. But it also recalls the following passages in Philo, *Q.R.D.H.* 265; *de Somn.* 1. 119; *Quod Deus Imm.* 3, in each of which Philo is speaking about inspiration, which he regards as the deposition of the natural reason by the power of God. In *Q.R.D.H.* 263-265, commenting on Gen. 15. 12, he says that the sun symbolizes the human mind (τὸν ἡμέτερον νοῦν); it is only when this sun sets (πρὸς δυσμὰς γένηται) that the light of God shines and we become possessed by God. Such is the experience of the prophets (the προφητικὸν γένος). In *de Somn.* 1. 119 he is dealing with Gen. 28. 11, and again the significant words are ἔδυ ὁ ἥλιος. This means the supersession of νοῦς and αἴσθησις by the divine Word (θεῖος λόγος); the two former must undergo, like the sun, a "setting" (κατάδυσις). Only in *Quod Deus Imm.* 3 is the word ἐπισκιάζω used; here the passage under discussion is Gen. 6. 4, and Philo argues that the community of darkness (οἱ τοῦ σκότους ἑταῖροι) gets its chance only when the light of the understanding is overshadowed (ὅταν ἀμυδρωθὲν ἐπισκιασθῇ τὸ διανοίας φῶς). It will be observed that this last quotation is really quite different from the first two and certainly has nothing to do with the overshadowing of the human reason by the divine Spirit; indeed, as the preceding paragraph shows, the Spirit here does not "overshadow" but illuminates.

The connection thus established between Lk. 1. 35 and the Philonic (? Hellenistic) notion of prophetic inspiration is not close, but Leisegang proceeds from it to inquire how the Spirit, thought of as prophetic inspiration, can be also the cause of Mary's conception. He says: [2] "Our question may be considered answered if it can be proved that in Greek ideology there existed a definite association between the bestowing of the πνεῦμα προφητικόν and the supernatural conception of a woman through precisely the same πνεῦμα, a conception leading to the birth of a son of a god." It must be said that Leisegang fails to establish the necessary relationship. It is true that the Pythian prophetess

---

[1] This word, however, is used of δύναμις ὑψίστου, not of πνεῦμα κυρίου.
[2] *Op. cit.* 32.

was believed to receive the πνεῦμα μαντικόν by means of her sexual organs,[1] and that Irenaeus[2] quotes the words in which the heretic Marcus promises to women the gift of prophecy by means of a sexual act.   But, as Leisegang himself points out, the gulf is not yet bridged between the "bearing" of prophetic speech and the bearing of a real child.

There is a further stage in the argument in which the chief link is Philo.   Leisegang instances the cases to which we have already referred, where Philo deals with Sarah, Leah, Rebecca and Zipporah; and connects them with *de Migr. Abr.* 33 ff. and *Q.R.D.H.* 36, where Philo describes his own experience of inspiration.   "It is always the same thing: a sexual act between God and man, only in manifold variations, moving between a concrete, sensual event and a spiritualized symbol, reduced almost to a figure of speech."[3]   "A clearly recognizable bond links together the myth of the birth of Dionysus,[4] the notions of the divinely caused prophecy of the Pythia at Delphi, the Lucan birth narrative, and the religious metaphor of a Philo."[5]   The mystical experience of union with God which was known to Philo, for example, was projected, according to Leisegang, into the heavenly world.   We have already given the relevant passages;[6] but it is questionable whether the parallelism between the earthly and heavenly events, which is so important as the culminating point in Leisegang's argument, is justified.   Even if the parallels were closer than they are, they would hardly establish the required connection between prophetical inspiration by the Spirit, inspiration caused by a sexual act, and the actual begetting of a real child by the operation of divine Spirit upon a woman.   It should be observed that in *Leg. Alleg.* 2. 49 Philo clearly speaks of God as the father of the universe (τῶν ὅλων) and of his Excellence—Wisdom as the mother of all things (τῶν συμπάντων).

Quite apart from his failure to establish a satisfactory connection between manticism and the begetting of a child, two further arguments may be brought against Leisegang's view.   The first is expressed very simply, but quite unanswerably, by Dr Bultmann,[7] who points out that Luke does not describe either Mary or Jesus as a prophet, though indeed the Magnificat might perhaps be called "Prophecy"; all possible connection, therefore, with Semele and Zeus, or with Hellenistic manticism in general, falls to the ground.   Second, there is the indisputable fact of the thoroughly Semitic character of Lk. 1 f.   Is it credible that the writer of these chapters was intimately acquainted with Greek folklore and mystical speculation?   If he had known these things would he have been capable of applying them to the "Lord Messiah" (Lk. 2. 11)?   And if he had, perhaps in ignorance, so applied them, would those of his fellow-

---

[1] Strabo, *Geogr.* IX. 3. 5, 6, 11; Origen, *c. Cels.* 7. 3; Chrysostom, *Hom.* XXIX. 1 (2), *ad 1 Cor. 12.*, Cf. also Aeschylus, *Agamemnon* 1202-8.

[2] *a. Haer.* 1. 13. 3.   [3] *Op. cit.* 47.

[4] Dionysus the prophet god was born of Semele and Zeus; at the time of her pregnancy Semele was in a state of enthusiasm—like Elisabeth and Mary.

[5] *Op. cit.* 49.   [6] p. 10.

[7] *Theologische Literaturzeitung* (1922), 426.

Christians who were capable of seeing their significance have admitted these demonic speculations, whose morality they loathed, into the canon? [1]

We shall not, then, agree with Leisegang in his conclusion that "Here a begetting by a prophet-god is made to precede the birth of a prophet. The production, observed in manticism, of ecstatic speech in consequence of conception through a πνεῦμα is combined with the idea of the birth of a divine child equipped with the gift of prophecy. Thus the woman becomes at the same time a prophetess and the mother of a prophet." [2] Nor need we yet suppose that the notion that a πνεῦμα should beget life in men is Greek rather than Jewish.

We have to consider next the view advanced by Dr Thomas Walker in *Is not this the Son of Joseph?*

According to Dr Walker, the present forms of the infancy narrative, which involve the notion of a virgin conception and birth, are due to a Greek misinterpretation of an originally Jewish story, in which Jesus was born in the ordinary course of nature, but which also stressed the Jewish belief that in all births in pious homes (and therefore in this one) the Holy Spirit was present and active. This belief he describes as follows: [3] "These people (the Jews) had come to regard themselves as the sacred offspring of the mighty Spirit of the Holy. In the conception of children of their religious community there was recognized one of the chief manifestations of His glory in their midst. In their ritual of thanksgiving this was given a place of very significant prominence. This sublime idea of the creative providence of Jehovah in the life of the family was in their day native to the pious mind of the Synagogue. Among them it was reverently taken for granted that neither male nor female could or should be conceived without the presence of the Shechinah with the man and the woman. The Holy One was piously thought by them to be an essential co-partner with the devout father and the devout mother in the production of the child." In support of this statement Dr Walker adduces three quotations from the Rabbinic literature:

Gen. R. 8. 9. R. Simlai said. . . . In the past Adam was created from the dust of the ground and Eve was created from Adam. Henceforward it is to be "in our image and after our likeness"—meaning, man will not be able to come into existence without woman, nor woman without man, nor both without the Shechinah.

Soṭah 17a. When husband and wife are worthy, the Shechinah is with them.

Niddah 31a. There are three partners in the production of the human being: the Holy One, blessed be He, the father and the mother.

The original birth narrative was written in this belief, without any suggestion of miracle. It was misunderstood and rewritten in the interests

---

[1] For an argument that Lk. 1. 35 is not a pagan Christian insertion into a Jewish Christian source, see Gunkel, *Zum religionsgeschichtlichen Verständnis des NT*, 67 f.
[2] *Op. cit.* 69.   [3] *Op. cit.* 23 f.

of a Church dogma.[1] Dr Walker concludes: ". . . a Greek mind, with its presuppositions concerning human nature so very different from those of the Hebrew mind, very readily misunderstood a Semitic conception story of really exquisite beauty. The Virgin Birth idea was an error of the Greek-minded leaders of the early Church in the second century, who, in spite of their professions to have done so, never really got entirely free from the erroneous notion of their upbringing, that the human body was the seat of evil for the soul. They lamentably misinterpreted a Semitic story of the conception of a child of Hebrew parents." [2]

There is much that is attractive in this theory; and it may be that the doctrine of the Virgin Birth did arise, or at least attained its present form, in the transition of the gospel from the Hebraic to the Hellenic world; for, as we have already seen, the OT has no parallel to offer for conception without the agency of a human father, and paganism, within limits, has many. Two considerations, however, may be advanced which make it necessary for us to go further than Dr Walker.

(i) Dr Walker does not expound at all the work of the Holy Spirit as it is represented in the documents we actually possess. He explains its place (a not very exalted one) in the narrative he presumes to underlie the present accounts, but we are left with no explanation of the part played by the Holy Spirit in the miraculous stories which lie before us in Mt. and Lk.

(ii) It is very doubtful whether there was ever a non-miraculous conception story. It must continually be remembered that the Evangelists were evangelists and not historians. They were not interested in what happened from a biographical point of view. The narratives and sayings which they wrote down they repeated in order to convince, to instruct, to edify; and especially to promote faith in Jesus as the one vehicle of God's revelation, the Son of God. There was no point in saying at so great length that the parents of Jesus were pious Jews: so were many other parents. The motive of combating slanders against Mary's chastity might indeed sufficiently account for some description of Jesus' home; but it is altogether inadequate to explain the most characteristic features of the infancy narratives, which throughout, by their language as well as by their content, proclaim that the time of the fulfilment of the OT has arrived. Moreover, if there was something extraordinary about the birth of the Messiah the circumstances might be related as an aid to faith. The miracle, whether it be fact or not, with its unescapable OT background, apart from which it cannot be understood, is the creative factor in the tradition, and it is therefore unscientific to press behind the present form of the Gospel narratives (here as elsewhere) in the hope of finding something less miraculous and offensive.[3]

[1] Dr Walker, following Streeter, makes the very improbable suggestion (33) that the original text of Lk. 1. 34 is preserved in *b*.

[2] *Op. cit.* 34.

[3] It should be emphasized that the intention is not to assert the complete credibility of the infancy (or any other) narratives as records of fact; their historicity is an entirely different question from the fact that the Church was interested in them only as miraculous history.

We must next proceed to examine the views advanced by Norden in *Die Geburt des Kindes*. In the part of his work with which we are concerned (76–92) Norden quotes a very important passage in Plutarch, *Numa*, 4. 4. The significant words are γυναικὶ μὲν οὐκ ἀδύνατον πνεῦμα πλησιάσαι θεοῦ καί τινας ἐντεκεῖν ἀρχὰς γενέσεως; but it will be well to take into account the whole context.   Plutarch is dealing with the legend that Numa, after the death of his wife, withdrew into solitude, not out of mere despondency, but in order to have intercourse with a divine being, Egeria.   Such a story, says Plutarch, is not unique, but should not be credited.   It is natural enough that gods should seek familiarity with men rather than with the lower creatures, but it is unreasonable to suppose that this extends to intercourse with the human body, and favour towards human beauty.   It is true, however, Plutarch adds, that in this matter the Egyptians make a distinction, and assert (in the words quoted above in Greek) that a god (πνεῦμα) may beget children by a woman, but not that a man may have intercourse with a goddess.   This distinction Plutarch does not think to be valid.

Before using this passage for our present purpose we may make two observations.   (i) The context (referring to Numa) makes quite clear that Plutarch is speaking of real physical intercourse.   Nothing else is thinkable in the case of Numa and Egeria, and this instance governs the whole context.   (ii) This fact must determine the meaning of the word πνεῦμα in this passage.   πνεῦμα must represent a personal divine being, a god; not merely rarefied matter (Plutarch was no Stoic) nor even undifferentiated divine essence.   This is confirmed by another passage of Plutarch (*de Is. et Os.* 36), cited by Norden, where it is said that the Egyptians call πνεῦμα Zeus, i.e., Amon, an equation which appears also in Egyptian documents.   We perceive at once an important difference between Plutarch and the Gospel infancy narratives.

Norden thinks that this notion of conception under the influence of πνεῦμα was developed in connection with a Hellenistic exaltation of virginity; this is not impossible, though the Philonic use of virginity as an allegorical symbol does not, as we have seen, bear strongly upon the question of the actual virginity of a woman who has given birth to a real child.   Norden's further treatment of the Annunciation in relation to the Egyptian Horus-myth and its possible descendants in Is. 7 and Vergil's Fourth Eclogue is very interesting but does not directly concern us. We must, however, reproduce his quotation from Hephaestion (p. 65, 17, ed. Engelbrecht), ὁ δὲ ἐπὶ τοῦ τρίτου γεννώμενος ἐκ θεῶν σπαρήσεται, καὶ ἔσται μέγας καὶ μετὰ θεῶν θρησκευθήσεται καὶ ἔσται κοσμο-κράτωρ καὶ πάντα αὐτῷ ὑπακούσεται, for the sake of the words ἐκ θεῶν σπαρήσεται.   Yet in this respect the passage does not go beyond other references to divine birth which we have shown above to be fundamentally irrelevant as parallels to the NT infancy narratives. Norden, it should be observed, follows Leisegang in his explanation of the word ἐπισκιάσει (Lk. 1. 35).

Norden, then, seems at first to promise more light on our subject than he actually affords. It is true, and it is very important, that he has drawn attention to a passage in which it is actually said that a woman's pregnancy is effected by $\pi\nu\epsilon\hat{\nu}\mu\alpha$; and much more important than the solitary reference to this belief in Plutarch is his statement that it was a popular superstition in Egypt. The belief is indeed strikingly akin to the Christian account of the birth of Jesus, and we need not hesitate to allow some point of contact between the infancy narratives and folk superstition. But two points remain to be accounted for: the use, in the Gospels, of $\pi\nu\epsilon\hat{\nu}\mu\alpha$ for impersonal, divine force, not a divine being; and the relation, which must be presumed to exist, between the notion of Spirit involved in conception "by the Holy Spirit" and that contained in the OT, since both Mt. and Lk. are clearly impregnated with OT ideas, and are dominated by them rather than by Hellenistic thought. That this is so may be briefly seen as follows. The Matthaean narrative points to the OT by direct reference. A genealogy ($\beta i \beta \lambda o s \ \gamma \epsilon \nu \epsilon \sigma \epsilon \omega s$, סֵפֶר תּוֹלְדֹת, book of generations, Gen. 5. 1; cf. Gen. 2. 4 et al.) is provided for Jesus, described as son of David and of Abraham. The genealogy neatly, though inaccurately, divides Jewish history into three equal sections, indicating thereby that with Jesus a new period, standing over against the prophetic past, began. The following narrative is supported by five proof texts.[1] Luke, though he adduces no proof texts, conveys even more powerfully than Matthew that in the events of the infancy the fulfilment of the OT was taking place. His style is closely akin to that of the LXX; and most of the phrases in the songs attributed to Mary,[2] Zachariah and Simeon are drawn directly from the OT. There is, indeed, in all these songs, a notable difference in view-point from the OT; for the constant burden of the Lucan Psalms is neither prophecy nor prayer, but the triumphant assertion that the Lord *has* visited and redeemed his people (1. 68), that he *has* put down the mighty from their seats (1. 52) and that the patient servant may now be dismissed, since his eyes have at last rested upon the promised Saviour (2. 29 f.).

CONCEPTION BY THE HOLY SPIRIT. It will be well at this point briefly to recapitulate the factors which must be taken into consideration if we are to give an account of the work of the Spirit in the birth narratives. First (and this is a point which distinguishes what is here said of the Holy Spirit from what is contained in the rest of the NT), the Spirit is said to act creatively upon matter; not merely to produce visible effects in the physical world, such as the casting out of demons or speaking with tongues, but to be itself productive. This essential element of the narratives is closely associated with the notion of divine begetting, which, as we have seen, is one that flourishes on pagan rather than Jewish soil.

---

[1] Is. 7. 14; Mic. 5. 2; Hosea 11. 1; Jer. 31. 14, and the source—whatever it may be—of the "Nazorean" prophecy.
[2] Or Elisabeth, if the Magnificat is to be attributed to her.

Allied again to this is the non-Jewish emphasis upon virginity. Finally we shall have to bear in mind the fact that the infancy narratives are written (and this is especially the case with Lk. 1 f.) in a style notably reminiscent of that of the Greek OT, and with frequent allusions and explicit references to the OT. Thus the infancy narratives produce a contradictory impression, since they seem at once Jewish and Hellenistic.[1] What is the explanation of this double appearance?

It will be necessary in the first place to examine the use of the word רוּחַ (ruaḥ) in the OT, bearing in mind what has just been said about the special aspect of the Spirit which is to be observed in the birth narratives, i.e., its creative influence upon physical nature. The results of the investigation are meagre. It is indeed true· that the Spirit is frequently connected, especially by the earlier OT writers, with physical as well as psychical phenomena: Samson and other judges perform warlike deeds, the prophets behave in striking and uncanny ways, through the influence of the Spirit. But this influence is not creative; material things are affected by it, but they do not come into being as the result of it. Only a few passages fall strictly within the class which we are considering.

Gen. 1. 2 (P). This is the most important passage of all. The word מְרַחֶפֶת (merraḥepheth) suggests the brooding or hovering of a bird (cf. Deut. 32. 11),[2] but it is probably incorrect to find here a trace, or at least to find more than the most superficial trace, of the ancient and widespread belief in the primeval world-egg from which proceeded the earth, sky, sun, moon and so forth; for this implies that the germ of world life was in the egg. The biblical idea is different. That over which the Spirit broods is not potential life; it is chaos.[3] The life is not in the chaos; it is in the Spirit (or breath, or wind). Milton in a frequently quoted passage paraphrases correctly:

> On the watery calm
> His brooding wings the Spirit of God outspread,
> And vital virtue infus'd, and vital warmth,
> Throughout the fluid mass.

> *Paradise Lost,* vii. 234 ff.

The רוּחַ אֱלֹהִים (ruaḥ 'elohim: however we should translate that phrase) was, along with the creative speech of God, the agent by which the present existing world was brought out of the inchoate primeval waste.[4] So at least, as we shall see, the creation myth [5] was understood by writers of other parts of the OT, and of some of the later apocryphal

---

[1] Cf. Gunkel, *op. cit.* 66 f.

[2] The meaning " to brood " cannot be demonstrated for the Hebrew word ; but there seems to be no doubt of it in the case of the cognate Syriac verb.

[3] Cf. other allusions to chaos in the OT, e.g., Job 38. 8-11 ; Ps. 65. 8 ; 77. 18 f. (with specific reference to the Red Sea, but the whole is described in cosmological language) ; 93. 3 f. Especially important are allusions to a return to the conditions of chaos as they were before the creation. See, e.g., Jer. 4. 23-26—there is no life in this picture, which (though not universally) is often taken to refer to primeval chaos ; see, e.g., BDB, *s.v.* תהו.

[4] Not out of non-being ; just as, of course, a child is not created out of *nothing.*

[5] Whether taken from Gen. 1. 2 as it now stands or from some earlier source not preserved in writing.

and pseudepigraphic works; though this is not the only possible way of understanding ruah 'elohim; the LXX, for example, took it to mean a wind.

Gen. 2. 7.   This verse does not contain the word Spirit, but it must be considered here.   It is not the words נִשְׁמַת חַיִּים (breath of life) that are significant but the fact of God's breathing (וַיִּפַּח, and he breathed), for what God breathes may be described as ruah 'adonai or ruah 'elohim. It is God's breath which supplies man with the breath of life, and makes him a living soul (נֶפֶשׁ חַיָּה, nephesh hayyah) distinguished from the dust of which he is composed (cf. 6. 17; 7. 15, 22).   Here too, therefore, we are justified in seeing a reference to God's Spirit in creative action—at the creation of the world.

Ps. 33. 6:
> By the word of the Lord were the heavens made;
> And all the host of them by the breath (ruah) of his mouth.

Ps. 104. 30:
> Thou sendest forth thy Spirit (רוּחֲךָ, ruhaka), they are created.

Ps. 147. 18:
> He sendeth out his word and melteth them:
> He causeth his wind (רוּחוֹ, ruho) to blow, and the waters flow.

In two at least of these passages ruah has a physical connotation, and none of them is very important for us, save that Ps. 33. 6 points back to the beginning of the world as the time when the ruah was active in a creative manner.

Job 27. 3; 32. 8; 33. 4.   These verses are more important.   27. 3 and 33. 4 may be taken together, especially if we adopt Peake's suggestion [1] and read 33. 4 after 33. 6, in what seems to be its rightful place.   If we do this we have a possible allusion to Gen. 2. 7, which the writer takes to apply to every man, as well as to the first.   But he probably thinks of the divine breath as a hereditary possession handed on from generation to generation rather than as a distinct gift of God to each man.   This is attested by 32. 8 where the special gift to Elihu (described in similar terms) is not that which makes him a living man but what gives him wisdom and speech.   Again we are brought back to the activity of the Spirit in the creation of the world and of man.

Prov. 8. 22 ff.; Wisd. 7. 22 f.; 15. 11.   In these books Wisdom, regarded as a distinct hypostasis, is said to have shared in the work of creation. There is no allusion to Spirit in Prov. 8, but the two conceptions of Spirit and Wisdom are closely related.   In Wisd. this relation becomes at times explicit, notably in 7. 22 f.   It is clear that though the πνεῦμα which is qualified by so many adjectives is said to be in Wisdom (ἐν αὐτῇ), yet there can be little distinction between the two.[2]   15. 11 seems to be a

---

[1] *Century Bible ad loc.*
[2] Cf. 7. 25 where Wisdom is said to be ἀτμὶς τῆς τοῦ θεοῦ δυνάμεως καὶ ἀπόρροια τῆς τοῦ παντοκράτορος δόξης εἰλικρινής.

further allusion to the creation of man by God and the Spirit.[1] We are therefore led back indirectly by the Wisdom literature to the creation narratives.

Judith 16. 14:

> Let all thy creation serve thee:
> For thou spakest, and they were made,
> Thou didst send forth thy spirit and it builded them,
> (ἀπέστειλας τὸ πνεῦμά σου, καὶ ᾠκοδόμησεν)
> And there is none that shall resist thy voice.

2 Baruch 21. 4:

O thou that hast made the earth, hear me, that hast fixed the firmament by the word,[2] and hast made firm the height of the heaven by the Spirit, that hast called from the beginning of the world that which did not yet exist, and they obey thee.

Both of these passages are akin to Ps. 33. 6, quoted above. In each case the activity of the Spirit in the creation at the beginning of time is closely linked with God's powerful speech.

Ezek. 37. 1-14. This is a very interesting passage for the study of the use of the word ruaḥ in Hebrew. We find it used in its subsidiary meaning (in the plural) of the four quarters of heaven, and, in addition, to mean breath, wind, the vital spirit of man, as well as the Spirit of God. The sense of the passage is quite plain. The dry bones must first be assembled and clothed with flesh and blood. When this has been done they are still corpses. They do not live and stand up upon their feet until the wind (ruaḥ) has put breath (ruaḥ) into them. The exiled people felt themselves to be in a state as hopeless as a pile of dry bones marking the site of an ancient battle. But God promises to restore the situation, to bring his people up out of their graves, to reconstitute Israel. "And I will put my spirit (רוּחִי, ruḥi) in you, and ye shall live." This is one of the most striking forms of the constantly recurring prophecy that God would visit and redeem his people. Redemption would be a new creation. God had once breathed into dust and made man a living soul; he would breathe again into a people who had forfeited their life, and make them live again. The new life of the redeemed Israel, of the Israel of the New Age, is God's life because it is the product of God's creative Spirit.

Is. 44. 3 f. God's Spirit outpoured will, in the promised time, promote the expansion of his people as water favours the growth of grass and willows. Little stress can be laid upon this passage.

From these passages we learn then that in the OT the Spirit appears to act creatively only [3] in relation to the primal creation of the world and man, and in the redemption of the people of God. This is a very striking and important fact.

It appears, however, that this view of the Spirit's activity was not

---

[1] Note the expression πνεῦμα ζωτικόν, and compare ἐμφυσήσαντα with ἐνεφύσησεν in Gen. 2. 7.
[2] Accepting (with Charles, *Ap. and Ps.* II. 493) Ryssel's very probable emendation.
[3] Except Ps. 104. 30, and here רוּחַ (ruaḥ) means breath rather than Spirit.

retained in the later periods of Palestinian Judaism. This was in part
due to the schematization and formulation of thought which was pro-
gressively carried through in the Rabbinic schools. For the Rabbis
the Spirit was pre-eminently the Spirit of prophecy, as is attested, for
example, by the phrase רוּחַ נְבוּאָה (ruaḥ neᵇbu'ah, or רוּחָא דַּנְבוּאָה, ruḥa'
danᵉbu'ah) which constantly recurs in the Targums in place of the
biblical ruah 'ᵉlohim or ruaḥ 'ᵃdonai.[1] It is for this reason that Str.-B.
have to write:[2] "πνεῦμα ἅγιον, רוּחַ הַקֹּדֶשׁ, signifies in Mt. 1. 18 the
life-giving, creative power of God; in this sense רוח הקדש does not
seem to be found in the older rabbinical literatuᵣe." Other meanings
are therefore found by the Rabbis for Gen. 1. 2, usually the simplest.
In one place (at least)[3] the obvious link (by means of רחף, r-ḥ-ph)
with Deut. 32. 11 is given; elsewhere the interpretation follows that
given by the Targum of Onkelos—וְרוּחָא מִן קֳדָם יְיָ מְנַשְּׁבָא עַל־אַפֵּי מַיָּא (a wind
(or breath) from before the Lord was moving over the surface of the
waters); the ruaḥ is simply a wind or breath. Much more interesting
is the saying of R. Shim'on b. Laqish, preserved in Gen. R. 2 (3b):
"The spirit of God moved (hovered); by this is meant the King, the
Messiah, as Is. 11. 2 shows, the Spirit of the Lord, etc."[4] But nowhere
(according to Str.-B.) is the spirit (in Gen. 1. 2) thought of as the creative
activity of God.

There are, however, a few passages in which the Spirit is spoken of as
the recreating, revivifying power of the days of the Messiah. Very
important for our purpose is a passage in Exod. R. 48 (102d) where the
functions of the Spirit in this age and in the age to come are distinguished.
"God said to Israel, 'In this world my Spirit has put Wisdom in you,
but in the future my Spirit will make you to live again, as it is said, I will
put my Spirit in you that you may live, Ezek. 37. 14'." The same
biblical reference is given to the same effect in Gen. R. 96 (60d).[5] The
Spirit of God was to be the creative power of the life of the age to come;
but here the Spirit's work does not seem to extend beyond the raising
from death of those who, having already lived, are to share in the blessings
of the days of the Messiah.

When we turn to Judaism that had come under the influence of
Hellenistic thought we find that the creation-myth is somewhat differently
treated—as we should expect. From the days at least of Anaxagoras
Greek philosophers had found the cause of the present movements and
aggregations of the elemental units of the physical universe in Mind
(νοῦς), which, whether we should call it a spiritual substance or a spiritual
being, was at least (in comparison with matter) spiritual and creative, and
which offered a clear point of contact with the divine Spirit of Gen. 1. 2.

The LXX follows the same rendering of Gen. 1. 2 which we have

[1] A few references are given in Str.-B. II. 129.   [2] I. 48.
[3] T. Ḥag. 2. 5 (234) ; see Str.-B. I. 124.
[4] Other parallel passages (and one in which רוח (ruaḥ) is said to be the soul of the first man)
are given in Str.-B. II. 351.
[5] Cf. p. Keth. 12. 35b. 5 (Str.-B. III. 828 f.).

already seen in the Targum, i.e., it drops the metaphor of a bird suggested by מְרַחֶפֶת (meraḥepheth), and translates πνεῦμα θεοῦ ἐπεφέρετο ἐπάνω τοῦ ὕδατος. This suggests the picture of a violent wind, but no more; it does, however, leave the way open to other interpretations of πνεῦμα. Philo refers to the passage in several places, and, after his manner, with no attempt at consistency. In *de Gigant.* 22 he distinguishes two meanings of the word πνεῦμα; the former signifies simply the third element, air, which flows away from the earth (i.e., upward);[1] the latter is pure knowledge (ἀκήρατος ἐπιστήμη) such as Bezalel received (Exod. 31. 2 f.). A different view appears in *de Opif. Mundi,* 29 f., where though Gen. 1. 2 is not cited it is clearly in mind. Philo points out that the two special features of the Mosaic creation narrative are Spirit (πνεῦμα) and light. Philo explains the importance of Spirit, and why it is called the Spirit of God, as follows: τὸ μὲν γὰρ (sc. πνεῦμα) ὠνόμασε θεοῦ, διότι ζωτικώτατον[2] τὸ πνεῦμα, ζωῆς δὲ θεὸς αἴτιος. Here πνεῦμα is much more than the third element of *de Gigant.* 22; it is a divine life-giving power. In *Leg. Alleg.* 1. 33 ff. Philo discusses Gen. 2. 7 in relation to Gen. 1. 2. Why does Moses in the former verse use πνοή while in the latter he has πνεῦμα?[3] The answer (42) is that πνοή is a gentler and milder power than πνεῦμα, more fitted to the weakness of the man who is moulded out of matter. πνεῦμα on the other hand is conceived κατὰ τὴν ἰσχὺν καὶ εὐτονίαν καὶ δύναμιν. On occasion, then, Philo can think of πνεῦμα as a powerful life-giving agent of God.

It is a very striking fact that we find the same concept of spirit in the Hermetic Corpus, where that literature has been influenced by Jewish thought. It has been proved by Professor Dodd[4] that the first Hermetic tractate, *Poimandres,* has been influenced by the Genesis cosmogony; and there is a close parallel in it to the LXX phrase πνεῦμα θεοῦ ἐπεφέρετο ἐπάνω τοῦ ὕδατος. In 5b we have κινούμενα δὲ ἦν (sc. γῆ καὶ ὕδωρ) διὰ τὸν ἐπιφερόμενον πνευματικὸν λόγον.[5] This πνευματικὸς λόγος, in a context such as this, where Jewish influence is undoubted, should be thought of in terms of such passages as Ps. 32. 6; 147. 7 (LXX) where πνεῦμα and λόγος are used in parallel, as we have seen, of God's creative work, rather than as a material and disseminated principle (after the manner of the Stoics). We find, then, in this Jewish-influenced Hellenistic tract, that an agent in creation is the πνευματικὸς λόγος, representing the πνεῦμα of Gen. 1. 2. There is a similar passage in the Third Tractate, 1b. This reads: ἦν γὰρ σκότος ἄπειρον[6] ἐν[7] ἀβύσσῳ,

---

[1] ὁ ῥέων ἀὴρ ἀπὸ γῆς, τρίτον στοιχεῖον ἐποχούμενον ὕδατι.

[2] Cf. Wisd. 15. 11, πνεῦμα ζωτικόν.

[3] Josephus (*Ant.* 1. 1. 2 (34)) says πνεῦμα ἐνῆκεν αὐτῷ.

[4] *The Bible and the Greeks,* 99-248.

[5] Scott, *Hermetica,* I. 118, reads . . . διὰ τὸν ⟨ἐπάνω⟩ ⟨τοῦ ὕδατος⟩ ἐπιφερόμενον πνευματικὸν λόγον, which is even nearer to the LXX text. But τοῦ ὕδατος, derived by Scott from the previous sentence, is required there, where, with Reitzenstein and Professor Dodd, we should read . . . ὡς μὴ θεωρεῖσθαι ⟨τὴν γῆν⟩ ἀπὸ τοῦ ὕδατος.

[6] Scott transposes ἄπειρον, reading it after ὕδωρ.   [7] Perhaps read ἐπ'.

καὶ ὕδωρ καὶ πνεῦμα λεπτὸν νοερόν, δυνάμει θείᾳ ὄντα ἐν χάει.[1] The whole section is strongly reminiscent of the LXX version of Gen. 1. 2, and of the description of Wisdom in Wisd. 7. 22 (especially the words νοερόν, λεπτόν). Here, even more clearly than in *Poimandres*, we see that the πνεῦμα of Gen. 1. 2 was understood as creative divine power, and that it was associated with the σοφία τεχνῖτις of Wisd.

We now have in our hands sufficient data to explain the phenomena which we find in the NT. We are directed by the Gospel narratives themselves to look to the OT. Doing so, we observe what the earliest Christians appear to have seen: that, just as the Spirit of God was active at the foundation of the world, so that Spirit was to be expected also at its renewal. The conclusion is easily drawn that the entry of the Redeemer upon the stage of history was the work of the Spirit, and this accounts for the introduction of the Spirit into the birth narratives. It was not introduced because it was natural to think of the Spirit, as known through the OT, as a male principle, capable (as Zeus or Apollo might have been supposed to be capable) of begetting children by mortal women. Ruah is generally feminine, and is God's activity, not a personal demigod. As Gunkel says, "Judaism, descended from the OT, could, it is rightly said, speak of a miraculous *creation* of the child, but not of a miraculous *begetting* by a divine agent. It will be recalled with what horror the union of the sons of God with the daughters of men is spoken of in Gen. 6." [2] The motives which introduced the Spirit into the infancy narratives were rather Messianic and eschatological.

It was in these categories that the earliest tradition found it necessary to express the significance of the work and teaching of Jesus, and it seems probable that he himself thought of his mission in these terms. Consistent recourse to the OT as a commentary upon the events of the New Covenant led to consideration of the work of the Holy Spirit as the creative power of God. But we have just seen that this genuinely biblical concept of the activity of the Spirit in the new creation was kept alive chiefly in Hellenistic rather than in Palestinian Judaism, and it seems therefore probable that the elucidation of the birth of Jesus in terms of the creative work of the Spirit took place on the basis of Hellenistic rather than Palestinian interpretation of the OT.

If this be true, another of the questions before us has been answered. How was the notion of a divine begetting by the Spirit able to enter Christian circles, when that notion was, as we have seen, Greek rather than Jewish, and the Christian circles (so far as we can infer their nature from the infancy narratives themselves) based their faith upon the OT? Precisely because the sphere in which Christian interpretation of the OT was able to work on the lines we have suggested was not Palestinian Judaism but Judaism influenced and permeated by Hellenism. The fundamental thought involved in the conception stories in their bearing upon the work of the Holy Spirit is legitimately derived from OT thought:

---

[1] Scott very plausibly suggests θείᾳ ⟨διῆκ⟩ον τὰ ἐν χάει.   [2] *Op. cit.* 66 f.

the Spirit is *Creator Spiritus* in both creations. But, in the first century, the circumstances were such that this OT doctrine throve in a Hellenistic atmosphere, in which it was possible for other Hellenistic concepts also—for example, that of divine begetting—to flourish.

Thus we find at length a reconciliation of the three factors with which we are chiefly concerned—the OT background and formulation of thought represented by the birth narratives, the Hellenistic and non-Jewish basis of the notion of divine begetting, and the unique and specifically Christian claims of the birth narratives which we possess. At the same time, in finding the explanation of the creative, procreative, power of the Spirit in a syncretized Judaism, we find incidentally that the non-Jewish stress on virginity is explained. The central, biblical, idea with which we have to deal is that the entrance of Jesus into the world was the inauguration of God's new creation and therefore has its only true analogy in Genesis; the means whereby the Church arrived at this end was Hellenistic Judaism, and a secondary product of this means was belief in the virginity of the mother.

The authors of the infancy narratives perceived what, as we shall see, was set forth in another form in the baptism narrative. The ministry of Jesus could only be properly explained on the basis of the OT, and this involved both the Messiahship of Jesus and the work of the Holy Spirit. Whether this activity of the Spirit excludes the possibility of procreation by Joseph is a question to which no one is able to give an answer, unless he has excluded all possibility of miracle on *a priori* grounds. But it is natural to suppose that if the transition from creation to begetting was effected by the migration of the gospel from Palestinian to Hellenistic Judaism, to an atmosphere where divine paternity was familiar, then at one step the birth became virgin birth, in accordance with the intellectual and religious climate in which the change was made.[1]

The part played by the Holy Spirit in the birth narratives is thus seen to be the fulfilment of God's promised redemption in a new act of creation, comparable with that of Gen. 1. This thought is fundamentally Hebraic; but before it took its present form it must have come under strong Hellenistic influences.

---

[1] Büchsel (*TWNT* I. 667) suggests a specific connection between God's ποιεῖν and his γεννᾶν in Philo, on the basis of *Leg. Alleg.* 3. 219. The same equation is made by Dr W. F. Howard, *Christianity according to St. John*, 198 f. But the passage quoted by Büchsel will not bear the weight he puts upon it. Philo is allegorizing Gen. 21. 6 and says that ἐποίησεν is equivalent to ἐγέννησεν. He does not say that ἐποίησεν is *always* equivalent to ἐγέννησεν, as Büchsel says—" All creation (ποιεῖν) by God he is able to term ' begetting ' (γεννᾶν)."

3

THE BAPTISM OF JESUS

WE have seen in the preceding section that the ascription of the conception of Jesus to the activity of the Holy Spirit was not based upon any purely general background of Jewish piety, nor upon a combination of notions derived from Hellenistic manticism, but that his birth was regarded as a unique operation, unique because it was, in the broad sense of the term, Messianic; i.e., it was a product of that activity of the Spirit which was expected to break forth at the inauguration of the New Age, at God's new act of creation. If this be the case with regard to the birth of Jesus, if, that is, this was the motive of the Evangelists Matthew and Luke in recording the birth narratives, we are led to propose a similar question concerning the second allusion in the life of Jesus to the Spirit, i.e., the baptism story. The question has in fact been put by Hoskyns in his essay on *The Christ of the Synoptic Gospels*.[1] He says: "It is claimed that the natural meaning of the narrative is that Jesus, conscious of the need of repentance, and therefore possessing a sense of sin, came to be baptized by John. At the moment of His baptism He passed through a religious experience, of which He alone was conscious, and that He then felt Himself called to associate Himself with the work of the Baptist. Thus, in spite of all the later Christological accretions, there is preserved in St Mark's Gospel a genuine reminiscence of the consecration of Jesus to the work of a prophet, in the light of which the claim to the Messiahship, if He did make the claim, must be interpreted. . . . But is the Marcan narrative really capable of such psychological treatment? . . ."[2] Or, in effect, is not the Messianic significance of the event rooted deep in the most primitive document we possess?

Not all the elements in the Synoptic account of the work of John the Baptist need be considered at this point; but it will be necessary, as a preliminary to the discussion of the baptism of Jesus, to examine the meaning of John's baptism, although it is important to observe that the baptism of Jesus cannot be held to stand in any direct causal relationship to the descent of the Spirit upon him, since many others were baptized by John and did not hear a voice from heaven or see a dove.

The following questions arise for discussion:

(a) What was the significance of John's baptism?

(b) Why did Jesus receive it?

(c) What is the meaning of the descent of the Spirit and the dove symbolism?

(d) What is the meaning of the voice from heaven?

[1] In *Essays Catholic and Critical*, ed. E. G. Selwyn, 151-178.   [2] *Op. cit.* 169.

B

(a) What was the significance of John's baptism ?

There are two sources for answering this question, the NT and Josephus, *Ant.* 18. 5. 2 (116-119); they seem to be independent witnesses. It has indeed been held that the passage in Josephus is a Christian interpolation into the original text; but this is unlikely. A Christian interpolation would have been more Christian, and, in particular, would have been more closely conformed to the tradition contained in the Gospels. Josephus uses the terms βαπτισμός, which is rare in the NT,[1] and βάπτισις, which does not occur in the NT at all. It is true that Josephus uses the word βαπτιστής without explanation; but this is not unlike his manner, and in any case the circumstances are met if we suppose the words τοῦ ἐπικαλουμένου βαπτιστοῦ to be a Christian explanatory insertion. Josephus does not use the word characteristic of the NT, βάπτισμα, nor does he describe John's baptism as a baptism of repentance (μετάνοια); and though he has an account of John's death at the hands of Herod it is quite different from that given in Mk.

Accordingly we are to recognize in Josephus and the NT two distinct sources for our knowledge of John.[2] It has been held by some that there is a third source, the writings of the Mandaeans, which do indeed contain numerous references to John. But all of these can be shown to be secondary, and derived from Nestorian Christian sources,[3] so that for our purpose Mandaism can be safely neglected.

When we turn to Josephus' account of John we find only a few sentences, introduced parenthetically. The historian notes a popular explanation of the defeat which Herod Antipas suffered in A.D. 36 at the hands of Aretas, King of Arabia. Many of the Jews (says Josephus) thought this defeat a well-deserved punishment for Herod's treatment of John.[4] Herod had killed John, though he was a good man and enjoined virtue.[5] The baptism which he commanded was not a means of pardon for sins, but was for the purification of the body (ἐφ᾽ ἁγνείᾳ τοῦ σώματος) where the soul had already been purified by the practice of the virtue John demanded (τῆς ψυχῆς δικαιοσύνῃ προεκκεκαθαρμένης). The popular movement which arose out of the great respect which the people had for John was broken off by his arrest; Herod, fearing what Josephus vaguely calls ἀπόστασίς τις and τὶ νεώτερον,[6] had the Baptist conveyed to Machaerus and there done to death.

This is not a very satisfactory piece of narrative. It raises at least three fundamental questions, which are by no means easy to answer on the

---

[1] Mk. 7. 4 ; Heb. 6. 2 ; 9. 10 ; nowhere used of John's baptism.

[2] Of course, several sources are contained in the NT itself.

[3] See Oepke, *TWNT* I. 534, and the literature there cited. Add S. A. Pallis, *Mandaean Studies*, Oxford, 1926.

[4] This, according to the NT, must have happened c. A.D. 29 ; however, it is not impossible that popular resentment at the tyrannical act may have smouldered seven years.

[5] ἀρετή, issuing in both δικαιοσύνη and εὐσεβεία.

[6] This means not " anything new which might come to his mind " (Klausner, *Jesus of Nazareth*, 240) but a rebellion, according to the customary usage of Josephus, and of other authors (cf. LS, new edition, 1173a).

basis of Josephus alone. First of all comes the most obvious question, with regard to John himself. What sort of person was he? In what category of men must he be placed? What was the purpose of his preaching and baptism? Josephus mentions other baptizers; there was, for example, his own teacher, Banus, who lived in the wilderness, used for food and clothing only what things he found growing, and washed himself day and night with cold water for purity.[1] But there are obvious differences between John and Banus. Banus washed himself; John baptized his converts. Banus was a solitary who fled from the world, and to whom Josephus had to attach himself; John also was in some sense a solitary, but all the world went after him and he became the leader of a popular movement. Again, Josephus speaks of the washings of the Essenes;[2] but, although the identification has been made, John was not an Essene as the Essenes are described by Josephus. We miss their exclusiveness, their communism, their demand of celibacy, their sun-worship.[3] John remains in Josephus an isolated and enigmatic person.

It is hardly easier to answer the question: Why did Herod kill John? A quick reading of Josephus suggests only that John was a good man who told the Jews to be virtuous, and that the Jews did as they were bidden. There was nothing in this to provoke the anger even of Herod. Closer examination reveals that behind Herod's fear lies something that Josephus has, no doubt quite consciously, concealed, namely, a Messianic movement not unrelated to revolution. Only one thing could have provoked John's Jewish hearers to an excitement so menacing that Herod was driven to murder its ringleader; John's demand of righteousness could have seemed treasonable only if it was directed (as the Gospels say it was) towards a Jewish Kingdom of some sort. But Josephus does not say this; probably he expected the well-informed reader to understand it.

Again, we may ask: Granted John's preaching of righteousness, granted also preaching of some sort about the Kingdom of God, why did the prophet employ the symbolism of washing? Again, Josephus has no answer. The bath, he says, did not convey pardon for sins, but was ἐφ᾽ ἁγνείᾳ τοῦ σώματος. It effected, then, a cleansing from ceremonial defilement. But from what defilement? For all the forms of ceremonial uncleanness that could be incurred there was provision in the ordinances of the current legal system. There was no need for a prophet to inaugurate a wholly new rite of lustration for a purpose which was already adequately fulfilled. In this instance also the obscurity of Josephus' narrative points to the fact that he has left out an essential factor in his story—the Jewish, Messianic, element in John's teaching and action which alone makes sense of the rest. Josephus' Hellenistic public would not understand—

[1] πρὸς ἁγνείαν, Josephus, Vita, 2 (11) ; cf. the ἐφ᾽ ἁγνείᾳ in the account of John's baptism.
[2] B.J. 2. 8. 5 (129) ; these too he calls ἁγνεία. He does not speak of this practice when he describes the Essenes in Ant. 18. 1. 5 (18-22).
[3] If this be the meaning of πρὶν ἀνασχεῖν τὸν ἥλιον οὐδὲν φθέγγονται τῶν βεβήλων, πατρίους δέ τινας εἰς αὐτὸν εὐχὰς ὥσπερ ἱκετεύοντες ἀνατεῖλαι (B.J. 2. 8. 5 (128)).

and in so far as it would have understood could not have approved—
anything that smacked of Jewish nationalism, so Jewish nationalism had
to disappear from Josephus' narrative; but it was so important a feature
of the history with which Josephus was dealing that (here and in many
other places) he could not but leave traces that the story had been
tampered with.   John the Baptist wears Greek dress with singularly ill
grace; he is at home in the prophet's mantle.   But just as we cannot
explain why Herod should put to death a Stoic preacher of righteousness
(and Josephus' John answers to this description), neither can we explain
the national act of cleansing which this strange person proclaimed, unless
we recognize a deeper motivation and inspiration than Josephus allows
us to see.   It is plain that the whole of Josephus' account of John is only
precariously held together, and is not easy to understand; the reason is
that Josephus has taken away the keystone of the arch, the clue to the
puzzle.

Accordingly we turn from Josephus to our second source, the NT.   We
have seen that the background of John's mission which Josephus has
almost but not quite completely concealed is that of the Jewish national
hope, and we may expect to see this background more clearly in the NT.
But it must be remembered that, though what Herod feared was no doubt
the political intentions of his unruly subjects, Jewish hopes were by no
means political hopes only.   Although from the earliest times they had
been framed and conditioned by political circumstances, they were
essentially religious.   It is not correct to speak as though the Messianic
expectation (using the term in its broadest sense) had two sides or aspects,
a political and a religious.   The political hope was religious; for the
hope was always of what God would perform.   True, there are frequent
traces, in the extant sources, of an expectation that God would act
through his people, even through their armies, but the work was his,
not theirs, and consequently even when the end hoped for was most
crudely expressed it was essentially a religious end.   Yet, in the NT, it is
from a religious standpoint that the Messianic hope as it flared up in
the person of John the Baptist is described.[1]   This appears in several
ways.   The Baptist is introduced by the quotation of Scripture (Mk. 1. 2 f.,
followed by Mt. and Lk.); he is God's messenger, the voice in the desert.
He is so described [2] as to suggest the OT prophets (cf. Zech. 13. 4;
2 Kings 1. 8).   His preaching contains the two notes characteristic of
the prophets, the threat of judgement, and the corresponding demand for
a radical repentance and trust in the mercy of God.

In particular, John is represented (in Mk., Q and L) as Elijah.   Several
Jewish sources reveal an expectation that the return of Elijah would

---

[1] John is spoken of in Mk., in the Q material, and in the matter peculiar to Lk., as well as in
the Fourth Gospel and Acts.   Mt. 11. 14 has no parallel, and should probably be regarded as
editorial.

[2] Perhaps the true text of Mk. 1. 6 is preserved by D and the Old Latin, in which case we
should say, by Matthew.

precede the advent of the Messiah.[1] By the time of the writing of the Gospels the equation of John with Elijah was accepted, and it appears in every source with which we have to deal. In the opening verses of Mk. it is suggested by the quotation of Mal. 3. 1. Later in the Gospel the identification is made even more explicit (9. 11-13). Mt. 11. 10 (Q=Lk. 7. 27) makes the same quotation of Mal. 3. 1 with regard to John, who is at the same time said to be more than a prophet (Mt. 11. 9=Lk. 7. 26). In the same context Matthew (11. 14) explicitly declares that John is the promised Elijah, but this verse is editorial and does not appear in Lk., though the saying to which it is appended (Mt. 11. 12 f.=Lk. 16. 16) appears in both Gospels and is important. The Lucan infancy narrative (L) relates John to Elijah in terms of Mal. 3. 1, 23 f. and 2 Kings 2. 9, 15 (Lk. 1. 13-17).

The preaching of John falls into two divisions. One element is that which, roughly speaking, is common to all the prophets. John demanded repentance in view of an approaching judgement, a day of the Lord which would be darkness and not light. The themes of repentance and judgement are not stressed in Mk., though of course they are reflected in the Marcan narrative of John's death (6. 17-29). They are, however, emphasized by the non-Marcan material which Mt. and Lk. have in common. Mt. 3. 7-10, 12 (=Lk. 3. 7-9, 17) demand repentance with its corresponding fruit, and set forth the judgement as close at hand. There is no defence to be had in ancestry or elsewhere; every tree will be judged by its fruit, and those which fail to stand the test will be cast into the fire. The distinctive element in John's preaching is his prophecy of the Coming One who would follow him, with greater power and dignity. This prophecy seems to have stood in both Mk. and Q, as a few minor agreements of Mt. and Lk. against Mk. suggest. It is referred to in a later Q passage, the question "Art thou the Coming One?" sent by John to Jesus (Mt. 11. 3=Lk. 7. 19).[2]

Both of these elements in John's preaching are related to the most striking and characteristic feature of his mission—his baptism. The repentance which he required in view of the judgement which he proclaimed to be immediately at hand was to be sealed by the act of baptism.[3] But the prophecy of the One who was to come was also conceived in terms

---

[1] See the detailed excursus in Str.-B. IV. 779-798. It is to be noted that, as Billerbeck points out, the expectation of the coming of Elijah belongs to Rabbinic literature rather than to the Apocrypha and apocalypses (but see Sir. 48. 10 ; 4 Ezra 6. 26 ; Justin, *Dial. c. Tryph.* 8, 49). Yet the prophecies of Mal. 3. 1 ; 3. 23 f. (LXX, 4. 4 f.) will always have been present to influence any who paid attention to them.

[2] Probably the source from which Matthew and Luke derived their information about John used in both cases the participle ἐρχόμενος, and we should suppose that in regard to this word Matthew (in 3. 11) reproduces the source more exactly than Luke.

[3] It is because the baptism rests upon this unique repentance in the presence of an immediately impending doom that it is generally taken to have been a single, unrepeatable rite, and so distinguished from the washings of such a baptist as Josephus' Bannus. This assumption seems, on this ground, to be justified ; but it should be made clear that there is no direct evidence, in the NT, Josephus, or elsewhere, to prove that John's baptism could not be received on several occasions. It is interesting to hazard the speculation that the Mandaeans, whose baptisms were unlike those of the Nestorian Christians only in that they were repeated, may in this one feature

of baptism, and the difference between his baptism and that of John was the measure of his superiority to the forerunner. The saying about the baptism of the Coming One is preserved in two forms (Mk. 1. 8; Mt. 3. 11=Lk. 3. 16); probably neither of them is original.[1]

What then was the baptism of John? What was its origin?

It is not necessary to make a detailed examination of the Hellenistic rites of lustration which have been adduced as parallels to and sources of John's baptism. An admirable account of many of these is given by Oepke (*TWNT* I. 528-532), and there is no need to repeat it, especially in view of his conclusion, which it seems impossible to dispute: "By this means (i.e., because John's baptism introduced a Messianic revival) its exact place in the history of religions is defined: Palestinian Judaism. There is not a single syllable in the Gospels to hint that it was the off-spring of Oriental syncretism." [2] It is, however, and for this reason, the more necessary to consider Jewish baptismal rites.

The older parts of the OT contain ample proof of the ancient, and very natural, connection between washing, which removes ordinary dirt, and the removal of ceremonial impurity. With this fact, however, we are not concerned, but with the developments of this primitive notion which appear in later Judaism. Brandt [3] summarizes the post-exilic lustrations under eleven heads, all of which are related to circumstances arising out of natural functions or disease—such as sexual intercourse, childbirth, leprosy. That is, the washing is still strictly ceremonial; it has no real ethical significance. The same is true of the elaboration of lustral rites which appears in the Rabbinic sources. It is manifestly impossible here even to summarize the rites which appear in the Mishnah. The require-ment of washing (טְבִילָה, t\ebilah) appears on innumerable occasions; a special tractate (*Miqwaoth*) is devoted to the bath (מִקְוֶה, miqweh) in which the act takes place. In spite, however, of a few passages where it is recognized that the mechanical performance of a rite is unavailing without true repentance,[4] the use of baptism is entirely ceremonial and in no way ethical. But John's baptism of repentance is not entirely without precedent. The metaphor of washing is not infrequently used in the OT to represent ethical purification. So for example it stands in the opening prophecy of Isaiah; the context of Is. 1. 16 makes it quite impossible to think that any ritual act is in mind. A precisely similar demand is made by Jeremiah (Jer. 4. 14); we may add Ps. 51. 4, 9. The same figure of speech is used eschatologically in Is. 4. 4 and

---

have preserved a genuine relic of Johannine baptism. But this is on the whole unlikely; it does not outweigh the argument from the particular repentance demanded by John, and the Mandaeans could easily have picked up the practice of repeated baptisms from many a source in their religious environment.

[1] See the discussion below, pp. 125 f.
[2] *Op. cit.* I. 534.
[3] *Die jüdischen Baptismen*, 20-22.
[4] *T. Ta'an.* 1, 8 (215, 23) : A man who has in his hand a reptile (causing uncleanness), even if he washes in the waters of Shiloh and in all the waters of creation, yet will he never be clean. But if he cast the reptile forth out of his hand, then a baptism in 40 *seah* is effective for him. The proof text is Prov. 28. 13. Cf. parallel passages cited in Str.-B. I. 171b.

Ezek. 36. 25. In all these cases a moral transformation is in question, not an actual physical bath. But we can take a step further in the direction of John's ethical baptism by means of the prophetic use of symbolism. It seems probable that the striking deeds performed by some of the prophets bear some relation to the older, magical level of religion. When, for example, Joash, his hands covered by those of Elisha, shoots an arrow in the direction of Syria and strikes with the arrows upon the ground (2 Kings 13. 15-19); or when Jeremiah breaks his earthen vessel (Jer. 19) and acquires the field at Anathoth (Jer. 32. 6-15); when Ezekiel portrays the besieged city on a tile (Ezek. 4. 1-3), we are reminded of the rites of mimetic magic. This is not to say that the great prophets really thought that they were controlling "action at a distance"; but it is likely that for them the symbolism meant more than mere illustration. How much more we need not here attempt to determine; by their acted prophecy the prophets supply a link between their teaching of moral cleanness and John's adoption of a practice which was often no more than a part of that formal ritualism which fell under their condemnation.[1]

One further baptismal rite, which stands by itself, must be considered at this point, namely, that administered to proselytes to Judaism. It can now be taken for granted that the antiquity of proselyte baptism [2] is sufficient to warrant its being compared with John's baptism and to prove that it did not arise by imitation of the Christian rite.[3] Three requirements were made of a male proselyte: circumcision, baptism and sacrifice. The last two were obligatory upon women also. The origin of the ceremony of proselyte baptism clearly lies in the sphere of ritual uncleanness. If the born Jew had continually to submit to various lustrations in order to be in a fit state to carry out the functions of his religion, it was inevitable that one coming into Judaism from the impure world of heathenism should be compelled to remove the taint of his former life by a similar bath. But, in the nature of the case, proselyte baptism was (as John's baptism appears to have been) an unrepeatable act; a man would only pass from paganism to Judaism once. Proselyte baptism, then, appears as a unique event, the significance of which must have included both purification and sanctification for admission to the people of God.

The significance of John's baptism may now, in the light of the facts which we have considered, be summed up under the following four heads:

(i) It bears a close relationship to proselyte baptism. This view is

---

[1] It is striking that one of the very few (four in all) places in the LXX where the verb βαπτίζω is used is that which describes the washing submitted to by Naaman in obedience to the prophet's command: 4 Kdms. 5. 14 κατέβη Ναιμὰν καὶ ἐβαπτίσατο ἐν τῷ Ἰορδάνῃ. The other references for βαπτίζω are Jdth. 12. 7; Sir. 31. 30; Is. 21. 4.

[2] See the careful discussion in Brandt, op. cit. 57-62.

[3] The four arguments (based on Epictetus, Diss. 2. 9. 19 ff.: Sib. Or. 4. 165: Mish. Pes. 8. 8 ; Ed. 5. 2 : b. Yeb. 46a) given by Oepke (op. cit. I. 533) seem to me to be conclusive.

taken by Oepke,[1] but denied by Lietzmann.[2] It is certainly necessary
here to be on our guard against taking analogy for genealogy; but
Lietzmann's objection seems strikingly ill-founded. He says: "This
last (i.e., the comparison of John's baptism with proselyte baptism) has
been asserted and we are presented with the strange paradox that John
demanded that the Israelite, who was proud of his nationality, should
have himself baptized and made clean, just as the unclean heathen must
do, before he could come to God; which is too paradoxical to be convincing." But in fact this paradox is one of the fundamental axioms of
John's preaching. "Think not to say in yourselves, We have Abraham
as our father; for I say to you that God is able to raise up of these stones
children to Abraham." Jewish descent is no guarantee of security in the
day of the Lord; Jews of pure descent are no better off than (not Gentiles
merely, but) stones. Hence the necessity for some act by which those who
had forfeited the right of membership in the chosen people of God might
regain their position. If John really thought, as he appears to have
thought, that Jews by descent were not as such Israelites indeed and heirs
of the Kingdom of God, there seems to be no new paradox involved in
taking the view that he required baptism, an initiatory baptism, from them
also. On the contrary, John's preaching fits admirably with the opinion
that his baptism constituted a parallel with the rite by which (along with
circumcision and sacrifice) proselytes were made full members of Judaism.

(ii) It is right to consider here the meaning of words used by Josephus
in his description of John,[3] βαπτισμῷ συνιέναι. This phrase may mean,
and it seems quite likely that it does mean, not "to come together for the
purpose of being baptized" but "to unite by baptism".[4] If this is a
correct translation, and if Josephus was well informed, John regarded
his baptism not as an act related merely to the individuals who submitted to it, but as one by which they were bound together. This is of
course perfectly understandable if what has just been said is true; that
John's baptism was related to proselyte baptism in that it was intended
as the means of entry into the true Israel. It also agrees with the way in
which John's mission as *Elijah redivivus* is stated in Lk. 1. 17, ἑτοιμάσαι
Κυρίῳ λαὸν κατεσκευασμένον.

(iii) John's baptism should be regarded as an instance of prophetic
symbolism. There can be no doubt (if our sources are to be trusted at all)
that John would have rejected altogether a baptism that was merely a
mechanically performed rite undertaken with no serious intention; this
was not the fruit worthy of repentance which he demanded. The repentance itself was his real requirement. But on the other hand he must
have insisted very strongly on the performance of the rite; such insistence
alone can explain the prominence given to it in all the accounts of his

[1] *Op. cit.* 1. 535.   [2] *The Beginnings of the Christian Church*, 51.
[3] *Ant.* 18. 5. 2 (117).
[4] Cf. Eisler, *The Messiah Jesus and John the Baptist*, 269; Marsh, *NT Baptism*, 64; see however
H. St J. Thackeray, *Josephus, the Man and the Historian* (1929), 132.

work, and the name βαπτιστής which is applied to him and no other. Josephus does not call his own master Bannus βαπτιστής, in spite of his regular washings.[1] John could not have laid so much stress upon a development, or variation, of legal ritual. His baptism belongs to the same class as the symbolic actions of the prophets mentioned above (p. 31). It is probably vain to speculate about the relation between the act of washing and the forgiveness of sins because it is very doubtful whether John or anyone else ever formulated it; in fact, it seems incorrect to separate the various components of the one complex event which included repentance, confession, immersion and forgiveness. Through his baptism the penitent became one of the prepared people of God, able to await the coming judgement without the fear of being cast into the fire. John, as we have seen, had abundant authority in the language of the prophets for adopting the metaphor of washing as a symbol of cleansing, and adequate precedent for turning the metaphor into a symbolic action.

(iv) The motivation of John's baptism lies in the eschatological necessity by which he was impelled to his prophetic ministry, his conviction, that is, that the remaining period of world history was short. The whole of his work rested (for him) under the shadow of the imminent judgement, when every unfruitful tree would be cut down. It was necessary to act, and to act quickly; to pluck, if possible, at least a few brands out of the fire; to assemble a remnant of Israel, truly prepared to meet their God. The purity which he preached, and towards which his baptism contributed, was no general requirement of goodness; it was an urgent necessity of the last times. As Dr Schweitzer truly points out, the rite of baptism in this context is closely akin to the marking of the faithful in Ezek. 9. 4-11 and in various parts of the NT.[2] We should recall, too, OT passages which we have mentioned earlier,[3] where a cleansing of the people with water is promised before the final coming of God to judgement and vindication.

The points that we have just made can easily be put together. John's baptism was, in the sense just defined, eschatological; we may with Dr Schweitzer [4] call it an eschatological sacrament. It was conceived under the influence of a vivid expectation of the End, of the coming of God to judgement. It is precisely for this reason that it deals with sin, and that it has a communal aspect. The only sort of Israel that could meet the judgement was an Israel that had been cleansed from its sin; and John knew from the OT that there was reason to hope that, before the time came, God would cleanse his people with water. To one who recalled the deeds of the prophets, or rather, who himself lived in the thought-world in which those deeds were still natural, it would be an easy step to translate the prophesied cleansing into a national act of re-

---

[1] It is, of course, possible, as was suggested above (p. 26), that the words τοῦ ἐπικαλουμένου βαπτιστοῦ are a Christian insertion into the text of Josephus; but the Christian evidence alone is sufficiently striking.   [2] *Mysticism of Paul the Apostle*, 229 f.
[3] Is. 4. 4; Ezek. 36. 25. Cf. pp. 30 f.   [4] *Op. cit.* 233.

pentance and washing. It is not too much to say that Mark was quite correct in saying that John's baptism was εἰς ἄφεσιν ἁμαρτιῶν (Mk. 1. 4); if the baptism had not dealt with sin it would entirely have failed of its purpose in preparing men for the judgement, at which sin, or its absence, was to be the decisive factor. At the same time, those who were in this way made secure against the eschatological future were banded together in the ranks of the true Israel; or better, their security lay in their membership of the purified people of God, which they had entered in a manner analogous to that in which a proselyte was initiated into the ordinary Judaism of the time.

(b) Why did Jesus receive John's baptism?

It is clear that this question caused some perplexity in the earliest days of dogmatic theology. To deal with it, Matthew inserted two verses (Mt. 3. 14 f.); John himself knew that the position was anomalous. Luke also, though he makes no such addition, seems by his rearrangement of Mark's words,[1] to take away the stress from the baptism of Jesus and to put it elsewhere, on the fact that Jesus was praying.[2] The Fourth Evangelist, though he deals at length with the Baptist, has nothing to say about the baptism of Jesus.[3] The Gospel of the Hebrews [4] deals even more explicitly with the problem. The reason for this evasiveness, argumentation and reticence is clear. It is only natural to suppose that an inferior person is baptized by a greater, who by his act confers a benefit upon the other; and confession and repentance on the part of a person supposed to be sinless are at the best unnecessary, and at the worst hypocritical. This objection must be considered, because Matthew and others have raised it. But whether they did well to raise it is another question.

The Marcan baptism narrative seemed to the later Evangelists open to the false interpretation that Jesus was a sinful man, inferior to John the Baptist; consequently they took precautions against such a mis-understanding. But it seems likely that they themselves had in the first place misunderstood Mk., and read into the story of the baptism more than it really meant. It is a very precarious assumption that the baptism narrative can be used as evidence for the psychological condition of Jesus, and Mark did not describe it as a piece of religious experience. It was, apparently, set forth at the beginning of the Gospel to assert that the person of Jesus could be understood only in terms of Messiahship and the Spirit of God; that is to say, Mark used the narrative as a Christological statement.

Mark's use of the baptism was Christological; yet the baptism was also a historical event, for it seems highly improbable that Church theologians should themselves have created the difficulty in which the

---

[1] The effect is the same if we suppose that Luke is here using a source independent of Mk.
[2] References to Jesus at prayer are especially characteristic of the third Gospel.
[3] He assumes, however, the story of the baptism in its Synoptic form (cf. Jn. 1. 32-34), and his silence is therefore the more impressive.   [4] Quoted by Jerome, Comm. on Isaiah, ch. 11. 2.

accounts of the baptism placed them. But even if we must presume an
earlier tradition which preserved the memory of the baptism as a historical
event, it is impossible on the basis of the evidence we now possess to
reconstruct the state of mind of Jesus as he went to the Jordan. Instead
of attempting to conjecture what motives may have led Jesus to baptism, it
will be more profitable simply to draw at once the one certain inference
which the relationship between Jesus and John thus set up offers.

Jesus' acceptance of John's baptism meant that he was moving in the
same circle of prophetic and eschatological concepts as the Baptist. We
have already suggested that John's baptism might be not improperly
described as the sacrament of the New Age, the means by which a holy
people of God was called out and prepared for its place in the coming
Kingdom. According to Mark, Jesus presented himself for baptism in
the same way as any other of the sons of Abraham who wished to break
with the disobedience and unfaithfulness which had brought upon them
destruction in the past and which were now holding back the promised
Kingdom, and who were minded to bind themselves together in a fresh
allegiance to God. This means that Jesus too (as of course we know was
the case) was concerned about the near approach of the Kingdom of God,
and the ethical demands which its imminence made.[1]

(c) What is the meaning of the descent of the Spirit, and of the dove
symbolism?

All the Evangelists insist that at the baptism of Jesus the Spirit descended
upon him as a dove,[2] and it is reasonable to suppose that this symbolism
had a particular significance for those who used it. Unfortunately it is
impossible now to discover certainly what that significance was. In
1910 Gunkel wrote[3] of the dove in the baptism: "This feature is so far
unexplained." After more than thirty years it remains unexplained.

Gunkel himself seems to have thought that the explanation might lie
in the field of pagan religion, for he adds:[4] "Here too there may be
mythical influence. There are ancient pictures of the gods with a dove
on their heads", and he refers to Schliemann, *Mykenae*, p. 209, and
Ohnefalsch-Richter, *Kypros*, pp. 229 f. It seems unlikely, however, that
we should look in this direction in order to understand the dove in the
Gospel narrative, though it is true that the dove was regarded as a holy
creature nearer to the Jordan than Cyprus; among the Syrians and
Phoenicians also it was regarded as a divine messenger and helper.
Direct borrowing from pagan sources on the part of Christian writers is
improbable; the tension between Christians and heathen society was by

---

[1] Matthew's variants in the baptism narrative, and his added verses, are secondary ; but the
motive supplied for the baptism—πληρῶσαι πᾶσαν δικαιοσύνην—is nevertheless worthy of consideration. It means complete obedience to every ordinance (as if δικαίωμα had been used—so
Klostermann *ad loc.*), which was according to some Rabbinic sayings necessary before the
Messiah could come (e.g. *Sanh.* 97a ; " the Messiah cannot come until the people repent and
perfectly fulfil the law"—Schürer, *Jewish People in the Time of Christ*, II. ii. 163).
[2] Mk. 1. 10 ; Mt. 3. 16 ; Lk. 3. 22 *in bodily form as a dove.*
[3] In the second edition of his *Zum religionsgeschichtlichen Verständnis des NT*, 70.   [4] *Loc. cit.*

no means such as to encourage it. There is no evidence that such ideas were transferred to Christianity by way of Judaism.

Leisegang [1] connects the descent of the Spirit with the Hellenistic idea of divine begetting which, as we have seen, he finds in the birth narratives.[2] His view may be summarized as follows. Corresponding to the account of the mysterious begetting of the body of Jesus (given in Mt. and Lk.) there is also an equivalent soul-begetting, associated with the baptism. Of this we have altogether six accounts, in Mt., Mk., Lk., Jn., the Gospel of the Ebionites and the Gospel of the Hebrews. In each of these the Spirit appears, either in the form of a dove, or as light, or as a spring, and in each case the presence of the Spirit is adduced as proof, or at least connected with the statement, that Jesus is the Son of God. The significance of the dove-form is to bring out clearly the fact that the Spirit (in Hebrew, ruaḥ) is a female principle, over against God the Father as a male principle.[3] "Nachweisbar ist es jedenfalls, dass der Geist gerade in der Gestalt einer Taube als ein weibliches Prinzip gedacht wurde." [4] This appears from the gender of περιστερά, and also from the *Acts of Thomas* 50 (47); cf. *Protev. James* 8. 1. In the canonical Gospels the mythology is suppressed, and consequently the dove is left over as an unexplained (and as it stands inexplicable) symbol. The apocryphal Gospels indicate that what originally lay behind the narrative was a begetting in the heavenly world of the aeon Jesus. The Gospel of the Hebrews makes Jesus speak directly of "My mother, the Holy Spirit". "In accordance with Hellenistic speculation we should therefore have to assume: God and the Spirit beget in heaven the spiritual (*pneumatischen*) Jesus; the spiritual Jesus flies down from heaven into the bodily Jesus after his baptism at the Jordan, which gives a mythical illustration of the words: καὶ ὁ λόγος σὰρξ ἐγένετο." [5] It is true that there is confusion here, since the dove is, in this quotation, said to represent the "spiritual Jesus", not the Spirit. But, Leisegang points out, a similar confusion may be noted in Philo. In *Q.R.D.H.* 126 the dove (τρυγών) represents divine Wisdom (θεία σοφία), and in the same book (234) the dove (τρυγών) signifies the Logos (ὁ θεοῦ λόγος). Further, baptism recalls death and resurrection: this is confirmatory evidence for the interpretation of the gift of the Spirit as an act of begetting: we may compare Acts 13. 33 where Ps. 2. 7 ("Thou art my son, this day have I begotten thee") is quoted in connection with the resurrection (if, in Acts 13. 33, ἀναστήσας refers to the resurrection—an assumption difficult to justify). "So Hellenistic mysticism weaves its threads equally into the birth, baptism and resurrection of Jesus. Each of these three events is interpreted in the same sense: as a mystical act of begetting, through which the new, spiritual (*pneumatische*) man is created, an act accomplished by the influx of divine πνεῦμα into the chosen human being, and at the same time accompanied

---

[1] *Op. cit.* 80-95. [2] Pp. 10-13.
[3] The Holy Spirit is so thought of in the Gospel according to the Hebrews.
[4] *Op. cit.* 88 f. [5] *Op. cit.* 90.

by the appearance of spirit-inspired enthusiasm. It is, however, just the motif (*Motiv*) of begetting, so closely bound up with the NT conception of the Spirit, that here radically distinguishes the πνεῦμα ἅγιον from the Spirit of God of the OT. In the OT all conceivable acts may be ascribed to the Spirit, but certainly not that of begetting." [1] Thus Leisegang proceeds with his proof that the NT conception of the Spirit was derived from pagan, non-biblical sources.

His views have been given at some length because, on one side, they are valuable and true; on another they are impossible and misleading.[2] The connection which is made between the birth, the baptism and the resurrection, by the stress laid, on each of these occasions, on the Sonship of Jesus, is important.[3] But to find in these events, or in the first two of them, a mythological sexual act, which links them with Hellenistic ideas, is to go further than the evidence warrants. It involves reading into the narratives of the canonical Gospels matter and thought derived from other sources; and to interpret the canonical by the apocryphal Gospels is historically quite unjustifiable, for the apocryphal works are demonstrably later. The Gospel of the Ebionites, for example, the only apocryphal Gospel (so far as we know) to refer to the dove, is manifestly dependent upon Lk., and perhaps on one or more of the other Gospels also. The process of manipulating the earlier canonical Gospels can be clearly seen in the conflate form of the voice from heaven; [4] in the magnification of the superiority of Jesus over John; [5] and in the confusion in the use of the dove symbolism, to which Leisegang himself refers.[6] It is quite impossible to base any serious argument on the words of the epiclesis prayer given in the late *Acts of James* 50: "Come, O communion of the male. . . . Come, she that manifesteth the hidden things and maketh the unspeakable things plain, the holy dove that beareth the twin young." These acts are Gnostic in origin, and in Gnostic circles imagination ran riot over the Holy Spirit and its relation to Jesus.[7] There is no indication

---

[1] *Op. cit.* 95.

[2] Cf. pp. 41 f.

[3] It was pointed out earlier by Harnack, *Date of the Acts*, 142-148.

[4] A voice from heaven saying: "Thou art my beloved Son, in thee I am well pleased": and again: "This day have I begotten thee."

[5] "And then John fell down before him and said: I beseech thee, Lord, baptize thou me."

[6] "The Holy Ghost in the likeness of a dove . . . he was called the Son of God from the Christ that came into him from above in the likeness of a dove." For these quotations see James, *Apocryphal NT*, 9 f.

[7] Cf., e.g., *Pistis Sophia*, 120 : (the mother of Jesus says to him) " When thou wast little, before the Spirit came over thee, there came the Spirit from on high whilst thou wert with Joseph in a vineyard. It came to me in my house in thy likeness, and I had not recognized it and I thought it was thou. And the Spirit said to me, 'Where is Jesus my brother, that I may meet him ? ' And when it said that, I was in doubt and thought it was a phantom come to tempt me. So I took it and bound it at the foot of the bed in my house, till I went out into the field to you, to thee and Joseph, and found you in the vineyard with Joseph putting up the stakes. And it came to pass that when thou heardest me tell the matter to Joseph thou didst understand and didst rejoice and say ' Where is he, that I may see him, for I am waiting for him in this place ? ' But when Joseph had heard thee say these words he was troubled, and we went back at once, we entered into the house, and found the Spirit bound on the bed. And we looked at thee and it, and found thee like it ; and the one that was bound on the bed was untied, he embraced thee and kissed thee and thou didst kiss him : you became one." This very fairly cancels out the references in the Gospel according to the Hebrews to the Holy Spirit as the mother of Jesus.

in the NT that the Spirit, whether symbolized by a dove or represented in any other way, is thought of as a female principle engaging in a sexual act; in fact, in the birth narratives, if we were to think of anything like a sexual union at all, the Spirit would have to be given the part of the male. Accordingly, we should recognize later Gnostic speculations for what they are, and find some other explanation for the data in the Synoptic Gospels.

It has been necessary, in pursuing Leisegang's theory, to digress to some extent from the question of the symbolism of the dove. It will be clear, however, that not paganism but Judaism must contain the source of this feature of the tradition.

Hellenistic Judaism offers us little material. Two passages of Philo (*Q.R.D.H.* 126 f., 234) have already been mentioned; in them the dove is allegorized as Wisdom and Logos. But it should be observed that in each case Philo distinguishes between τρυγών and περιστερά (the word used in the Gospels). The former bird, he says, loves solitude, and therefore represents the divine Word or Wisdom; the latter is domesticated and frequents the cities of men; it therefore stands for human reason. Consequently, we cannot assume any direct borrowing from Philo on the part of the Evangelists; nor is any indirect contact probable.

The metaphorical use of the dove in Palestinian Judaism is well summed up by Str.-B. [1] as follows: "In Rabbinic literature, the dove several times represents the community of Israel; that it was also treated as a symbol of the Spirit of God appears probable only to a very limited degree." The few Rabbinical references, however, which are relevant are very important and suggestive; and they are set out more convincingly by Abrahams [2] than by Str.-B. The following passages may be quoted:

Targum to Cant. 2. 12 (the voice of the turtle-dove), "the voice of the Holy Spirit of salvation ".

Bab. Ḥag. 15a [3]: Rabbi Joshua the son of Hananiah was standing on an ascent on the Temple Mount, and Ben Zoma saw him but did not stand before him. He said to him: Whence comest thou and whither go thy thoughts, Ben Zoma? He replied: I was considering the space between the upper waters and the lower waters, and there is only between them a mere three fingers' breadth, as it is said, And the Spirit of God was brooding on the face of the waters like a dove which broods over her young but does not touch them.

Rashi on Gen. 1. 2 says: The Spirit of God was moving: the Throne of glory was standing in the air and moving on the face of the waters by the Spirit of the mouth of the Holy One, blessed be he, and by his Word like a dove that broods on the nest, in French *acoveter*.

The passage in Rashi, who usually represents "orthodox" Rabbinic opinion, is cited by Abrahams against those who have understood the

---

[1] I. 123.   [2] *Studies*, I. 47-50.   [3] For other parallel references see Str.-B. I. 124.

Talmud as in general deprecating Ben Zoma's idea. "If anyone understood the spirit of the Talmud it was Rashi, and the fact that he (like other Jewish commentators) adopts the simile of the dove is of itself enough to show that Ben Zoma's simile was not considered objectionable." [1]

The connection between the Holy Spirit and the dove is thus perhaps closer than is suggested by Str.-B.; though it is certainly true that the dove has usually a different meaning, and, as Str.-B. say,[2] "In any case, there is in the older literature no passage in which the dove is plainly and clearly *a symbol* of the Holy Spirit" (my italics). Consequently, we cannot hold that the precise meaning of the dove-symbolism has been certainly determined. But it is very important that the evidence, such as it is, points to the text which we found fundamental in our discussion of the birth narratives, to Gen. 1. 2; that is to say, here too we have to deal with the creative activity of the Spirit; a new thing was being wrought in the waters of baptism comparable with the creation of heaven and earth out of primeval chaos.

It is impossible to carry further our discussion of the descent of the Spirit without consideration of the words of the voice from heaven by which it was accompanied, and which supplies a partial interpretation of it. Accordingly we must turn to our fourth question.[3]

(*d*) What is the meaning of the voice from heaven?

The notion which is conveyed by the words φωνὴ ἐκ τῶν οὐρανῶν is similar to that which is frequently described in the Rabbinical literature in the words בַּת קוֹל (*bath qol*): Aramaic בְּרַת קָלָא (*bᵉrath qala'*) or בְּרַת קָל (*bᵉrath qal*). The expression means literally "daughter of the voice" and implies the indirect hearing of a voice uttered in heaven.[4] About the use of the term *bath qol* two preliminary points must be mentioned, before the words of the voice themselves are considered.

(i) The revelation given by means of a *bath qol* is a substitute for, and is inferior to, the direct Word of God which was formerly given by the Holy Spirit (very frequently in Rabbinical sources, the Holy Spirit *of prophecy*) to a prophet. Since the days of the last prophets the Spirit had

---

[1] *Op. cit.* 49.   [2] I. 125.

[3] Eisler (*The Quest*, 1912) suggested that the Messiah was thought of as a second Noah who was to inaugurate the new era by punishment and effect a purification by a second flood; the dove in the baptism narratives becomes on this theory a clear Messianic allusion. Dr Telfer (*JTS* xxix. 238 ff.), referring to Mt. 10. 16, regards the dove as a "fitting emblem (not of God the Holy Ghost, nor of an outpouring of heavenly power, but) of the unique moral character of the ministry of Jesus". In a similar suggestion Büchsel (*Geist Gottes*, 170) says: "Perhaps it is worthy of note that Jesus appears as the lamb and his spirit as a dove, neither of them warlike animals, but both defenceless, both sacrificial, animals; both the opposite of the lion and the eagle, the warlike and royal beasts. In Mt. 10. 16 simplicity is the quality in which the dove is an ideal for the disciples of Jesus."

[4] The expression is clearly explained in Str.-B. I. 125, where the Tosaphist on *Sanh.* 11a is quoted: "One would hear not the sound which proceeded from heaven, but another sound proceeded from this sound; as when a man strikes a powerful blow and a second sound is heard, which proceeds from it (the blow) in the distance. Such a sound would one hear; hence it was called 'Daughter of the voice'." That is, the *bath qol* is an echo.

not spoken directly; Israel had only the *bath qol*. Abundant evidence for these statements is supplied in Str.-B. I. 125-128. See, for example, *T. Soṭah* 13. 2 (318): When Haggai, Zechariah and Malachi, the last prophets, died, the Holy Spirit ceased out of Israel; yet he (i.e., God) permitted it to hear the *bath qol*. Targum to Lam. 3. 38: Evil never proceeds directly out of God's mouth, but it is signified by a *bath qol* because of the deeds of violence of which the earth is full; but when God is determined upon good for the world, then it proceeds out of his holy mouth. Thus the usual notion of the *bath qol* or voice from heaven is that of an inferior substitute for inspiration by the Holy Spirit.

(ii) The sound of a *bath qol* is sometimes compared to the cry of a bird. Some evidence is given for this in Str.-B. I. 124 f., but there is a fuller treatment in Abrahams, *Studies*, I. 47-49. It is not necessary to quote at length, but we may note *Midr. Qoheleth Rabba* on Eccles. 12. 7 (explaining 12. 4): "Said R. Levi, For 18 years a daughter of the voice was making announcement and chirping[1] concerning Nebuchadnezzar." *T. b. Berach.* 3a: "I heard a *bath qol* moaning as a dove and saying: Woe to the children through whose iniquities I laid waste my Temple."

These two points help to explain the use of the dove-symbolism, and at the same time make clear that the descent of the Spirit is a unique element in the baptism story; many Rabbis had heard a voice from heaven, but the Holy Spirit had not been sent since the days of the prophets.[2] Jesus is thus brought at once out of the category of the Rabbis and into that of the prophets.

The voice is variously reported in the Synoptic Gospels. We have:

Mk. 1. 11: Thou art my son, the Beloved, in thee I am well pleased.[3]

Mt. 3. 17: This is my son, the Beloved, in whom I am well pleased.

Lk. 3. 22: Thou art my son, the Beloved, in thee I am well pleased.[4]

Two titles are ascribed to Jesus in this saying; he is the son, the only, the chosen son of God; and he is the elect servant of God. The latter

---

[1] מצפצפת (mᵉzaphzepheth)—used of a bird.

[2] Cf. the saying in *j. Soṭa* 9. 12 about Hillel: "There came forth a *bath qol* and said: There is among you a certain man worthy of the Holy Spirit, but the generation is not worthy thereof."

[3] Some MSS read "in whom" for "in thee", but this reading is due only to assimilation to Mt. Here, and in the Lucan and Matthaean parallels, I take ὁ ἀγαπητός as a Messianic title; see J. A. Robinson, *Ephesians*, 229-233; cf. R. H. Charles (quoting Robinson) on *Asc. Is.* 1. 4.

[4] Here too the reading "in whom" for "in thee" is due to assimilation to Mt. There is a much more important variant preserved in D a b c ff² l r and a considerable number of early Fathers. These authorities give, as the voice from heaven, "Thou art my son, today have I begotten thee" (i.e., a quotation of Ps. 2. 7). As we have seen above (p. 37) the Gospel of the Ebionites attests the existence of the saying in this form by giving a composite version of the voice from heaven. It has often been argued that the Western reading is the true one, and that the other is due to assimilation; but it may well be asked why, in this case, the text of Lk. has been assimilated to that of Mk. and not to that of Mt., as is usually the case in assimilations. Both forms of the saying are susceptible of an Adoptionist interpretation and we cannot therefore rule out either as an orthodox "improvement" of the other. Accordingly, our judgement in this instance must be governed by our view of the Western text as a whole; my opinion coincides with that of Dibelius (*From Tradition to Gospel*, 231 n.): "I . . . regard this form (the Western) as old, but as precanonical and unjustifiably introduced into D from the unregulated tradition."

title arises from the unmistakable allusion to Is. 42. 1; 44. 2.[1] It is not relevant to our purpose to discuss the use and significance of these titles in the NT. All that need here be attempted is to make clear the connection between them and the gift of the Spirit which is recorded in the baptism narrative. This is easy enough in the case of the Servant; for Is. 42. 1 reads: "Behold my servant, whom I uphold; my chosen, in whom my soul delighteth: I have put my spirit upon him."[2] Along with this passage should be taken Is. 11. 2; 61. 1, which were no doubt thought (by men for whom there were no Proto-, Deutero-, and Trito-Isaiahs, but only one Isaiah the son of Amoz) to refer to the same person. The declaration that Jesus is the Servant of God is inevitably accompanied by the gift of the Spirit, since the Servant must be equipped with the Spirit for the performance of his service.

It is not so easy to find any connection between the Spirit and the Son of God. It will be recalled that Leisegang[3] sought to establish such a connection by the hypothesis that the baptism narrative signified the begetting of the heavenly Christ by God and the Spirit, and the descent of this heavenly Christ upon the man Jesus. Several considerations have already been advanced which make against the probability of this view; but the most important of all may here be put forward. The words which refer to Jesus as the Son of God do so in language which is closely related not to an act of begetting, but to the process of adoption. This is suggested with much plausibility by Gunkel.[4] The pronouncement "Thou art my son" is an adoption formula; similar formulae are known to have been in use among other Semitic people.[5] The further saying in the Psalm (which becomes relevant if we accept the reading of D in Lk.), "Today have I begotten thee", in its context and by reason of the use of the word "today", must also refer to adoption, and not to actual birth. Gunkel says: "The poet has given a new meaning to (umgebogen) the word about begetting. From 'today' onward, that is, from the day of accession, the ruler will be treated by God as if he were his own child. He means that, up to the present, it was a man who was his father: from today it will be Yahweh himself."[6] This means that, in the Psalm, the speaker becomes God's son, not through an act of begetting or any analogous divine process, but by adoption on the occasion of his elevation to the throne of David.[7] Similarly, in the Gospel, Jesus at the baptism becomes, or is revealed as, Son of God, not as the result of a divine begetting but because he is then installed as King Messiah, the true successor of David. There is accordingly no need for us to find, with

---

[1] ὁ ἀγαπητός is equivalent to ὁ ἐκλεκτός, as a comparison of Is. 42. 1 and 44. 2, and the variants in Lk. 9. 35, show.

[2] We should probably see the influence of this "upon" (LXX ἐπί) in the change of Mk.'s εἰς into ἐπί which is made in both Mt. and Lk.

[3] Op. cit. 47-49.   [4] Die Psalmen (1925), 6 f.

[5] E.g., Code of Hammurabi, 170: "If . . . the father has said to the sons which the maid-servant has borne him, ' My sons ', has numbered them with the sons of his wife . . . the sons of the wife and the sons of the maidservant shall share equally." Other references in Gunkel, loc. cit.   [6] Op. cit. 7.   [7] Cf., e.g., 2 Sam. 7. 14.

Leisegang, any allusion to a Hellenistic notion of an actual begetting in the heavenly world. Our view, that the significance of the baptism is Messianic, is confirmed.[1]

If, then, the words "Thou art my son" are addressed to Jesus in virtue of the Messianic office which from the time of his baptism he assumes, their connection with the descent of the Spirit becomes easier to understand. This is suggested by several considerations.

The word מָשַׁח (mashaḥ; whence the word Messiah is derived) means *to smear*, and hence *to anoint*.[2] It is rarely used metaphorically;[3] the anointing is nearly always with a physical medium, oil, and the expression "to anoint with the Holy Spirit" is unknown in the OT. Yet the use of such language must have been very near at hand for readers of the OT, if only because of such a passage as Is. 61. 1: "The spirit of the Lord is upon me, because (יַעַן, ya'an) the Lord has anointed me." Moreover, in more primitive parts of the OT the same connection is found. When Saul, and again when David after him, is anointed (with oil) the immediate consequence is that the Spirit of the Lord begins to work upon him (1 Sam. 10. 1, 6, 10: 16. 13). Closely connected with the literal anointing with oil is a (metaphorical) anointing with Spirit.[4] Accordingly, it is not strange to find it said in Acts 10. 38 (apparently with direct allusion to the baptism) that God anointed (ἔχρισεν) Jesus with the Holy Spirit (cf. Acts 4. 26 f., where the words χριστός, χρίω are closely associated with the description of Jesus as the Servant, precisely as in the baptism narrative).

Some passages in later Jewish literature show that the obvious step of linking the person of the Messiah, the Anointed, with the "Messianic" gift of the Spirit was not omitted. The following passages may be quoted:[5]

1 Enoch 49. 3:

> In him [sc. the Elect One] dwells the Spirit of wisdom,
> And the Spirit which gives insight,
> And the Spirit of understanding and of might,
> And the Spirit of those who have fallen asleep in righteousness. (Cf. 62. 2 and Is. 11. 1 f.)

This passage is in the Similitudes of Enoch. In the same book (52. 4) the term "the Anointed" is used.

Pss. Sol. 17. 42:

> And relying upon his God, throughout his days he will not stumble;
> For God will make him mighty by means of [his] Holy Spirit,
> And wise by means of the Spirit of understanding, with strength and righteousness. (Cf. 18. 7.)

---

[1] Ps. 2. 7 was applied to the Messiah by the Rabbis; see Str.-B. III. 15-22, especially 19.
[2] See BDB 602 f.
[3] Ps. 45. 8.
[4] Cf. 1 Kings 19. 16—the anointing of Elisha to be a prophet.
[5] It is not to be supposed that the writers of all of these passages intended to refer to the Holy Spirit in anything like the Christian, or even the OT, sense. Their importance is the sense which could have been, and was, given to them by their readers.

Zadokite Fragments 2. 10:
> And through his Messiah he shall make them know his Holy Spirit.[1]

The most striking of all is in *Test. Lev.* 18. 2-14, a Messianic hymn, dating, according to Charles, from between 109 and 108 B.C. These verses are so important that it will be necessary to transcribe them in full.

2. Then shall the Lord raise up a new priest
And to him all the words of the Lord shall be revealed;
And he shall execute a righteous judgement upon the earth for a multitude of days.

3. And his star shall arise in heaven as of a king,
Lighting up the light of knowledge as the sun the day.
And he shall be magnified in the world.

4. He shall shine forth as the sun on the earth,
And shall remove all darkness from under heaven,
And there shall be peace in all the earth.

5. The heavens shall exult in his days,
And the earth shall be glad,
And the clouds shall rejoice;
And the knowledge of the Lord shall be poured forth upon the earth, as the waters of the seas;
And the angels of the glory of the presence of the Lord shall be glad in him.

6. The heavens shall be opened,
And from the temple of glory shall come upon him sanctification,
With the Father's voice as from Abraham to Isaac.

7. And the glory of the Most High shall be uttered over him,
And the spirit of understanding and sanctification shall rest upon him in the water.

8. For he shall give the majesty of the Lord to his sons in truth for evermore;
And there shall none succeed him for all generations for ever.

9. And in his priesthood the Gentiles shall be multiplied in knowledge upon the earth,
And enlightened through the grace of the Lord.
In his priesthood shall sin come to an end,
And the lawless shall cease to do evil.
And the just shall rest in him.

10. And he shall open the gates of paradise,
And shall remove the threatening sword against Adam.

11. And he shall give to the saints to eat from the tree of life,
And the spirit of holiness shall be on them.

12. And Beliar shall be bound by him,
And he shall give power to his children to tread upon evil spirits.

13. And the Lord shall rejoice in his children,
And be well pleased in his beloved ones for ever.

14. Then shall Abraham and Isaac and Jacob exult,
And I will be glad,
And all the saints shall clothe themselves with joy.

---

[1] Bacher proposes to read " by his Holy Spirit ".

With this passage we may compare *Test. Jud.* 24. 2 f. The latter passage is preserved in two texts:[1]

αβ S 1:

2. And the heavens shall be opened unto him,
   To pour out the spirit, (even) the blessing of the Holy Father;

3. And he shall pour out the spirit of grace upon you;
   And ye shall be unto him sons in truth,
   And ye shall walk in his commandments first and last.

A:

2. And the heavens shall be opened unto him,
   And the blessings of the Holy Father shall be poured down upon him.

3. And he will pour down upon us the spirit of grace.
   And ye shall be his true children by adoption,
   And ye shall walk in his commandments first and last.

These passages from the Testaments seem to bear a close relationship to the Gospels, not merely in respect of the baptism narrative but in other particulars also. Charles, however, in his commentary does not consider that the verses in question are a Christian interpolation (except the words "in the water" in *Test. Lev.* 18. 7b, which are omitted by one MS). It is true that there is nothing in them that could not have been written by the original author of the Testaments. If they are to be considered pre-Christian, we must see here very important evidence that the Messianic office was associated with a particular endowment of the Spirit; and at the same time we should recognize a document which, as it influenced Christian literature in other respects, may also have helped to mould the baptism narratives into their present form.[1]

We may note also at this point the saying ascribed by Justin to Trypho the Jew, that the Messiah would not become known until he had been anointed by Elijah.[2]

The connection between the sonship of Jesus and the descent of the Spirit may now be said to be established. Jesus is addressed as the newly established son of God in virtue of his installation as Messiah; this Messianic office involves a personal endowment of the Holy Spirit which it was believed would be poured out in the last days. Accordingly, it appears that the Messiahship, since it underlies the office of Jesus as the Servant of the Lord, his status as son of God and the descent upon him of the Spirit, is the key to the understanding of the baptism narrative, and apart from it the whole event, as it is recorded in the Gospels, is meaningless. It is impossible to take away this element and discover a coherent account of a baptism, an inspiration, otherwise conceived. Even in form, as Dr Bultmann has shown, the narrative is different from the prophetic "calls" which are found in both OT and NT.[3]

[1] See note on p. 45.
[2] See Charles, *Ap. and Ps.* II. 324, for the symbols used.   [3] Justin, *Dialogue* 8.
[4] Bultmann, *GST* 263 f. : "One ought not, however, to psychologize and speak of the narrative of a call (*Berufungsgeschichte*) or even describe its content as a call given through a vision (*Berufungsvision*). It is characteristically distinguished . . . from the narrative of a call

It is perhaps too much to hope that final answers should be given to the questions which have been raised here. We have, however, surveyed the relevant evidence, and it suggests results which may be tentatively stated as follows:

The work of the Spirit is to call into being part of the New Creation of the Messianic days, namely, to inaugurate the ministry of the Messiah, and this Messianic conception underlies the whole intention and significance of the narrative, and stands in a closely interlocking unity with the conception of the Spirit involved. Here, as in the birth narratives, the Spirit is the creative activity of God which calls into being the conditions of the Messianic era. If, with Mark, we trace the origins of the Messiah to the beginning of his ministry, they must be described in the terms of the baptism—the descent of the Spirit upon Jesus and his inauguration thereby to the office of Messiahship. If, with the later Evangelists, we consider an earlier stage of the Messiah's career, his birth as a human being, we find precisely the same essential features, the descent of the Spirit (Lk. 1. 35) and the formation, by the power of the Spirit, of the Messiah—Son of God (Lk. 1. 35b; Mt. 1. 20).[1]

such as Is. 6. 1-13; Jer. 1. 5-19; Ezek. 1 and 2; Acts 9. 1-9; Lk. 5. 1-11; Rev. 1. 9-20; Jn. 21. 15-17; not only is there no word about the inner state of Jesus, but there is also lacking any word of commission to the person called, and any answer from his side—features so characteristic of real narratives of call. Nor indeed is Jesus' real mission referred to, which is the preaching of repentance and salvation, but his Messiahship or divine sonship, which cannot be described as a mission. . . . The legend narrates Jesus' initiation to the Messiahship, and is thus fundamentally not a biographical legend but a legend of faith."

[1] The Fourth Evangelist begins his Gospel at an even earlier stage, and speaks of the pre-existence of the Word in language which recalls speculation about the Logos, Sophia, and the Spirit.

Note. The question of the Christian editing of the Testaments is more complicated than appeared when this book was first published. The serious consideration it deserves cannot, however, be given to it here.

4

CONFLICT WITH EVIL SPIRITS—TEMPTATION AND EXORCISM

WE have now considered the activity of the Spirit of God in the conception and at the baptism of Jesus. We have seen reason to believe that here the work of the Spirit has a profound theological significance, that is to say, it was regarded as an important factor in God's dealing with the world, and one which had its place in the eschatological world-view; but the effects of the Spirit were not those commonly attributed to it and observable as activities of the human mind. This is plainly so with regard to the birth of Jesus; the new-born child cannot be called inspired.[1] It is true also in the baptism; for, as we have suggested, the baptism is to be thought of as the installation of the Messiah rather than as a prophetic calling and endowment. Now, however, as we proceed to consider the ministry of Jesus, psychological expressions of the possession of the Spirit come into view. In the primitive Church the gift of the Spirit was certainly accompanied by psychological activities expressed in speech or act, such as prophecy, glossolalia, and the other gifts described by St Paul.[2] One might well expect it to be the same with Jesus; and so it was.

It might be said rather more accurately that in this section of the Gospel material, which deals with the conflict between Jesus and the powers of evil, the two categories of thought, theological and psychological, overlap, since the conflict is represented from both points of view. There is on the one hand the conflict between God and Satan, between the Kingdom of God and the power of Beelzebul; and on the other the manifest disorders of the human spirit ascribed in the time of Jesus to demon possession. In these two ways the tension of good and evil is expressed, in the one instance theologically, in the other psychologically; and both are taken up in the passages of the Gospels which fall now to be considered. The theological aspect of the conflict is stressed in the temptation narrative, the psychological in the exorcisms.

THE TEMPTATION: Mk. 1. 12 f.; Mt. 4. 1-11; Lk. 4. 1-13. Cf. the Gospel according to the Hebrews in Origen, *On John*, 2. 12, and *On Jeremiah*, hom. 15. 4.

It appears that there are two narratives of the Temptation with which we have to deal, one given by Mark, the other contained in a source used by both Matthew and Luke. The Marcan account is much shorter

---

[1] Contrast the inspiration of the other characters in the nativity stories, who, being filled with the Spirit, prophesy and praise God.
[2] See 1 Cor. 12, 14.

46

than that which Mt. and Lk. have substantially in common, and it is sometimes held that what Mk. presents is merely an abbreviated version of that which is given by the other Evangelists *in extenso*. But this seems unlikely in view of the facts that (*a*) Mt. and Lk. both use the word (ἀν)άγω, against Mk.'s ἐκβάλλω (which in Hellenistic Greek need not be regarded as a strong and unsuitable word); (*b*) Mk. has no reference to the fasting and hunger which are an integral part of the narrative in Mt. and Lk.;[1] (*c*) Mk. does not use the term διάβολος, which occurs in the opening sentences of both Mt. and Lk.; (*d*) Mk. includes the two features of Christ's being with the wild beasts and his being served by angels, the former of which is found in neither Mt. nor Lk., the latter in Mt. only.

From these facts we ought to conclude[2] that we possess two independent accounts of the Temptation, one given by Mk., the other belonging to the Q material; though Matthew may have taken from Mk. the ministry of the angels, and Luke, perhaps, the phrase (4. 2) πειραζόμενος ὑπὸ τοῦ....

There is no difference in motive and meaning between the two temptation narratives, and it is particularly striking that both begin with a reference to the Holy Spirit; unless indeed this feature has been derived by Matthew and Luke from Mk. and not from their common source. In any case, Matthew and Luke must have thought such a reference not inconsistent with their non-Marcan material. We may begin by considering the longer and more explicit account, that of Mt. and Lk.

The temptations of Jesus have often been explained as due to a natural mental reaction to the events of the preceding narrative of the baptism. So (to choose one example out of many) Plummer[3] says: "It is the common experience of mankind that times of special spiritual endowment or exaltation are followed by occasions of special temptation. The Messiah is no exception. No sooner is He anointed with the Spirit for the work of the Ministry than He has to undergo a fierce conflict with the great personal power of evil." In the Q narrative there is some apparent justification for this view, for the several temptations are described in pictorial-psychological form.

By other scholars[4] the temptations are regarded as similar to those ascribed in other religious literature to other holy men. Thus Abraham is tempted (Gen. 22. 1); Buddha is tempted by Mara.[5] The motive for the inclusion of the temptation narrative in the Gospel tradition would then become that of the example story; the Christians are to resist and overcome temptation as did the Lord (and in the same way—by the use of Scripture, Jas. 4. 7; 1 Pet. 5. 9). Another motive which should not be ignored is that of apologetic. The Church had to face such questions as, Why was the alleged Messiah poor and in physical need? Why did he not afford unmistakable signs of his power and authority? Why did

---

[1] Note the first temptation.
[3] *Exegetical Commentary on St Matthew*, 35.
[5] *SBE* X. ii. 69-72.
[2] With Streeter, *Four Gospels*, 187 f.
[4] E.g., Bultmann, *GST* 270 ff.

he not unite his nation for the purpose of world conquest? To these questions the temptation narrative supplied convenient answers.

Nevertheless, we have not yet arrived at a sufficient understanding of the temptations as they stand in the Synoptic tradition. To regard the temptations as mental reaction from a spiritual illumination, a trough of doubt and despondency following a crest of certainty, is a quite inadequate view of the Evangelists' intention. They were not novelists of the psychological school, and they very rarely or never pause to depict the inner mind of Jesus and to discuss his feelings. Besides, the more strongly we hold the baptism to be an event used by the Evangelists to explain the person of Jesus, that is, for a theological purpose, rather than a zenith of religious experience, the less justification is there for regarding the temptations as the corresponding nadir. Again, it seems improbable that the temptations were recorded simply as moral paraenesis. They are not well adapted to this end. Early Christian ethical instruction was usually quite pointedly applied to the particular situations to which it was directed; and, though some of the believers may, as has been suggested, have been inclined to overestimate the importance of the miraculous, it is unlikely that they were tempted to turn stones into bread or to fly down from a pinnacle of the Temple. In the OT, moreover (and this, rather than Buddhist literature, is decisive for NT interpretation) the righteous, or the people of God, are tested not by any of the powers of evil, but by God himself.[1] The suggestion that the temptation narratives have an apologetic motive is more cogent, and may possibly represent part of the truth;[2] but it hardly supplies a complete motivation, and leaves unexplained the most characteristic features of the narratives.

The true interpretation of the temptations is succinctly expressed by Montefiore:[3] "Both in Mk. and in Q the temptation is 'Messianic,' i.e., it is the temptation of the Messiah, not of an ordinary individual." The psychological form of the narrative is only superficial, and is the medium of a myth, in its essentials not uncommon in religion, which deals with a battle among divine beings for dominion over the world. The victorious protagonist is the newly appointed Messiah. It is he who is attacked by Satan as no other could be; he only could be tempted to establish himself over against God as an independent divine being. His opponent is variously described as ὁ διάβολος, ὁ πειράζων and ὁ Σατανᾶς. The first and third of these terms (and no doubt the second also) are synonyms in the usage of both the NT and the LXX, where διάβολος wherever it occurs (except in two places) does so as a rendering of שָׂטָן

[1] See, for example, Gen. 22. 1; Exod. 15. 25; 16. 4; 20. 20; Deut. 8. 2; 13. 4; Judg. 2. 22; 3. 1, 4; the case of Job, where the word "tempt" (נִסָּה, niṣṣah; πειράζω) is not used, is no exception, for there Satan is not regarded as a distinct evil power, but as a subordinate minister of God himself; elsewhere, the "proving" is done by an evil power, e.g., in Judg. 3. 1 ff., the Canaanites, but even so, this lies within the purpose of God.

[2] The suggestion would carry greater weight if the temptation narratives had ever been used apologetically by early Christian writers; but apparently this was not so.

[3] *Synoptic Gospels*, 2nd ed., I. 20.

(saṭan). There is no need to trace in detail the history of this word, or to decide whether its accepted derivation and meaning, "accuser", is or is not to be preferred to the etymology given by Dr Torczyner,[1] who explains it as originally the roving eye of God, i.e., his travelling police officer who reports on the political loyalty of his subjects.[2] It is sufficient to remark that in the beginning the Satan was a member of the heavenly court, i.e., a spiritual being, and that in course of time his office developed from public prosecutor to public enemy. Under various names (Beliar, Sammael, Mastema) a Satan, or prince of evil, appears in later Jewish literature as an opponent of God, or as an Antichrist.[3]

If it be true (and further evidence will be brought to show that it is) that the Q temptations are essentially Messianic, the same is a fortiori true of the Marcan temptation, which has no psychological or ethical motivation. Wellhausen indeed said:[4] "The temptation of Jesus has in Q a definitely Messianic character. . . . In Mk. the temptation at this place (1. 12, 13) is not Messianic. The Messianic temptation, according to Mk., does not come after the baptism, but only after the confession of Peter." But, though there is an important parallel between the Q temptation and Mk. 8. 32 f., this position cannot be maintained; if the Marcan temptation be not Messianic it is impossible to understand it at all.[5]

We may turn next to examine the details of the two temptation narratives, with regard first to their setting, then to the temptations themselves (in Q).

(a) In all three Gospels Jesus at the time of the Temptation is under the influence of the Spirit. Mk. has τὸ πνεῦμα αὐτὸν ἐκβάλλει; Mt. ἀνήχθη . . . ὑπὸ τοῦ πνεύματος; Lk. πλήρης πνεύματος ἁγίου . . . ἤγετο ἐν τῷ πνεύματι. The expressions in Mt. and Lk. seem to indicate that Jesus acted under the constraint of the Spirit, perhaps even implying, as Easton[6] says, "an ecstatic condition". Jesus faces his opponent fully and manifestly equipped with divine power.[7]

(b) The scene of the Temptation is the wilderness (ἡ ἔρημος), a favourite habitation of demons.[8] The temptations, carried out by the chief of the demons, are thus brought into contact with the exorcisms.

(c) Jesus (according to Mk.) was with the wild beasts. This feature of the narrative has been explained in several ways.[9] (1) It may be a reminiscence of the friendly relation between Adam and the beasts in the Garden of Eden before the fall.[10] The Messiah in his victory over Satan restores the blissful conditions of primeval times, before the entry of sin into the world. (2) The presence of wild animals may be intended

---

[1] ET 48, 563 ff.   [2] Justin (Dial. c. Tryph. 103) has another very curious etymology.
[3] See R. H. Charles, Revelation (I.C.C.), ii. 76-87.   [4] Einleitung, 1st ed. 74 ; 2nd ed. 65 f.
[5] Cf. Harnack, The Sayings of Jesus, 195 n. 2.   [6] Gospel according to St Luke, 46.
[7] πλήρης πνεύματος is a characteristically Lucan phrase.
[8] See the evidence in Str.-B. IV. 516d.   [9] Cf. Klostermann on Mk. 1. 13.
[10] Cf. Joachim Jeremias in TWNT I. 141, s.v. Ἀδάμ.

simply to emphasize the loneliness of the place; the struggle took place in the complete absence of human beings, attended only by brutes. Cf. Is. 13. 21; 2 Macc. 5. 27. (3) Dominion over the beasts is sometimes (see the passages cited below) associated with conquest over Satan; this may be the case here. The Messianic prophecies in Is. 11. 6; Ezek. 34. 25 are important here, and we should also compare Ps. 91. 11-13 and Job 5. 23. In all these passages the wild beasts have, in different ways, ceased to be dangerous. In the Testaments of the XII Patriarchs, which seem to have influenced the NT so widely, we find side by side the discomfiture of evil spirits and the submission of the animals.

Test. Issach. 7. 7 :

> Every spirit of Beliar shall flee from you,
> And no deed of wicked men shall rule over you;
> And every wild beast shall ye subdue.

Test. Benj. 5. 2 :

If ye do well, even the unclean spirits will flee from you, and the beasts will dread you.

But we may note especially *Test. Napht.* 8. 4 :

> If ye work that which is good, my children,
> Both men and angels shall bless you;
> And God shall be glorified among the Gentiles through you,
> And the devil shall flee from you,   [cf. Jas. 4. 7]
> And the wild beasts shall fear you,
> And the Lord shall love you,
> And the angels shall cleave to you.

The last line is omitted by Charles for reasons of parallelism; but the association of angels, beasts and the devil is very striking; cf. Ps. 91. 11-13.

There is no reason why (1) and (3) should not be combined in the exegesis of this reference to the wild beasts. It is precisely as the Second Adam, the Heavenly Man, that Jesus effects the eschatological conquest over Satan, which results in a salvation that means the restoration of primeval bliss. This interpretation is attractive, but it would be dangerous to pronounce definitely in favour of it against (2).

(*d*) With regard to the angels, the essence of the true interpretation was given by Clement of Alexandria : [1] ὡς ἂν ἤδη βασιλεὺς ἀληθὴς ὑπ' ἀγγέλων ἤδη διακονεῖται. As King Messiah, Jesus is attended in his war with Satan by angels; cf. Mt. 26. 53. Mk., who says nothing about a fast, and whose imperfect tense διηκόνουν seems to imply a constant ministry throughout the forty days, probably had such a service in mind; cf. Mk. 8. 38; 13. 27, and the passages from the OT and Pseudepigrapha quoted above under (*c*). Mt., on the other hand, who places the service of the angels at the close of the forty days (4. 11), may have thought of a miraculous feeding by angels, such as Elijah enjoyed (1 Kings 19. 5). We may compare also the gift of Manna in the wilderness, referred to

[1] *Exc. Theod.* 85.

in Ps. 78. 25 as the food of angels (אַבִּירִים, 'abbirim). The angels are the counterpart of the wilderness-demons.

(e) Jesus (according to Mt. and Lk.) fasts during the temptations. The detail is probably added as a motivation for the first temptation; it may also have been intended to recall the fasts of Moses (Exod. 34. 28; Deut. 9. 9) and of Elijah (1 Kings 19. 8).

(f) The period of forty days (in any case, a biblical round number) is probably a further reference to the fasts just mentioned, which also lasted forty days. A parallel may be intended also with the forty years of temptation which Israel underwent in the wilderness.[1]

(g) All the Gospels agree in using the word $\pi\epsilon\iota\rho\dot{\alpha}\zeta\omega$ to describe the temptation of Jesus. This word is used in the LXX as an equivalent of נִסָּה (niṣṣah). The Hebrew and Greek words precisely correspond. Both mean "to make trial of", "to attempt", and "to test"—a person. The last of these meanings is, of course, that which is used in the temptation narratives. In the OT we must distinguish two chief classes among the passages in which the word is used. First come those in which God tempts, i.e., tests, men. We may mention as examples Gen. 22. 1, where God tests Abraham by requiring the sacrifice of the son who was the only vehicle of the promised seed; Deut. 8. 2, which refers to the forty years of trial in the wilderness, and the Manna; and Ps. 26. 2, where the Psalmist, conscious of his own integrity, calls upon God to test him. In the second class the rôles are reversed, and man (presumptuously) puts God to the test. Here we may quote Exod. 17. 2; Num. 14. 22; Deut. 33. 8; Ps. 78. 41, 56; 95. 9; 106. 14, all referring to the period of wandering in the wilderness. It is probably not wrong to see a reference to both of these forms of temptation in the forty days' trial of Jesus in the wilderness. As man he is tempted by the agent of God, that his faithfulness, his dependence upon God, may be revealed; at the same time, in tempting Jesus, Satan is tempting God (Mt. 4. 7=Lk. 4. 12, $\dot{\epsilon}\kappa\pi\epsilon\iota\rho\dot{\alpha}\zeta\omega$). There is no eschatological reference in the use of either $\pi\epsilon\iota\rho\dot{\alpha}\zeta\omega$ or $\pi\epsilon\iota\rho\alpha\sigma\mu\dot{o}\varsigma$ in the OT. But in the NT itself there is some suggestion that the word had an apocalyptic connotation. This is particularly clear in 2 Pet. 2. 9 where $\pi\epsilon\iota\rho\alpha\sigma\mu o\hat{v}$ seems to be used in parallel with $\dot{\eta}\mu\dot{\epsilon}\rho\alpha\nu$ $\kappa\rho\dot{\iota}\sigma\epsilon\omega\varsigma$; cf. Rev. 3. 10. But if we are to find eschatological significance in the temptation narrative it must be on the basis of what takes place, not on the mere use of the word $\pi\epsilon\iota\rho\dot{\alpha}\zeta\omega$.

We need not consider at so great a length the details of the temptations which are actually set before Jesus. They are unmistakably Messianic. The first (as the reply shows) points back to the giving of Manna as food for the people of God; and it was expected that in the Messianic Kingdom

---

[1] The parallel between the testing of Israel, God's son, and that of Jesus, also God's son, is stressed by Dubose, *The Gospel in the Gospels*, 35-41.

the supply of Manna would be renewed.[1] To explain the second temptation (Matthaean order) another tradition has been noted, that "When
the King Messiah reveals himself, he comes and stands on the roof of
the Temple".[2] But there is no need to suppose that the Gospel depends
upon this tradition. The temptation is simply to perform a compulsive
sign, to put the fact of the Messiahship beyond all possible doubt. The
third temptation (Matthaean order) is also peculiarly Messianic. The
high mountain is neither "a visionary conception as Rev. 21. 10; Apoc.
Bar. 76. 3", nor "an originally mythical mountain of the gods", nor a
"fairy-tale motif".[3] It is Pisgah, the mountain whence Moses viewed
the promised land. So from this mountain Jesus has in prospect a possible
kingdom [4] which he rejects: the Messianic Kingdom was not to be
acquired by submission to Satan.

The temptations are all answered by Jesus (and one of them is addressed
to him) in terms of Scripture. The conversation between Jesus and the
devil reads almost like a Rabbinic controversy, in which the missiles are
proof texts. It is true that the Torah was thought of as in some sense a
weapon against the angel of death,[5] but the form of the temptation
narrative is certainly much more akin to a debate in the Schools than to
a war of gods and spirits.

The temptation narratives are indeed compounded of very diverse
elements. Their basis is mythical; it is the old story of a war of the gods,
adapted to a particular Messianic conflict. The devil is defeated, but
he is not destroyed. The Church was too well acquainted with his
devices to suppose that Satan had died. The Messianic Kingdom had an
activity neither unrestricted nor unopposed. The mythical, Messianic
basis of the narratives is treated in a psychological manner. Jesus faces
the devil under the inspiration of the Spirit, which leads him to the
conflict, thus transferred from the world of the gods to the field of the
mind. The ancient saga (which appears in various forms) of a battle
between God (or the gods) and the devil, and the account of an inward
experience of the human mind, are both pictorial, and inadequate,
means of setting forth the conflict between good and evil which was
brought to a crisis in the ministry of Jesus. In the conflict itself he
appears in the rôle which we know he filled, that of a teacher, arguing
from Scripture. The outcome of the struggle, which clearly points
toward the exorcism narratives which we shall shortly consider, is what
may conveniently be described as the Messianic secret. He who from
the time of the baptism *is* Messiah cannot by any outward sign declare
his title, or enter forcibly upon his Kingdom. This is apparently the
force of his refusal to work compulsive Messianic signs. Hence, as we

---

[1] We need not distinguish between the two views which were held : (i) fresh supplies of
Manna were prepared in the third heaven : Ḥag. 12b, 2 Baruch 29. 8 ; (ii) the golden pot of
Manna, which, with the ark, had disappeared, was to be restored : Tanḥ. 83b, et al.
[2] Psiq. R. 36 (162a) ; Str.-B. I. 151.   [3] Klostermann, Matthäusevangelium, 29.
[4] All the kingdoms of the earth ; cf. Rev. 11. 15.   [5] Str.-B. I. 149.

shall see, he commands the demons to be silent, and keeps his cures secret. From this point, with the exception of one or two instances, we hear no more of Jesus acting in, or under the influence of, the Spirit. He is a *hidden* Messiah, not revealed by specifically Messianic works or an evidently Messianic endowment of the Spirit.

THE EXORCISMS

Examination of the OT reveals very little that is parallel to the NT stories of the exorcism of demons. The stories of Elijah and Elisha furnish miracles enough which both in content and in form have not a little in common with the pericopae of the Gospels; but neither casts out an evil spirit. The OT passage most closely resembling the exorcisms of the Synoptic Gospels is 1 Sam. 16. 14-23. The Spirit of the Lord, which formerly had governed Saul's activity as King of Israel, was removed from him, and its place was taken from time to time by an evil spirit (also from the Lord) which seems to have produced periods of melancholy. It was suggested that these attacks might be cured by music and David was called to play on the harp. "And it came to pass when the spirit from God was upon Saul, that David took the harp and played with his hand: and so Saul was refreshed, and the evil spirit departed from him" (16. 23). Even this, however, is a poor parallel, though it does represent a spirit or demon taking possession of a man and being driven from its dwelling.

The reason for this paucity of parallels is very probably the simple one that OT thought was deficient in a convenient demonology. Belief in spirits, malignant as well as beneficent, was no doubt common from the earliest times,[1] but the demons were associated with particular natural objects and territories rather than thought of as free to take up their abode in a human being from whom they might in turn be ejected by a stronger spiritual power. A fuller demonology does not seem to have arisen until the Persian period, and under foreign influence.[2]

It is interesting to observe that Josephus, in his paraphrase of the incident recorded in 1 Sam. 16, regards it as the expulsion of demons. Saul, he says,[3] was subject to $\pi\acute{a}\theta\eta$ $\tau\iota\nu\grave{a}$ $\kappa\alpha\grave{\iota}$ $\delta\alpha\iota\mu\acute{o}\nu\iota\alpha$[4] and the demons which caused his trouble were removed by David's playing. Elsewhere[5] the same incident is referred to and the spirits are called $\pi o\nu\eta\rho\grave{o}\nu$ $\pi\nu\epsilon\hat{v}\mu\alpha$ and $\delta\alpha\iota\mu\acute{o}\nu\iota\alpha$. Josephus speaks also of Solomon's pre-eminent power over demons ($\tau\grave{\eta}\nu$ $\kappa\alpha\tau\grave{a}$ $\tau\hat{\omega}\nu$ $\delta\alpha\iota\mu\acute{o}\nu\omega\nu$ $\tau\acute{e}\chi\nu\eta\nu$), and adds that his skill can still be used, giving as an example a cure performed in the presence of Vespasian, in which a demon ($\delta\alpha\iota\mu\acute{o}\nu\iota o\nu$— Josephus seems to use $\delta\alpha\acute{\iota}\mu\omega\nu$ and its diminutive synonymously) is

---

[1] See, for example, Robertson Smith, *Religion of the Semites*, Lectures II and III.

[2] No different result is obtained by using the Greek instead of the Hebrew OT; for $\pi\nu\epsilon\hat{v}\mu\alpha$ is used as an almost exact equivalent of רוח (ruaḥ), and $\delta\alpha\acute{\iota}\mu\omega\nu$ and $\delta\alpha\iota\mu\acute{o}\nu\iota o\nu$, which occur but rarely, are not used of spirits said to possess men. [3] *Ant.* 6. 8. 2 (166).

[4] Both Josephus ($\pi\nu\iota\gamma\mu o\grave{v}s$ $\alpha\grave{v}\tau\hat{\omega}$ $\kappa\alpha\grave{\iota}$ $\sigma\tau\rho\alpha\gamma\gamma\acute{a}\lambda\alpha s$ $\epsilon\pi\iota\phi\acute{e}\rho o\nu\tau\alpha$) and the LXX ($\epsilon\pi\nu\iota\gamma\epsilon\nu$ ... $\pi\nu\acute{\iota}\gamma\epsilon\iota$, 1 Sam. 16. 14 f.) seem to take בעת (b-'-th) =strangle. [5] *Ant.* 6. 11. 2 (211).

drawn out of a patient's nose by a ring having under the seal a root
mentioned by Solomon. The demon attests its departure by upsetting
a bowl of water.[1]

The OT Apocrypha and Pseudepigrapha, though later and more
exposed to foreign influence than the greater part of the OT, supply
hardly any exorcism narratives, though 1 *Enoch*, for example,[2] reveals
the same background of demonology as is manifest in the NT. The
one real story of demon expulsion (Tobit 6. 4 - 8. 3) is frankly magical:
the demon succumbs to the smoke of the heart and liver of a fish, applied
under the direction of the angel Raphael.[3]

In the Rabbinical literature, however, we find a wealth of allusion to
demons and their harmful activities among men. Here, too, methods
of dealing with evil spirits are known, and Solomon, as in Josephus,
is the most notable of exorcists. The demons are the cause of illness,
and exorcism means restoration to health. These points, with many
others, are illustrated at length in Str.-B. IV. 501-535, and there is no
need here to repeat the evidence.[4] But it is very important to note the
observations of I. Abrahams:[5] "It is in the Babylonian Talmud that
we find an appalling mass of demonology which, though it stands in relation
to earlier beliefs—Biblical, Apocalyptic and Rabbinical—cannot properly
be cited as applicable to the time of Jesus in the Holy Land. . . . Probably,
therefore, the Pharisees were amazed at the attitude and actions of
Jesus, so that it is intelligible that Jesus was afterwards called a 'magician'
(Sabbath, 104b), though subsequent schools of Pharisaism would have
been less amazed than his contemporaries were. . . . There was between
the years 150 and 450 a great increase in Jewish circles in the belief in
demons and their influence." Nevertheless, full weight on the other
hand must be given to the saying in the Gospels, "By whom do your sons
cast them out?" (Mt. 12. 27; Lk. 11. 19). The facts to which Abrahams
draws attention account (as we shall see) for silence in Rabbinic literature
on some subjects where otherwise it would not, perhaps, have been
expected.

Demons were equally well known in the pagan world, and there is
abundant evidence for belief in demon possession in both literary and
non-literary texts. In the latter category we are now well supplied with
charms and other instructions for exorcists in the different collections
of magical papyri which have been published.[6] Some of the best illustra-
tions in the former class are to be found in Philostratus' *Life of Apollonius
of Tyana*,[7] many of whose miracles are not unlike those related about
Jesus. For example, at Athens,[8] a youth who, unknown to himself, was

---

[1] *Ant.* 8. 2. 5 (45-48).   [2] See Charles, *Ap. and Ps.* II. 185.
[3] This, as Joh. Weiss (*RE* 4, 417) pointed out, is not properly a case of possession.
[4] Cf. also Oesterley, *Jews and Judaism during the Greek Period*, 278-289 ; and in *Judaism and
Christianity : The Age of Transition*, 100-209.   [5] *Studies*, I. 110 f.
[6] E.g., A. Dieterich, *Eine Mithrasliturgie* (1903), and the same author's *Abraxas* (1891) ; and
see Deissmann, *Light from the Ancient East*, 251 ff., 304 ff.
[7] It is possible that the " Life " was a conscious parody, or " improvement," of the Gospels.
[8] *Life*, 4. 20.

possessed by a demon, mocks at Apollonius. The latter recognizes what is taking place and says: "οὐ σὺ ... ταῦτα ὑβρίζεις, ἀλλ' ὁ δαίμων ..." A description of symptoms is given, and Apollonius then commands the demon to leave the youth, giving a sign of his departure. The demon submits: "τὸν δεῖνα, ἔφη, καταβαλῶ ἀνδριάντα." The statue is duly overturned, to the astonishment of the onlookers, and a further proof of the completeness of the cure is given by the fact that the young man himself from that time dons the philosopher's cloak. There is no need here to point out how many of the details of this narrative may be paralleled in the NT. We might compare also Lucian, *Philopseudes*, 16.

The Gospel Narratives. In analysing these narratives it is important to distinguish clearly between the features which the NT exorcisms have in common with similar Rabbinic and pagan stories, and those which are peculiar to them. Almost all the Synoptic narratives of exorcisms occur in Mk. Most of them are taken over by at least one (often both) of the later Evangelists, but there seem to have been only one or two such narratives in Q and none in M or L,[1] though there are important sayings about the conflict with the powers of evil in Q and L. Many of the Marcan references to exorcisms are to be found in the summaries which occur frequently in that Gospel (e.g. Mk. 1. 34, 39; 3. 11 f.).

The general features of the exorcism narratives may be summarized as follows. Almost without exception they have parallels in non-Christian documents.

(a) Details are given to prove that the demoniac is in a very grievous state, or that he has been possessed for a long time. Thus in Mk. 5. 2-5 the plight of the Gerasene demoniac is described: he lives, solitary, in the tombs; he cannot be bound, but breaks any fetters that are fastened upon him; he shouts, and cuts (? beats) himself with stones. In Mk. 9. 17 f. the symptoms of the epileptic boy are narrated, and it is also pointed out that the disciples had been unable to cure him—so bad was his case. The deformed woman of Lk. 13. 10-17 had been bound by Satan eighteen years (13. 11, 16). There are corresponding descriptions in pagan stories. It will be sufficient to notice Philostratus, *Life of Apollonius of Tyana*, 3. 38: a demon, subsequently to be expelled by Apollonius, drives a boy into the wilderness (ἐς τὰ ἔρημα τῶν χωρίων ἐκτρέπει).

(b) The demons recognize in Jesus their destroyer, himself a supernatural being. This feature is frequently attested in the Gospels; see Mk. 1. 24; 3. 11; 5. 7. It appears also in other literature; we need refer only to the incident in the life of Apollonius just mentioned, in which the demon, without even seeing Apollonius, knows his power. That the demon should speak to the exorcist appears to be a normal event; cf.

---

[1] In Lk. 13. 10-17 the woman suffering from curvature of the spine (? συγκύπτουσα) is said to have a πνεῦμα ἀσθενείας, and to have been bound by Satan; her cure therefore approximates to an exorcism.

Lucian, *Philopseudes*, 16, ὁ μὲν νοσῶν αὐτὸς σιωπᾷ, ὁ δαίμων δὲ ἀπο-
κρίνεται ἑλληνίζων ἢ βαρβαρίζων ὁπόθεν ἂν αὐτὸς ᾖ, ὅπως τε καὶ
ὅθεν εἰσῆλθεν εἰς τὸν ἄνθρωπον.

(c) Jesus addresses the demon, often to rebuke it, and enjoin silence:
Mk. 1. 25; 3. 12; 4. 39 (since the wind is regarded as a demon); 9. 25.
Once Jesus inquires the demon's name—Mk. 5. 9. With these features
Bultmann [1] compares Lucian, *Philops.* 16; *Acts of Thomas*, 31-33; 45 f.;
75-77; Pap. Osl. Fasc., I. 1925, No. 1, 7. 164; cf. also Rohde, *Psyche*,
II. 424. See also the *Life of Apoll.* 3. 38, 4. 20.

(d) The demon is expelled by a word of command. In Mk. 1. 25
Jesus says, φιμώθητι καὶ ἔξελθε ἐξ αὐτοῦ; in Mk. 5. 8, ἔξελθε τὸ
πνεῦμα τὸ ἀκάθαρτον ἐκ τοῦ ἀνθρώπου; in Mk. 9. 25, τὸ ἄλαλον
καὶ κωφὸν πνεῦμα, ἐγὼ ἐπιτάσσω σοι, ἔξελθε ἐξ αὐτοῦ, καὶ μηκέτι
εἰσέλθῃς εἰς αὐτόν. [2] Similarly, in Mk. 4. 39 Jesus says to the wind and
sea, σιώπα, πεφίμωσο. [3] This form of command, and even the words themselves, may readily be paralleled. For ἔξελθε see M^e*ila* 51b: "R. Simeon
b. Yochai (c. 150) said: Ben T^elamyon (the name of a demon), go out,
Ben T^elamyon!". [4] Here the Hebrew word אצ (*za*) is used; the Greek
ἔξελθε occurs in address to a demon in the great Paris magical papyrus, f.
33 recto, l. 3013. φιμόω [5] is a magical word and means "to bind with a
spell". Evidence for this use is given in Rohde, *Psyche*, II. 424 (*ET* 604)
and in Moulton-Milligan s.v. Cf. also the Jewish formula in *T. b.*
Shab. 67a (Str.-B. IV. 532).

When the exorcisms are not performed by Jesus himself, they are done
in his name: Mk. 9. 38-40; Lk. 10. 17; Mt. 7. 22; cf. Acts 19. 13. For
the use of the formula of the "name" also there is good attestation in
pagan literature. See, for example, Lucian, *Philops.* 10, 12. Bultmann [6]
refers also to Josephus, *Ant.* 8. 2. 5 (46-48), but we do not find here the
use of the *name* of Solomon. But the formula was used in Judaism. On
the Hellenistic side we may refer again to the Paris magical papyrus, ll.
3069-3072, ὁρκίζω . . . τῷ ὀνόματι αὐτοῦ τῷ ἁγίῳ, and the Adrumetum
tablet quoted by Deissmann, [7] which runs ὁρκίζω σε δαιμόνιον πνεῦμα
. . . τῷ ὀνόματι τῷ ἁγίῳ. . . . On the Rabbinical side we may repeat
the reference to *T. b. Shab.* 67a: ". . . be cursed . . . in the name of
Morigo, Moriphath and his seals." [8]

(e) Sometimes an unmistakable sign is given that the exorcism has been
effective; e.g., in Mk. 5. 13 the swine, into whom the demons have
removed, rush down the cliff into the sea. Good parallels to this event
are afforded by passages which we have already used; in the *Life of*

---

[1] *GST* 239.   [2] Cf. ἐφφαθά in Mk. 7. 34.
[3] For demons in the winds cf. 1 *Enoch* 60. 11 ff.; Jub. 2. 2; Rev. 7. 1.
[4] Cited Str.-B. I. 760, IV. 534 f.
[5] Unless it means simply " to silence ", as Creed (*Luke*, 70) takes it.
[6] *GST* 238.   [7] *Bible Studies*, 274-277.
[8] Jewish sources are aware, but disapprove, of cures in the name of Jesus : *Tos. Hullin* 2, 22 f.
(503), quoted Str.-B. I. 36.

Apollonius, 4. 20 the demon overturns a statue;[1] in Josephus, *Ant*. 8. 2. 5 (48) the demon upsets a bowl of water.

(*f*) As happens in most miracle narratives of all sorts, the story ends by emphasizing the astonishment of the onlookers: Mk. 1. 27 f.; Mt. 9. 33; 12. 23; Mk. 5. 15. As an illustration of this feature, the same passage of Philostratus, *Life of Apollonius*, 4. 20, will serve.

It is also to be observed that the scene sometimes ends (in the Gospels) with a command that the event shall not be publicly revealed, just as (cf. (*c*) above) Jesus commands the demons to be silent: Mk. 1. 25, 34; 3. 12. To this there seems to be no true parallel.

It has seemed worth while to draw attention to these parallels (which might of course have been greatly increased in number) because their significance has been minimized by Canon Richardson in his valuable book, *The Miracle Stories of the Gospels* (see 20-28). It would not do to ignore the fact that the parallels exist, or to deny their importance; in fact, we are driven to the conclusion that there is hardly anything in the Gospel exorcisms which cannot be paralleled in more or less contemporary pagan or Jewish literature (or in both). Yet it remains true that, in comparing the three classes of story—Christian, Jewish and pagan—one is at once aware of the uniqueness of the narratives about Jesus, while the parallels have to be sought for. The reason for this is simply the fact that the NT exorcisms draw their significance not from their content, which is commonplace enough, but from their context; it is the Christological setting in which they are placed which completely differentiates them from other narratives which, both in content and in form, are similar, and indeed almost identical. The Evangelists tell us that the demons, with their supernatural knowledge, recognized Jesus in his relation with God. It is true that Jesus must have presented a "demonic", a "pneumatic" figure as with authority he rebuked the unclean spirits, but so did the legendary Solomon, and the half-legendary Apollonius of the *Life*; and so too did the perfectly real Rabbis who exorcised demons, and the equally real magicians who hawked the magical spells which we have considered. The narratives themselves, with nothing further, are enough to show that Jesus was a "pneumatic" person; but this is by no means enough to make him unique. The striking fact is that his power over demons is held to be a sign of the Kingdom of God, and it is the particular Messianic nature of the spiritual power wielded by Jesus that distinguishes him. Consequently, if we are rightly to understand the exorcism narratives, we must consider also the sayings explanatory of them.

It will be convenient, however, first to notice such evidence as there is to suggest that the Messiah, when he came, was expected to deal with evil spirits. The evidence is not large in bulk but is suggestive. We may

---

[1] And cf. Mk. 5. 18 with this story, in which the young man takes the philosopher's cloak.

refer first to a book which we have already had occasion to use several times, the Testaments of the Twelve Patriarchs.

Test. Lev. 18. 11 f.:

> And he shall give to the saints to eat from the tree of life,
> And the spirit of holiness shall be on them.
> And Beliar shall be bound by him,
> And he shall give power to his children to tread upon the evil spirits

Test. Reub. 6. 10-12 :

And draw ye near to Levi in humbleness of heart . . . because him hath the Lord chosen to be king over all the nation. And bow down before his seed, for on our behalf it will die in wars visible and invisible, and will be among you an eternal king.

Test. Jud. 25. 3 :

> And ye shall be the people of the Lord, and have one tongue;
> And there shall be there no spirit of deceit of Beliar,
> For he shall be cast into the fire for ever.

Test. Zeb. 9. 8 :

> And healing and compassion shall be in his wings.
> He shall redeem all the captivity of the sons of men from Beliar;
> And every spirit of deceit shall be trodden down.[1]

Test. Dan 5. 10 f. :

> And there shall arise unto you from the tribe of Judah and of Levi the
>   salvation of the Lord;
> And he shall make war against Beliar,
> And execute an everlasting vengeance on our enemies.
> And the captivity shall he take from Beliar, the souls of the saints,
> And turn disobedient hearts unto the Lord,
> And give to them that call upon him eternal peace.

A heavenly judgement of Azazel and his demons is depicted in *1 Enoch* 55. 4:

Ye mighty kings who dwell on the earth, ye shall have to behold Mine Elect One, how he sits on the throne of glory and judges Azazel, and all his associates, and all his hosts in the name of the Lord of Spirits.

On the other hand, God's Kingdom on earth is dealt with in *Ass. Moys.* 10. 1, 3:

> And then his kingdom shall appear throughout all his creation,
> And then Satan shall be no more,
> And sorrow shall depart with him. . . .
> For the heavenly One will arise from his royal throne,
> And he will go forth from his holy habitation
> With indignation and wrath on account of his sons.

It is to be noticed that this conquest of Satan is described as taking place before such apocalyptic signs as the trembling of the earth and the falling of the hills.

---

[1] These words are, according to Charles, a Jewish expansion. They do not occur in the majority of MSS. But it should be noted that the same verse contains what must be a Christian expansion (God in the fashion of a man), and it may be that the whole of the additional material in the MSS b d g is of the same (Christian) origin.

There is little (if we may depend on Str.-B.—see IV. 527) evidence in the Rabbinic literature that the Messianic age was expected to witness the overthrow of the demons. The reason for this is probably that hinted at above;[1] the influx of demonology into the Talmud took place after the Messianic hope had lost its earlier vigour. Str.-B. cite two passages:[2]

S. Lev. 26. 6 (449a) :
I will cause evil beasts to cease out of the land (Lev. 26. 6). R. Yehuda (c. 150) said: He (God) causes them to disappear out of the world. R. Shim'on (c. 150) said: He brings them to rest so that they do no more harm. R. Shim'on said: When is God honoured? At the time when there are no Mazziqin [demons] at all, or at the time when there are Mazziqin but they can no longer do any harm? So says Ps. 92. 1: A Psalm, a song for the Sabbath day, that is for the day that brings the Mazziqin in the world to rest so that they do no more harm.

P^siq. Rab. 36 (161a) :
What does Ps. 36. 10, In thy light shall we see light, mean? What light will the people of Israel see? It is the light of the Messiah; cf. Gen. 1. 4, God saw the light, that it was good. That teaches that God looked upon the Messiah and his deeds before the world was created, and he hid it (the primeval light of creation) for the Messiah under the throne of his glory. Then said the Satan before God: The light which was hidden under the throne of thy glory, for whom is it? He answered him: For him who one day will once more put you to shame with confusion of face. He said to him: Lord of the world, show him to me. He answered him: Come and see him. When he saw him, he trembled and fell on his face and said: Truly this is the Messiah, who one day will hurl into Gehinnom me and all the angel princes of the peoples of the world, cf. Is. 25. 8, He hath swallowed up death for ever, etc.

It is, of course, clear that the divine victory over evil in the days of the Messiah must include the overthrow of Satan and the inferior tormentors of mankind; but the evidence which we have reviewed suggests that this inference, though sometimes, was yet infrequently drawn. The argument of Jesus, however (see below), that his exorcisms were a sign of the proximity of the Kingdom of God, would be perfectly comprehensible even to those who disagreed with its assumptions.

We must now discuss the passages which bear upon the meaning of the exorcisms. They fall into two classes, (a) those which relate to the specifically Messianic works of Jesus himself, and (b) those which relate to the casting out of demons by others in the name or by the authority of Jesus.[3] The first class comprises the following:

Mk. 3. 20-30 and parallels. The Marcan section opens (3. 20 f.) with a brief reference to Jesus' activity, and then states that his own people (οἱ παρ' αὐτοῦ) went out to arrest him because they (or people generally?) thought that he was mad (ἐξέστη). The scribes who had come down from Jerusalem made the further charge that Jesus had Beelzebul and cast out demons in the power of the ruler of demons (3. 22). There follows a parabolic discourse from Jesus (3. 23-27) on divided kingdoms

---

[1] P. 54. [2] *Loc. cit.* [3] See below, pp. 65 f.

and houses, and on the security of a strong man, leading to the conclusions that (i) Satan's kingdom shows (in the exorcisms) signs of falling, but (ii) its fall is due not to internal dissension but to aggression from without. There is appended the saying about sin and blasphemy in general, and blasphemy against the Holy Spirit in particular (3. 28 f.); and finally the editorial comment: ὅτι ἔλεγον· πνεῦμα ἀκάθαρτον ἔχει (3. 30).

The corresponding Lucan section is 11. 14-23. This opens with the exorcism of a dumb demon, and the astonishment of the crowds. The accusation of casting out demons in the power of Beelzebul follows, and a tempting request for a sign. Jesus then makes the parabolic reply about divided kingdoms and houses. There follow here the saying about Jewish exorcists and the statement that the exorcisms of Jesus are a sign of the approach of the Kingdom of God. Then comes the brief parable of the strong man, and the saying, "He that is not with me is against me, and he that does not gather with me scatters." In Lk. 12. 10 there is a logion about speaking a word against the Son of man and blasphemy against the Holy Spirit.

It is apparent that, for the most part, Mk. and Lk. are saying the same thing. It is therefore a little surprising to discover that they use almost entirely different words for the purpose. Lk. opens with an exorcism; Mk. has no parallel. The accusation of the satanic origin of Jesus' work is then set out in almost the same terms in the two Gospels; but after this point they diverge again. In the section on division the only words the Evangelists have in common are βασιλεία, ἐφ' ἑαυτήν, εἰ, καί, ὁ σατανᾶς; without which the parable could not have been told at all. There is no Marcan parallel to the following section in Lk. (Jewish exorcists, etc.). In the parable of the strong man the only coincidence is in the use of ὁ ἰσχυρός (Lk. has the nominative, Mk. the genitive). In the concluding section on blasphemy (put by Lk. in a different place) the only common words are εἰς τὸ ἅγιον πνεῦμα and οὐκ; Mk. and Lk. have different parts of the verb βλασφημεῖν, and Mk. uses the noun ἄφεσις, Lk. the verb ἀφίημι.

Clearly Luke is not using Mk. here as his source, except possibly in a very subsidiary way. Clearly, too, from a comparison with Mt., Luke is here giving Q material. For Mt. has close parallels with both Mk. and Lk., and indeed there are few words in Mt. 12. 24-32 which do not correspond with words in Mk. or Lk., either exactly or with simple grammatical variation.[1] Matthew therefore offers us a conflation of the Marcan and Q traditions.

We therefore have to examine the two sections as they appear in Mk. and Lk.[2] Although the verbal differences which we have considered are very important in that they reveal to us an overlapping of Mk. and Q, they are not such as to prevent our considering at the same

---

[1] The exact proportion (in Mt.) of words with to words without parallels is 147 to 40.
[2] Lk. 11. 23 is a separate logion which may here be left out of account; the saying on blasphemy against the Holy Spirit is postponed until pp. 103-107, 133 f.

time the parallel versions of the several parts of the paragraph, and we can put together what we learn from Mk. and Q. Doing so, we find the following points :

(1) Divided Kingdoms.
(2) The Strong Man.
(3) Jewish Exorcists.
(4) The true power in Jesus' Exorcisms.

It is fairly clear that the sayings relating to these points cannot originally have been spoken at the same time, and that their present arrangement is due to editorial activity on the part of the Evangelists (or their predecessors) who wished to bring together such material as they had on the subject of demons and their expulsion.[1] For the same reason the logion about the return of the demon with seven others stands at this point in Lk. (and in Mt., though the controversy about signs is inserted). The four points, if we are to press their presuppositions and consequences by a rigorous logic, are not entirely consistent with one another. Thus (1) (Mk. 3. 24-26 and parallels) might be paraphrased: "I am accused of using demonic powers for the expulsion of demons. But this would involve the complete break-up of the demonic world, in accordance with usual human experience of seditious activity. Now it is clear that the empire of Satan still holds out (this assumption is necessary to the argument): therefore I do not cast out demons by Beelzebul, but in some other way." (2) (Mk. 3. 27 and parallels) may similarly be rendered: "A strong man can only be overcome by a stronger. The ruler of demons is strong and armed, and can only be cast out by one stronger than he. If, then, he is in fact being visibly overcome, it must be because he has been assailed by a stronger, e.g., by the Messiah." The disharmony between the two arguments is evident.

Again, (3) and (4) follow one another rather inconsequentially. In (3) (Mt. 12. 27 and parallel) the works of Jesus are declared to be no more works of the devil than those of other Jewish exorcists. In (4) (Mt. 12. 28 and parallel) the Jewish exorcists are at once left out of consideration, and the acts of Jesus, now no longer compared with but entirely differentiated from all other similar acts, are declared to be a sign of the approach of the Kingdom of God.

Nevertheless the Evangelists (as Evangelists, not historians) were right in grouping these sayings together, for in spite of their disharmony in detail they present an inward coherence and unity, which may be summarized in the following points :

(1) The exorcisms were not wrought by magic. No doubt there was need for this disclaimer, because the therapeutic methods employed by Jesus [2] did not differ in form from those of magicians. Here the contrary is flatly stated. There is no need to stress the logic of Mk. 3. 24-26 so as

---

[1] Bultmann, *GST* 10-12 ; Albertz, *Die synoptischen Streitgespräche*, 48-50.
[2] See above, pp. 55-57.

to make it contradict 3. 27; the argument is simply, Satan is not casting out Satan, because "Satan is not such a fool".[1] Some other power than that of Beelzebul is needed to explain the works of Jesus.

(2) While it is implied (by Mt. 12. 27 and parallel) that Jewish exorcists also cast out demons, the whole context implies, both in the accusation made by the Jews and in the defence of Jesus, that there were important differences between the two classes of exorcist. As we have seen, these differences did not lie in the external details of the cures. These first two points are negative.

(3) The unique element in the exorcisms of Jesus is that they are special signs of God's power and of his Kingdom. (Mk. 3. 27 and parallels; Mt. 12. 28 and parallel.) In Mk. 3. 27 the language used seems to be based upon Is. 49. 24 f., which in the LXX reads: μὴ λήμψεταί τις παρὰ γίγαντος σκῦλα; . . . ἐάν τις αἰχμαλωτεύσῃ γίγαντα, λήμψεται σκῦλα· λαμβάνων δὲ παρὰ ἰσχύοντος σωθήσεται.[2] That this prophetic expression had become proverbial is held by Ryle and James to be probable in view of Ps. Sol. 5. 4: οὐ γὰρ λήψεται σκῦλα παρὰ ἀνδρὸς δυνατοῦ.[3] Whether this be so or not, the meaning of the logion is clear. The strong man is the same person as Beelzebul (for the most probable interpretation of Beelzebul is בְּעֵל זְבֻל, i.e., Lord of the dwelling), and Jesus claims that, though his house· is not divided, it is nevertheless on the point of destruction because its master has met one stronger than himself—who can only be God himself or his representative.

This thought is carried further by the saying of Mt. 12. 28 and parallel. From the visible acts of exorcism Jesus argues (ἄρα) that ἔφθασεν ἐφ' ὑμᾶς ἡ βασιλεία τοῦ θεοῦ. The meaning of the word ἔφθασεν is, as is well known, contested.[4] It is sufficient that at this point we should notice that the exorcisms and the Kingdom of God are intimately related to one another, whatever the exact nature of the relationship may be. They may be signs that the Kingdom has come, or proleptic manifestations of it; or, perhaps, not exactly either of these things; but certainly it is meant that the exorcisms are taking place in virtue of the divine Kingdom. They are not magic or thaumaturgy; they are not occasional miracles granted in answer to the prayer of a sage or holy man; they are a particular and unique event in God's fulfilment of his promise of redemption in his Kingdom.

(4) The manner of God's activity is described more precisely in Mt. 12. 28a (=Lk. 11. 20a). Mt. speaks of the Spirit of God, Lk. of the finger of God. The difficult question is at once raised: Which Evangelist has preserved the earlier form of the tradition of this saying?

---

[1] Manson, in Major, Manson and Wright, *Mission and Message of Jesus*, 377.

[2] Cf. also Is. 53. 12, καὶ τῶν ἰσχυρῶν μεριεῖ σκῦλα.

[3] See their commentary *ad loc.*, 54. Cf. also Judg. 6. 12, where ἰσχυρὸς τῶν δυνάμεων = גִּבּוֹר הֶחָיִל (gibbor heḥail); 2 Kdms. 22. 31, 32, 33, 48; 23. 5 where ἰσχυρῶν = אֵל ('el, as also several times in Nehemiah and Job); Jer. 27/ 34; 39. 18; Dan. 9. 4; 2 Macc. 1. 24.

[4] Cf. C. H. Dodd, *Parables of the Kingdom*, 43 f.; J. Y. Campbell, *ET* 48, 91–94; Dodd, *ET* 48, 138–142; cf. J. M. Creed, *ET* 48, 184 f.

In favour of the priority of the Lucan form it may be urged that Luke, who speaks more frequently of the Holy Spirit than any other of the Synoptic Evangelists, would not have altered the phrase πνεύματι θεοῦ had he read it in his source, and that πνεύματι was substituted by Matthew for δακτύλῳ as an introduction to the saying about blasphemy against the Holy Spirit (Mt. 12. 31 f.). On the other hand, it could be argued that Luke is fond of such archaic and OT anthropomorphisms as "the finger of God" and that Matthew must have been following his source closely at this point since he retains the (for him) unusual expression, "Kingdom of God".[1] The arguments in favour of Lk.'s δακτύλῳ θεοῦ seem the better; and accordingly we must see one of the few references to the Spirit disappear from the earliest stratum of the Gospel tradition. Of course, it is true that there is no real difference of meaning between finger of God and Spirit of God: both are metaphors used to denote the mighty power of God.[2] This was recognized by so acute a biblical scholar as Augustine,[3] and similarly a modern scholar [4] writes: "even if, in the saying about the βασιλεία in Mt. 12. 28=Lk. 11. 20, the expression δακτύλῳ θεοῦ should be original, nevertheless it must denote an organ of power that belongs to the sphere of the Holy Spirit". That is to say, if Matthew's word is not original, it is nevertheless a legitimate interpretation of the more primitive expression. As Dr Manson points out,[5] the Lucan phrase contains a direct allusion to Exod. 8. 15 where, according to the interpretation of *Exod. R.* 10, Moses is contrasted with the Egyptian magicians, and the finger of God with the power of demons; consequently Luke, no less than Matthew, intends us to think of a divine might residing in Jesus, making him a "pneumatic", a spiritual person, and potent against evil spirits. It is a particular power, comparable with that by which God delivered his people from Egypt and gave them the Law (Exod. 31. 18);[6] and the context suggests that Jesus possessed it in virtue of his Messiahship.[7]

Lk. 10. 17-20. Jesus' communication of the power to cast out demons to his disciples is considered below, as part of the question whether Jesus foretold the gift of the Spirit to the Church. Here we are chiefly concerned with *vv.* 18 and 20. It is very questionable whether the link made by Luke between *v.* 18, the vision of the fall of Satan, and the report of the apostles that they had found the demons subject to them when they

---

[1] It is not legitimate to cut the knot by the hypothesis that Mt. and Lk. had different sources; for although, as I hold (cf. *ET* 54, 320-323), Mt. and Lk. did not derive all their Q material from a single common source, *at this point* their agreement is so close as to make it probable that their sources were identical. In any case, the question would remain, Does " Q₁ " or " Q₂ " retain the earlier form of the tradition?

[2] Cf. the use of hand and Spirit in Ezek. 3. 14.

[3] Cf. *De Spiritu et Littera*, 28 (xvi) : " Hic Spiritus Sanctus per quem diffunditur charitas in cordibus nostris, quae plenitudo legis est, etiam digitus Dei in Evangelio dicitur. Unde quia et illae tabulae digito Dei conscriptae sunt, et digitus Dei est Spiritus Dei per quem sanctificamur, ut ex fide viventes per dilectionem bene operemur ; quem non moveat ista congruentia ibidemque distantia ? "

[4] Windisch, *op. cit.* 229.   [5] *Teaching of Jesus*, 82 f.   [6] Cf. also Deut. 9. 10 ; Ps. 8. 4.

[7] Cf. Mk. 1. 27, where, after an exorcism, the people marvel at the exceptional authority of Jesus ; see below, pp. 85 f.

used the name of Jesus, is original. *V.* 18 may well have been an isolated
saying which was inserted at this point.[1] Its meaning, however, is clear.
Jesus, speaking as a prophet, recounts a vision [2] of the fall of Satan from
power. The fact that a past tense (ἐθεώρουν) is used of the vision does
not mean that the fall has taken place—the vision might have been seen
before the event. Yet it is entirely congruent with other passages of the
Gospels (e.g., Mk. 3. 27) to suppose that the fall belongs to the period of
the Messianic work of Jesus.[3] The setting of the saying in Lk. associates
the vision (? and the fall) with the success of the disciples in casting out
demons; the saying is in that case parallel to Mt. 12. 28=Lk. 11. 20.
The defeat of subordinate members of the Kingdom of evil is a proof
of the sovereign activity of God, that is, of the defeat of Satan. If, however, we isolate the verse, it may refer (as has been suggested by J. Weiss
and Zahn) to the Messianic overthrow of Satan at the Temptation. It
is probably best not to attach it to any particular event but to see in it a
general reference to the eschatological salvation wrought by Christ;
as Dr Bultmann [4] says, "It is, however, possible that the saying only
expresses pictorially the view that 'the end of the devil's power is now
being experienced' (Klostermann), in which case it would be a parallel,
in substance, to Mk. 3. 27." There seems to be no reason why this should
not be combined with the view adopted by Bultmann in his text, that
the verse is a "Visionsbericht". It is an eschatological saying expressed in
a visionary form, possibly resting upon a real visionary experience, and
formulated by Is. 14. 12.

The importance of *v.* 20 is that it minimizes the importance of the
exorcisms. They are no doubt a sign of the approaching salvation, but
they are necessarily of less import than the fact that the disciples are
elect participants in the salvation itself.

Mt. 12. 43-45 and parallel. A few words will suffice to deal with this
short passage. With the demonological details which it supplies we are
not concerned. It is clear that Matthew understood the description of
the man who falls back into the power of demons as something like an
allegory; this he shows by the words, "Thus shall it be with this wicked
generation too"; words which are not in the Lucan parallel and which
were probably not in Matthew's source. Even when the Matthaean
addition has been discounted, it seems that the saying must have more
than the bald meaning assigned to it by Jülicher [5]—it is not enough
to cast out an evil spirit; its place must be taken by the Spirit of God.[6]
If it is a parable it must be interpreted in the light of the critical period

---

[1] Cf. Bultmann, *GST* 174 : "The impression that it is a fragment is strong."
[2] "An ecstatic vision on the part of Jesus is suggested."—Creed, *ad loc.*
[3] It is interesting that most of the Fathers regards this verse as a reference to the pretemporal
fall of Satan ; so, for example, Chrysostom, *de Poen. Hom.* I. 2 ; *Ecloga de Poen. Hom.* XXXV.
(in each case he has εἶδον not ἐθεώρουν). But this exegesis is now generally abandoned. It is
much more likely that the fall of Satan to which Jesus referred was a lapse not from holiness
but from power.   [4] *GST* 113 n. 2.   [5] *Gleichnisreden Jesu,* II. 239.
[6] Bultmann, *GST* 176 f., who thinks the saying may have come from a Jewish writing, takes
a similar view.

which the ministry of Jesus precipitated. Its meaning would be, perhaps, to the effect that the Jews, if they do not take full advantage of the deliverance made available for them by Jesus, will find their last state worse than the first. Luke, however, appears to place the saying in the context of Christian experience—this is what happens to those who do not "hear the word of God and keep it".

Mk. 7. 24-30 and parallel. A similar motivation underlies this story, of which the details do not now concern us. The point of the reply made by Jesus, when he is asked to perform an exorcism for a Gentile, is that his powers are the privilege of the Jews; they may not be indiscriminately used. That is to say, it is not a general but a particular spiritual power, and one that is associated with the Jewish race; the reader naturally infers that it is the power of the Messiah, of the Kingdom of God, as our chief passage, Mk. 3. 20-30 and parallels, expressly states. Matthew strengthens the impression given by Mark. He brings out (15. 24) the Messianic purpose of Jesus, and, in 15. 27, changes "children" into "masters".

We must now turn to consider very briefly the second class of sayings about exorcisms, those which deal with the casting out of demons by others than Jesus.[1]

Mk. 3. 15; 6. 7, 12 f. and parallels. In these passages (and it seems that here too there was overlapping between Mk. and Q) it is stated quite generally that Jesus gave his disciples authority over unclean spirits (ἐξουσίαν ἐκβάλλειν, ἐξουσίαν τῶν πνευμάτων).[2] No indication is given of the means by which Jesus communicated this power. But the context of the mission (whether it be historical or not) is distinctly Messianic, and the disciples (according to Q) are bidden to accompany their miracles with the proclamation, "The Kingdom of God has come upon you". These facts suggest a great difference between Jesus' authorization of his followers to expel demons and the communication of magical charms. The deeds of the apostles, like his own, were an activity of the Kingdom of God.[3]

Mk. 9. 28 f. and parallels. In Mk. 9. 28 the disciples inquire why they were unable to cast out the dumb demon from the boy whom Jesus had just cured. To this verse there is a close parallel in Mt. 17. 19, but no parallel in Lk. In Mk. 9. 29 the reply is given: "This sort can come out by nothing but prayer". In Mt. 17. 20 the reply is quite different.[4] The disciples are told that if they had faith as a grain of mustard seed nothing would be impossible to them. Parallels to this saying in another place in Mt. (21. 21), in Mk. (11. 22 f.) and in Lk. (17. 6) suggest that it was contained in both Mk. and Q: i.e., Matthew has rearranged Mk., or conflated a Q saying with a Marcan miracle. The connection of the

---

[1] These passages will be more fully discussed below, pp. 127-130.
[2] For a discussion of the word ἐξουσία see below, pp. 78-82.
[3] Cf. what was said above (pp. 63 f.) about Lk. 10. 17-20.
[4] We must neglect v. 21, which is a harmonizing insertion, and not part of the original text.

saying about faith with the casting out of demons is therefore due to the editing of Matthew.[1] Of course, Mk.'s statement that the power to exorcise depends on prayer involves faith (cf. Mk. 11. 24), and thus sets forth as the basis of NT exorcisms the interlocking sources of faith and prayer. The effect of this is to remove the activity of Jesus and of his disciples as far as possible from the sphere of magic, and to cause it to depend simply and immediately upon God's power, brought into human life by these media of faith and prayer.[2]

Mk. 9. 38-40 and parallel. Mk. is quite closely followed by Lk. (9. 49 f.); there is no parallel in Mt., perhaps because the pericope contains matter which seemed latitudinarian to this "homme d'Église".

Its importance here lies in the fact that it attests the use of the *name* of Jesus as a means of exorcism. There are a few similar uses of this formula in the Gospels. They are Mt. 7. 22; Mk. 16. 17; Lk. 10. 17. All of these have a secondary appearance. Mt. 7. 22 is an elaboration of a logion which has been preserved in a simpler form in Lk. 6. 46 (and in 2 *Clem.* 4. 2). Lk. 10. 17 is apparently an editorial introduction to the saying of the next verse. Mk. 16. 17 belongs to the certainly unauthentic and secondary conclusion of the second Gospel. With regard to Mk. 9. 38 f., it has been said by Creed:[3] "It is most unlikely that exorcism in the name of Jesus would be practised in his lifetime on earth. It may be inferred that the question had arisen in the community as to what attitude should be adopted towards those who, though not strictly members of the Church, successfully exorcised in the name of Jesus." The objection to this view is that there is little trace of such tolerance as is suggested by the incident in the early history of the Church. We may compare the fate of the Jewish exorcists in Acts 19 and the enjoyment with which the narrator tells the story. We have already referred to a Talmudic passage (*Tos. Ḥullin* 2. 22 f. (503)) which shows that the name of Jesus was found to have power over demons.

Before we leave the subject of the conflict of Jesus with evil spirits one further point demands attention; the passion narrative may be considered from this point of view.[4] It was so regarded by St Paul; for in 1 Cor. 2. 8 the rulers of this world are evil spiritual powers, who, in their ignorance, were responsible for crucifying the Lord of Glory. The

---

[1] Matthew elsewhere adds the element of faith to Marcan miracles.

[2] We have neglected here the reading καὶ νηστείᾳ which is given in Mk. 9. 29 by a number of MSS. It is clearly an assimilation to the secondary verse in Mt. The existence of the reading attests a more magical strain of thought, for though in some Jewish circles fasting was thought of as a means of purification and atonement, it is introduced here either to support a new Church discipline or as a physical means of compelling the obedience of a spiritual being.

[3] *Luke*, 138 f.

[4] It is not irrelevant to point out that throughout the Gospels Jesus is engaged in controversies with various adversaries (see Albertz, *Die synoptischen Streitgespräche*), and Weinel (*Die Wirkungen des Geistes und der Geister*, 18-20) shows that similar disputes in the early Church were thought of as spiritual conflicts with evil powers. But Jesus for the most part uses (as in the temptations, see above, p. 52) argumentative methods (see Albertz, *op. cit.* 67-74, on Jesus' means of combat—comparison, question, antithesis, proof from reason, proof from Scripture). It is, however, important to notice also Mk. 8. 33, where Peter is addressed as a tempting minister of Satan. On this, cf. Wellhausen and Harnack, above, p. 49.

Synoptic passion narratives bear evident traces of the same view, in the following passages:

Mk. 14. 32-42 and parallels. The experience of Jesus in Gethsemane, as set forth by the Evangelists, is not quite an ordinary experience of fear; nor is Otto [1] entirely right in saying: "What is the cause of this 'sore amazement' and 'heaviness', this soul shaken to its depths, 'exceeding sorrowful even unto death', and this sweat that falls to the ground like great drops of blood? Can it be ordinary fear of death in the case of one who had had death before his eyes for weeks past and who had just celebrated with clear intent his death feast with his disciples? No, there is more here than the fear of death; there is the awe of the creature before the '*mysterium tremendum*', before the shuddering secret of the numen." Jesus is not so much in awe before the mystery of God; for him, even in Gethsemane, God is still Abba.[2] He is rather at grips with the mystery of the devil. He is entering upon the decisive struggle with evil. Matthew's insertion into the narrative of the arrest (26. 53) emphasizes the same interpretation; Jesus might have been reinforced by more than twelve legions of angels, i.e., the real enemy is not of flesh and blood, men with their swords and staves, but angels, principalities and powers. Lk. 22. 43 (if it be a genuine part of the text) suggests that Luke understood the Gethsemane story in the same way. The Lucan passion narrative, indeed, in several places refers quite clearly to the activity of Satan. The whole series of passion events is set in motion by the entry of Satan into Judas Iscariot (22. 3), and we are reminded of Lk.'s remark that, after the temptation in the wilderness, the devil left Jesus "until his time" (ἄχρι καιροῦ, Lk. 4. 13). He now returns for the decisive struggle. It is Satan also who lies behind the denial of Peter; so much at least can be based on the difficult verses 22. 31 f. Finally, Jesus says at the time of his arrest that "This is your hour and (? that of) the power of darkness" (22. 53).

Mk. 15. 33, 37 f. and parallels. The closing scene of the life of Jesus is depicted upon a supernatural background. Darkness falls upon the earth; the veil of the Temple is rent. According to Mt. (27. 51 f.), there is an earthquake, tombs are opened, the saints are raised and enter the Holy City. Whatever connotation these occurrences may have in detail, the general impression which they convey, and were no doubt intended to convey, is of a unique event in this world, which nevertheless belongs as much to the other, spiritual, world as to this; in fact, of a cosmological act (a defeat of Satan) whose decisive actor was yet visible in the world of space and time.[3]

---

[1] *Idea of the Holy*, 88.   [2] On this word see Kittel, *TWNT* I. 4-6.
[3] It is possible that the name Golgotha (Mk. 15. 22 and parallels) is significant here. The name Golgotha (גולגולתא) is correctly interpreted by Luke as "Skull-place". Dalman (*Sacred Sites and Ways*, 347) says: "According to Origen (*In Matth.* 126 Cat.—MPG 13. 1717) and Epiphanius (41. 5—MPG 41. 544 f.) the name was derived from the skull of Adam who was buried there. . . . As, according to the Jewish legend, Adam lived on Mount Moriah (*Pirke R.E.* 20; *Midr. Tehill.* 90. 5; *Targ. Jer.* i. on Gen. 3. 23), a place in Jerusalem called after Adam's

8 CONFLICT WITH EVIL SPIRITS

Thus we should note the clear hints of the Evangelists that the crucifixion was by them regarded as a struggle between Jesus and the powers of evil (and death). And we may observe also that in this part of the Gospels there are no exorcisms (and, indeed, in the earliest strata of the tradition, no miracles at all).

A full discussion of the results of this chapter must be deferred till a later point; [1] but it is necessary here briefly to draw out a few conclusions which may be deduced from it.

We have now seen some of the evidence which indicates that Jesus was a "pneumatic" person; he seems to have exercised the same control over spiritual conditions which other exorcists employed, and to have made use of similar means to that end. Moreover, there is at least the suggestion that he was also a visionary (the temptations and Lk. 10. 18).

Yet these facts, strangely enough, seem to be depreciated by the Evangelists. They are in themselves not stressed, and no pains are taken to describe Jesus in impressive terms as a potent bearer of the Spirit of God. The Spirit is in fact mentioned only once (and that in a secondary form of a saying) in connection with demons. In Lk. 10. 17-20 the depreciation is very apparent. It is only by reading between the lines of the Gospels that we discover Jesus as a "pneumatic" person.[2] This is simply because Jesus as a "pneumatic" person did not particularly interest the Evangelists or those for whom they wrote; such persons were by no means rare, and in no way significant. The visions of Jesus and his power to cast out demons did not *differentiate* him from other men.

Yet, when once his ministry had been understood as Messianic, the exorcisms were seen to have great significance. They were a signal instance of the power of the Kingdom of God in subduing the empire of the adversary. The meaning of the fact that Jesus was a "pneumatic" person now comes into sight. His spiritual power was not simply a means of revealing his Messiahship—"so great an exorcist must be the Messiah". It was rather at the same time both a revelation and a concealment. In it some saw merely the magical manœuvres of a thaumaturge, and were thereby hardened against him; only those who possessed the mystery could understand its true significance. The theme of the Messianic secret is thus so closely and intricately worked into the temptations (as well as the baptism) and the exorcisms that it is difficult to believe that it was imposed upon them by Mark—or by any other historian or theologian.[3]

---

skull would not, in itself, have been impossible." Jerome, we know (*Ep.* 46 *ad Marcellam*), drew the obvious contrast between the first and last Adam from this tradition, and it is conceivable that the early Gospel tradition had in mind a renewal of the conflict between Man and Satan (as in the temptation narratives). But, as Dalman (*ibid.*) goes on to say, " It is more probable that a bare rock formation, several examples of which are to be found in the environs of Jerusalem, suggested the name ' Skull '."   [1] Pp. 113-121.

[2] This fact is clearly brought out by Windisch, *op. cit.*, though not all his conclusions from it are valid.

[3] It will be seen that two reasons have now emerged why the Synoptic references to the Spirit are so few : (*a*) The Evangelists were not interested in " pneumatic " men ; (*b*) The Spirit was concealed with the Messiahship of Jesus. See pp. 118-120. The statements just made bear also upon the question of the Spirit and eschatology ; see pp. 120 f., 154-162.

JESUS AS MIRACLE-WORKER—THE WORDS ΔΥΝΑΜΙΣ AND ΕΞΟΥΣΙΑ

WE have discussed how the narratives of Jesus' exorcisms contribute to our understanding of the Evangelists' conception of the work of the Holy Spirit. Exorcism was, of course, not the only form of cure that he effected; nor were his miracles restricted to the healing of the sick. Along with the casting out of demons went the restoration of sight to the blind, of hearing to the deaf and of speech to the dumb; lepers were cleansed and other forms of disease remedied; the dead were raised; and Jesus exerted power not only over human beings, but also over, for example, the sea, or a fig tree. Now it is comparatively clear that, when Jesus exorcised an evil spirit, some inference is at hand about the Spirit of God, for there is a presumption that that which overcomes spirit is spirit. But the relevance of the other miracles to our subject is not so evident; and certainly it is not made explicit in the Gospels. Nevertheless, the miracles are relevant.

In the first place, Jesus as a worker of miracles appears unmistakably as a "pneumatic" person, working by the immediate exercise of non-material, supernatural authority. His cures are obviously effected by spiritual power. The question whether they are to be regarded as authentic historical events, of course, remains open; but in most instances the narratives given to us by the Evangelists cannot be rationalized without being completely transformed. Jesus is represented not as using natural laws and forces but as transcending and overriding them. He acts as he teaches—as one having authority. This fact, of the spiritual authority of Jesus, will be brought out most satisfactorily by an examination of the words δύναμις and ἐξουσία.

Secondly, as we observed in the exorcisms, this external, visible characteristic of Jesus is rooted, for the Evangelists, in their theological presuppositions. The narratives in general are bound up with both the Messiahship and the Messianic secret. This will appear in the course of the discussion that follows. For the present it will suffice to note the miracles in the first two chapters of Mk.

(a) The demoniac in the Synagogue at Capernaum, 1. 21-27. The demon recognizes Jesus as the Holy One of God, who has authority to destroy demons. Jesus commands the demon to be silent. The crowd note something "new" (καινή).

(b) Simon's mother-in-law, 1. 30, 31. No comment is given.

(c) Cure of many sick people and demoniacs, 1. 32-34. The demons know Jesus (to be Christ, several MSS add, no doubt interpreting correctly). Jesus refuses to let them speak.

(*d*) A leper, 1. 40-45. Jesus forbids the leper to tell anyone what has happened. Yet the healed man does in fact begin to spread abroad the word (τὸν λόγον), probably understood by the Evangelist as the Christian Gospel.

(*e*) A paralytic, 2. 1-12. Jesus not only heals the sick man, but also claims to have authority to forgive sins.

It is not too much to say that the spiritual might possessed and wielded by Jesus depended not upon any particular quality of his own personality, but upon the relation of his ministry to the powers of the Kingdom of God; and yet that spiritual might was no infallible and unmistakable proof of his claims, but in some cases served to conceal them.

Both of these assertions are justified by examination of the background which comparative study of the NT miracle stories reveals. The parallels between the miracle stories of the Gospels and those of more or less contemporary Jewish and Hellenistic literature have been set forth by Dr Bultmann [1] with a wealth of learning, and there is no need here to repeat what has already been so admirably said.[2] Jesus, in the miracle stories, is a character comparable with the thaumaturges of the ancient world, an uncanny figure, living in a numinous atmosphere.

At the same time, the unique OT and Messianic background of the Synoptic narratives must not be ignored. There is important evidence of the belief that miracles were to be expected of the Messiah. Fundamental is the well-known saying of *Midr. Qoh.* 73, 3 : גּוֹאֵל רִאשׁוֹן כֵּן גּוֹאֵל אַחֲרוֹן.[3] The Messiah would resemble Moses and, like him, execute mighty acts in God's name in the deliverance of the people. According to *Tanh.* 54. 4 the Messiah was expected to raise the dead, after the analogy of Elijah and Elisha. The Gospels themselves draw attention, by explicit quotation, to Is. 61. 1 :

The spirit of the Lord God is upon me; because the Lord hath anointed me to preach good tidings unto the meek; he hath sent me to bind up the broken-hearted, to proclaim liberty to the captives, and the opening *of the prison'* (*mg., opening of the eyes*) to them that are bound.[4]

Is. 35. 5 f. :

Then the eyes of the blind shall be opened, and the ears of the deaf shall be unstopped. Then shall the lame man leap as an hart, and the tongue of the dumb shall sing—

is alluded to; see for example Mk. 7. 32-37, where the rare word μογιλάλος is used, as in the LXX of Is. 35. 6.[5] We may add also Is. 29. 18 f. :

[1] *GST* 236-241, 247-253.
[2] Some parallels have been given in the section on exorcisms, pp. 55-57.
[3] " As was the former redeemer, so is the latter." Cited by Bultmann, *GST* 245.
[4] Lk. 4. 18 f. refers this more definitely to miracles : " to proclaim ... recovery of sight to the blind, to set at liberty them that are bruised ".
[5] Cf. Hoskyns in *Mysterium Christi* (ed. Bell and Deissmann), 72-74. It is not suggested that the author of Is. 35 had in mind the actual healing of blind, deaf or dumb men, by a personal Messiah or otherwise ; but that (i) uncritical readers, with no historical sense, might think so, and (ii) the writing of the NT authors was profoundly influenced (perhaps at times even unconsciously) by the LXX.

And in that day shall the deaf hear the words of the book (*or* a book, *or* writing), and the eyes of the blind shall see out of obscurity and out of darkness.

Of later literature we may quote at this point—

4 Ezra 7. 27 :
And whosoever is delivered from the foresaid evils, the same shall see my wonders.

ibid. 13. 50 :
And then shall he show them very many wonders.

Test. Zeb. 9. 8 (b d g) :
And healing and compassion shall be in his wings.
He shall redeem all the captivity of the sons of men from Beliar;
And every spirit of deceit shall be trodden down.

Test. Sim. 6. 6 :
Then shall all the spirits of deceit be given to be trodden under foot,
And men shall rule over wicked spirits.

Not only does this aspect of the Messianic hope lie behind the conception of Jesus as a wonder-worker; numerous details of the miracle narratives are only fully to be understood in the light of the OT. This fact is worked out by Canon Richardson.[1] Our attention is thus drawn to the double fact which we have already observed; Jesus is a "pneumatic" man, after the manner of many others; yet at the same time he differs radically from them, and his spiritual power is but a sign of a more fundamental fact of his office.[2]

We may now turn to a more detailed discussion of the points which have been raised.

THE WORD ΔΥΝΑΜΙΣ IN THE SYNOPTIC GOSPELS

The word $\delta \acute{v} \nu a \mu \iota s$, which is found in all classes of Greek literature from the time of Homer, means *strength, might, power, ability*.[3] About its use in the LXX there is little to remark. It is several times used as the equivalent of צָבָא (zaba'), and hence is sometimes associated with $\kappa \acute{v} \rho \iota o s$ in the rendering of the divine name יהוה צְבָאוֹת ('adonai zᵉba'oth, $\kappa \acute{v} \rho \iota o s \ \delta \nu \nu \acute{a} \mu \epsilon \omega \nu$). But this fact does not seem to have any particular theological significance, save that, in the title, $\delta \acute{v} \nu a \mu \iota s$ is used (as it might well have been used in any case) for the heavenly host, and the way was thus prepared for its application to individual divine beings (cf. (iv) below).

In the Synoptic Gospels $\delta \acute{v} \nu a \mu \iota s$ has a number of special uses which may be classed as follows:[4]

(i) $\delta \acute{v} \nu a \mu \iota s$ *as miracle*. That $\delta \acute{v} \nu a \mu \iota s$, from meaning "might", should

---

[1] *Op. cit.* 81-99 ; cf. also Hoskyns, *loc cit.*
[2] Opposite sides of this twofold situation are taken by Bultmann and Richardson respectively. The latter (*op. cit.* 20-28) minimizes the significance of the Hellenistic and Jewish parallels adduced by Bultmann, and stresses the OT background of the miracles (see especially ch. V of his book). Bultmann, on the other hand, considers that the formative influence of the OT has been exaggerated (*op. cit.* 245). It seems that we have no need to quarrel with the positive statements of either of these scholars. [3] See LS s.v.
[4] Its use in Mt. 25. 15 is obviously unimportant for our purpose ; all other Synoptic uses of the word are considered in our discussion.

come to signify a mighty act, seems no more than a natural development of usage, though it seems to be a use almost entirely restricted to the NT and later Christian literature.[1] It might therefore very tentatively be suggested that the development was not quite so simple as appears, and that this signification of δύναμις may have arisen by way of (vi) or (vii) below. It is certainly not uncommon in the Synoptic Gospels, though Luke seems to have had an objection to it—possibly because it did not belong to current Hellenistic or LXX usage. In Lk. it occurs only once (Lk. 10. 13), in a Q passage, while in the Matthaean parallel (Mt. 11. 20-23) it occurs three times. It appears also in another Matthaean Q passage (Mt. 7. 22), where the Lucan parallel is, at this point, decidedly different. In addition to these cases, this use of δύναμις is found three times in Mk.; twice (Mk. 6. 2, 5) in the short section dealing with the preaching of Jesus at Nazareth (taken over by Matthew in 13. 54, 58), and once (Mk. 9. 39) with reference to the man who was not in the company of the disciples of Jesus but cast out demons in his name (the whole section is omitted by Mt.). In the former of these cases Lk. has a pericope about the preaching at Nazareth which, whatever be its origin, differs widely from that in Mk., and which does not contain the word δύναμις (though it refers to the miracles and contains the important reference to Is. 61. 1). In the latter, Luke retains the incident but omits the use of δύναμις. Possibly we should include here Mk. 6. 14 (=Mt. 14. 2); but see (vi) below.[2]

(ii) δύναμις *as a periphrasis for God*. This is found in Mk. 14. 62, which is followed by Matthew in 26. 64. Luke also (22. 69) copies Mk. at this point, but adds, after δυνάμεως, τοῦ θεοῦ, thereby showing that he did not understand (or wished to interpret) the Jewish reverential periphrasis used by Mark.[3] The idiom is fully explained and illustrated by Dalman, *Words of Jesus*, 200-202; see also Canon Richardson on the Biblical designation of God as power, and Christ the power of God.[4]

(iii) δύναμις *in a doxology*. δύναμις forms part of the ascription to God in the doxology found in many MSS at Mt. 6. 13.[5] It is evident that the doxology is not a genuine part of the text. McNeile[6] suggests that the Matthaean doxology is a combination of a Hellenistic form (the power and the glory—as in the *Didache*) and a Hebraic form (the Kingdom and the glory). It is difficult to see why this distinction should

[1] The inscription from Buresch, *Aus Lÿdien*, 113, quoted by Moulton-Milligan and LS (new edition, 452a) is too broken to be of much value.
[2] Lk. 19. 37 is an apparent exception to what has been said about Luke's disuse of the word δύναμις in the sense of miracle, for here (according to the WH text) Luke uses δύναμις = miracle, without even a parallel to account for his doing so. But the exception is apparent only. The original text is probably preserved in the Old Syriac, which presupposes a Greek text περὶ πάντων ὧν εἶδον. The word δυνάμεων was then inserted (possibly by accidental repetition of the last three letters of εἶδον, or simply through a quite natural interpretation), and the curious reading περὶ πάντων ὧν εἶδον δυνάμεων is actually to be found in the MS B. This was emended in all other MSS to the well-known text περὶ πασῶν ὧν εἶδον δυνάμεων. See J. H. Moulton, *Prolegomena*, 3rd ed., 244.   [3] Luke does not refer to a δύναμις of God in the Philonic sense.
[4] *Op. cit.* 1-5, 16-19.   [5] Cf. the *Didache* 8. 2.   [6] *Commentary, ad loc.*

be made, especially since Ps. 145. 11 f. and 1 Chron. 29. 11, which
McNeile quotes to illustrate his Hebraic form, both contain the word
"power". Str.-B. quote a Rabbinic passage (*Berakh.* 58a) which comments on 1 Chron. 29. 11 and refers the power there mentioned (נבורה,
geburah) to the deliverance of the people from Egypt, quoting
Exod. 14. 31, "And Israel saw the great work (ר׳, yad) which the Lord
did upon the Egyptians". A little later in the same passage a *Baraita*
of R. Aqiba is quoted which connects the "power" with the killing of the
first-born in Egypt. There is no need to find in the ascription of power
to God anything not thoroughly Hebraic.

(iv) δυνάμεις *as heavenly beings.* Mk. 13. 25 (= Mt. 24. 29=Lk. 21. 26).
Part of the apocalyptic picture painted in Mk. 13, and taken over by
Matthew and Luke, is that in the time after the great affliction, but
before the parousia of the Son of man, signs shall appear in the upper
world; the stars will fall from heaven, and the powers which are in
heaven will be shaken. There is nothing new in the use of the word
δυνάμεις for heavenly beings, spiritual powers; [1] and the various celestial
bodies were often thought to be such powers. For this use of δυνάμεις
cf. Is. 34. 4; 4 Kdms. 17. 16; Dan. 8. 10 (Theodt.). Disorders in the
heavenly sphere were also a regular feature of apocalypses, [2] and the
notion was probably derived from the OT. [3] There is nothing here that
is important for our purpose; though the δυνάμεις and such-like beings
were important inhabitants of the spirit-world of St Paul. It is possible
that we should include under this head Mk. 6. 14 (=Mt. 14. 2) and
Lk. 1. 35; but cf. (vi) and (vii) below.

(v) δύναμις *as eschatological power.* Several important passages use
δύναμις in describing the outpouring of God's power at the end of time.
The most notable are Mk. 9. 1; 13. 26. The former verse is altered by
both Matthew and Luke so that the word δύναμις is omitted by them
(though Matthew has probably rightly interpreted Mk. by referring
explicitly to the parousia of the Son of man). Mk. 13. 26, taken over by
both the later Evangelists (Mt. 24. 30; Lk. 21. 27), also helps to determine
the meaning of 9. 1. These passages both imply that the earlier coming
of Jesus, and the first appearing of the Kingdom of God, were *not* μετὰ
δυνάμεως, ἐν δυνάμει. The Son of man was humiliated, his secret was
hidden, his end was to be the complete and incomprehensible poverty and
powerlessness of the cross. Similarly, the Kingdom was obscure and
unobservable; [4] it was leaven, hidden in a large quantity of flour, a
tiny seed sown in the earth, so small and insignificant that men did not
notice it. But the time would come for the Son of man to appear on the
clouds, with great power and glory, and all men would see him. The

---

[1] See above, p. 71, for the title κύριος δυνάμεων.
[2] See, e.g., 4 Ezra 5. 4 f.; 1 *Enoch* 80. 4-7; *Ass. Moys.* 10. 5; *Sib. Orac.* 3. 796-806;
2 Baruch 32. 1.
[3] Amos 8. 9; Joel 2. 10; 4. 15; Ezek. 32. 7 f.; Is. 13. 10; 34. 4.
[4] This seems to be the meaning of the difficult saying, Mt. 11. 12 (cf. Lk. 16. 16).

time would come when the trifling quantity of leaven should have permeated the whole mass of dough, when the minute seed should have become a tree in which the birds could nest; that is, when the Kingdom of God should come in power. This temporal contrast is by no means all there is to say about the person of Jesus and nature of the Kingdom; but it is one element of fundamental importance.

Lk. 10. 19 should perhaps be included here; Jesus promises his disciples authority over all the power of the enemy ($\tau\grave{\eta}\nu$ $\delta\acute{\upsilon}\nu\alpha\mu\iota\nu$ $\tau o\hat{\upsilon}$ $\grave{\epsilon}\chi\theta\rho o\hat{\upsilon}$). This is the power temporarily allowed by God to Satan: cf. Lk. 4. 6; 22. 53; Rev. 20. 7. It is the same quality of power as that which is connected with the Kingdom and the Son of man, but is of course exercised on the opposite side in the eschatological struggle.

It is possible that we should add also Mk. 12. 24 (=Mt. 22. 29; Lk. has the pericope but not this sentence). The clause read simply as it stands means that the Sadducees, who deny the resurrection, err and show that they do not know the Scriptures, which, as Jesus has just shown in Rabbinic fashion, prove that the dead are raised, and that they do not recognize the power of God; if he has the might properly ascribed to him, obviously he is able, *inter alia*, to make dead men live again. But the reply of Jesus was perhaps more pointed than this suggests.[1] The first two Benedictions of the Amidah prayer (which is very ancient; it is very likely that the parts with which we are concerned were in existence before the time of Jesus, perhaps in the second century B.C.) are known respectively as *Aboth* and *Geburoth*. The former is so called because it addresses God as the "God of Abraham, God of Isaac, God of Jacob, . . . who rememberest the pious deeds of the Patriarchs". The latter received its name because it addresses God as "mighty for ever" (נבור לעולם, gibbor le'olam) and later as "Lord of mighty acts" (בעל נבורות, ba'al geburoth). The mighty acts specified are: "Thou causest the wind to blow and the rain to fall. Thou sustainest the living with loving-kindness, quickenest the dead with great mercy, and keepest thy faith to them that sleep in the dust." With regard to this Benediction Abrahams says: "In its primitive form, this Benediction probably referred to the Omnipotence of God in more general terms, but when the Sadducees disputed the resurrection, the Pharisees (perhaps in the reign of John Hyrcanus, 135-104 B.C.E.) introduced into the Amidah this emphatic statement of belief in the dogma." [2] It seems not impossible that the first, Scriptural, argument of Jesus may have been suggested by the reference in the First Benediction to the Patriarchs.[3] But it is more than possible, it is quite likely, that in disputing with the Sadducees about the resurrection Jesus would think of the first of the "test benedictions", which had been

---

[1] I heard this interpretation given by the late Mr H. M. J. Loewe, of Queens' College.
[2] Israel Abrahams, *Companion to the Authorised Daily Prayer Book*, lix.
[3] Cf. a prayer attached to this benediction for use during the Ten Days of Penitence : " Remember us unto life, O King, who delightest in life, and inscribe us in the book of life, for thine own sake, O living God." But this prayer belongs to the Gaonic age.

introduced to deal with this very point, and that he would refer to it, perhaps by its name, Powers (gᵉburoth), which would naturally be changed into the singular (the δύναμιν of our Gospels) by anyone who did not recognize the allusion. The argument of Jesus, if this suggestion be true, is based both on Scripture and the liturgy; and his attack on the Sadducees may be paraphrased, "You know neither the Bible nor the Prayer Book". Now the powers of God in *Geburoth* include the power to raise the dead, and accordingly, if the saying in the Gospels is based upon *Geburoth* (and the suggestion seems plausible), this use of δύναμις also contains a specific reference to the powerful acts of God in the last days. The reference in the prayer to rain is thought by some to have eschatological significance. The evidence for this is set out in Str.-B. IV. 215b.

(vi) δύναμις *as miraculous power.* The Evangelists several times describe Jesus as possessed of a power for the working of miracles which resided in him almost as a physical fluid transferable to others by touch; in fact, very much like an electric charge, or mana in primitive thought. This is suggested by the instances [1] in which a cure is worked by Jesus by means of a physical contact set up between him and the sufferer, as when, for example, he touches the leper in Mk. 1. 40-45. This impression, based on the actions recorded in the healing miracles of Jesus, is abundantly confirmed by several statements of the Evangelists. The healing of the woman with an issue affords a particularly clear instance. She herself believes that if she can touch the clothes of Jesus she will be cured. Her belief is justified by the event, and Jesus is able to feel, without having seen the woman, that power (δύναμις) has drained away from him into her sick body (Mk. 5. 30, cf. Lk. 8. 46). There is no indication of this use of δύναμις in Q or in Mt., but Lk. 6. 19 is a precisely similar case; δύναμις, as it were, exudes from Jesus for the healing of the people. According to Lk. 9. 1 this power was transferable; Jesus was able to hand it on to the disciples.[2]

Probably we should quote here (and not in (i)) Mk. 6. 14, although the plural is a little strange. Miracle-working faculties are active in Jesus—as one would expect if he is indeed John the Baptist raised from the dead. But, as Dr Torrey [3] points out, only a very slight change of pointing is required in a presumed Aramaic original to give the equivalent of ἐνεργοῦνται αἱ δυνάμεις ὑπ' αὐτοῦ, in which case the passage falls under (i). We should note also Lk. 4. 36, though, as we shall see later (pp. 78, 81 f.), Luke[4] has here inserted the word δύναμις, not very happily, into a Marcan context which did not originally contain it.

In these passages we have the clearest possible evidence that Jesus was thought of as a "pneumatic" man, equipped with supernatural spiritual power. The picture drawn in many passages is so consistent

[1] See below, pp. 83 f.
[2] That this was Luke's view is confirmed by Acts 5. 15; 19. 11 f. (note especially the use of δύναμις in Acts 19. 11). [3] *Our Translated Gospels*, 98.
[4] This use of δύναμις is evidently characteristic of Lk.

and uniform that it is hardly likely not to represent the impression made by Jesus upon the minds of his contemporaries. Again it must be emphasized that we are not here concerned with the question whether the miracles happened or not, or rather with the question precisely what happened in them, or how they may be explained to the modern scientific mind. The chief point upon which the historian must seize is that Jesus acted as if he wielded an exceptional power over the natural and super-natural worlds, and that this power was conceded to him by both his friends and his adversaries. He acted with spiritual authority, and this fact is as well attested by those who said, "He has Beelzebul, or an unclean spirit", as by those who wrote the baptism and temptation narratives.

(vii) δύναμις *as the power of the Spirit.* In a few cases it is clear (either directly or indirectly) that δύναμις is not merely God's power in general, but power exerted by or through the divine Spirit. The expression "power of the Spirit" is used explicitly in Lk. 4. 14: after the baptism and the temptations Jesus returned to begin his ministry in Galilee ἐν τῇ δυνάμει τοῦ πνεύματος. The source of his power was his anointing with the Spirit at the time of his baptism by John (=Elijah).[1]

The connection between δύναμις and πνεῦμα is equally clear, in quite a different context, in Lk. 24. 49. At this point the third Evangelist is evidently preparing for the transition from the first to the second volume of his history. The second chapter of the Acts, the event of Pentecost, was in his mind as he wrote the last verses of the Gospel. The endowment with power of which he speaks can refer only to the descent of the Spirit on the day of Pentecost.

There are two equally clear passages in the first chapter of Lk. In 1. 17 it is prophesied that John the Baptist will do the work of the fore-runner in the spirit and power of Elijah. Now in this passage "spirit" means the Spirit of God,[2] and the parallel between δύναμις and πνεῦμα is close. Again, in 1. 35, the two clauses "Holy Spirit shall come upon thee" and "The power of the Most High shall overshadow thee" are certainly to be taken as members of a synonymous parallelism, and there is probably no difference in meaning between them.

One passage remains in which we may perhaps see, though not with the same certainty, the equivalence of spirit and power. In the description of the healing of the paralytic, Lk. says (5. 17) "the power of the Lord was with him to heal". It will be remembered that Lk. has only just quoted (in 4. 18 f.) Is. 61. 1, "The Spirit of the Lord is upon me . . . he hath sent me to proclaim . . . recovery of sight to the blind", etc. But this parallel cannot be pressed and 5. 17 is perhaps simply another instance of the use of δύναμις for miraculous power.

In these passages we see the "pneumatic" power of Jesus, which

[1] Luke obviously intends this description of Jesus as a "pneumatic" man, revealing and employing the immediate power of God, to be applied to at least the whole of the first part of the Gospel ; cf. Acts 10. 38.

[2] Cf. 2 Kings 2. 9. The Spirit meant is that which causes prophetic activity, i.e., the Spirit of God.

revealed itself in his prophetic and miracle-working ministry, ascribed directly to the Spirit of God; this it is that causes him to preach the Gospel and to heal the sick.

We have now examined every use of the word δύναμις in the Synoptic Gospels. From this discussion emerges one very important point for the doctrine of the Holy Spirit.

The last three sections which have been considered, (v), (vi) and (vii), are particularly significant. (v) and (vii) both represent quite familiar biblical concepts, the unveiling of God's power in a final act of salvation, and his mighty activity through the Spirit which effects his immanence. Nor, again, is there anything surprising in (vi), in the assertion that exceptional power was revealed in him who was believed to be the Son of God. But the question must now be asked, How is this miraculous power, residing in the person of Jesus, to be conceived? Is it related to these other power-concepts of the Bible to which we have just alluded? That is to say, Is it regarded as an anticipation of the future demonstration of God's power, a proleptic realization of his future blessing? Or is it thought of as the result of a special endowment of the Spirit of God? Unfortunately this question is not capable of a simple answer. The passages quoted in (vii) were all derived from Lk.; that is, the third Evangelist seems to have regarded "power" as the energy of the Spirit, while the characteristic connotation of δύναμις in Mk. is eschatological, that is to say, it is used (9. 1; 13. 26) in prophecies about the last days. We find in the Synoptic Gospels themselves the tension, which is certainly evident in the NT as a whole, between the view of Jesus as a herald of the divine consummation of history, and that which sees him as the founder of a universal and spiritual religion. This tension is concentrated in the use of the word "spirit", since an outpouring of the Spirit, in itself timeless, belongs to the last days (Joel 3. 1 ff.). Faith in Jesus as the eschatological redeemer, and faith in him as the "pneumatic" founder of a "pneumatic" community, are at once brought together and transcended by the actual emergence in the life of Jesus of the δύναμις of God. That in him which the Evangelists had to explain exhausted and overflowed the categories that were at their disposal; this accounts for much of the confusion and many of the apparent contradictions in their language. In him the age to come will not be shut out in the future; the Spirit will not be quenched. The words the Evangelists use, both in what they say and in what they are manifestly inadequate to say, reveal the writers' faith in the uniqueness of the events they describe. The "Other", which is no less "other" whether it be thought of as future and not present, or as spirit and not flesh, invades this world; and to its invasion the miraculous power of Jesus bears witness. Yet always the fully worked out future is qualified by the existing present (e.g., Mk. 9. 1), and the spiritual significance of the acts of Jesus remains concealed (Mk. 8. 17-21).[1]

---

[1] Cf. 2 Cor. 12. 9. This point will be resumed below, pp. 158 f.

THE WORD ΕΞΟΤΣΙΑ IN THE SYNOPTIC GOSPELS

We have seen that the word δύναμις is frequently used in the Synoptic Gospels to describe the mighty activity of God, especially as it was revealed in things done by Jesus of Nazareth. It has a sense quite close to that of ἐνέργεια (cf. Eph. 1. 19 f.); that is, it is not merely the power of God, but the power of God in action, force doing work. In comparison with this kinetic energy, as it were, ἐξουσία corresponds to potential energy; it is the divine authority which may at any moment become manifest as power, δύναμις, through the impulse of God's will. This contrast between δύναμις and ἐξουσία is, of course, not peculiar to biblical Greek, but is involved in the proper meaning of each word. For this reason, ἐξουσία could be used for an office, or magistracy, which afforded authority, the capacity for wielding δύναμις. Thus ἐξουσία belongs to a stage of effectiveness which lies behind δύναμις, which δύναμις reveals and on which δύναμις depends; although, as we shall see, there are cases in which ἐξουσία is used in substantially the same sense as δύναμις.

The use of ἐξουσία in the LXX is not distinctive.[1] It is, as might be expected, ascribed to God, though not very frequently; see, e.g., Dan. 3. 100.[2] But there is nothing peculiarly biblical in the ascription of authority to God.

Ἐξουσία is used five times in the Synoptic Gospels without immediate theological significance: Mk. 13. 34; Lk. 12. 11; 19. 17; 20. 20; 23. 7. These all fall within the sphere of normal Greek usage. The remainder we may treat as follows:

(i) *Cases where ἐξουσία has substantially the same meaning as δύναμις.* The signification of ἐξουσία seems to be different in the case of the different Evangelists; or perhaps it should be said that Luke is not careful in his use of the word. This appears from an examination of the Lucan parallels to certain Marcan uses of ἐξουσία. Mk. 1. 27 itself will be discussed in (iii) below; but the Lucan parallel (Lk. 4. 36) seems to treat δύναμις and ἐξουσία as synonymous. Similarly with Mk. 6. 7 (cf. 3. 15). Luke in his parallel (Lk. 9. 1, cf. 10. 19) again puts δύναμις and ἐξουσία together without distinguishing between them. The same observation may be made with regard to a Q passage, Lk. 12. 5. It could hardly be said of this passage that Luke is concerned to distinguish between the authority to cast into Gehenna and the exercise of this authority; and the Matthaean parallel, which has (Mt. 10. 28) δυνάμενον in place of ἐξουσίαν ἔχοντα, makes the equivalence of the words in this case clear.[3] We have already referred to Lk. 10. 19 (peculiar to Lk.) where the power of the disciples, variously described as δύναμις and

---

[1] Cf. *TWNT* II. 561 f.

[2] It seems that the word was used only in the later stages of the LXX translation; it is not found in the Greek Pentateuch.

[3] It is quite likely that the two expressions are translation variants, though it might be difficult to say at what stage of the tradition the variants were introduced.

ἐξουσία, is in question. For Lk. 22. 53 we may refer back again to
Lk. 10. 19; there is no real difference between ἡ ἐξουσία τοῦ σκότους[1]
and ἡ δύναμις τοῦ ἐχθροῦ.

Rather more doubtfully we may here quote Mt. 9. 8, which perhaps
ought to be dealt with as another reference to the ἐξουσία of Mt. 9. 6
(see (iv)). But probably Matthew was simply providing an equivalent
to Mk. 2. 12 and was not referring specifically to the authority to forgive
sins. Cf. Creed, *Luke*, 80.

(ii) Ἐξουσία *the authority antecedent to* δύναμις, i.e., ἐξουσία in its proper
sense. Here we should quote the Marcan passages (3. 15; 6. 7) where
authority is given by Jesus to the disciples for their healing and exorcistic
ministry. Jesus gives them authority that they may exert δύναμις. No
doubt this careful distinction was not in Mark's mind, but the right word,
according to Greek usage, is used.

An interesting case occurs in the Q miracle of the healing of
the centurion's servant. The ground of the centurion's confidence
in Jesus is that he himself is a man ὑπὸ ἐξουσίαν (Mt. 8. 9; Lk. 7. 8 adds
τασσόμενος), and therefore knows the meaning of authority. As a
centurion, he is in a subordinate position; nevertheless, those who in
their turn are under him obey his orders instantly. Jesus, to whom he
appeals, is on the contrary in no subordinate position; his absolute
authority will therefore be all the more certain of an immediate response
in the healing of the sick man. The argument is not made very clear by
the centurion's words—one would not expect him to mention his own
subordinate position without making clearer his *a minori ad maius* argument.[2] The emendations which have been suggested are not convincing,
but in any case the idea of authority remains unaltered. Jesus may be
expected to work a miracle because he is in a position to command the
events of nature.

In Lk. 4. 6 the devil claims authority over all the kingdoms of the
world; or perhaps rather that the several "authorities" of the several
kings of the earth are in his gift. The authority has been committed
(παραδέδοται) to him, and he can hand it on[3] to whomsoever he wishes.

(iii) Ἐξουσία *and* רשות (reshuth). An important article has been
written on the use of ἐξουσία in Mk. 1. 22, 27 (with reference also to
Mk. 11. 27-33) by Dr Daube.[4] His explanation of Mk. 1. 22, 27 may
be summarized in his own words: "(1) ἐξουσία in *vv.* 22 and 27 may
correspond to the Hebrew רשות [reshuth] or the Aramaic רשותא [reshutha']
in its technical sense, i.e., רשות [reshuth] or רשותא [reshutha'] *qua* authority
to lay down such doctrines and decisions as are of binding force. (2) The
γραμματεῖς, the סופרים [sopherim], as opposed in *v.* 22 to those teaching
with רשות, may be the inferior teachers who are not entitled to introduce

---

[1] But cf. Lk. 4. 6 in (ii) on this page.
[2] For example, by using instead of the indicative εἰμι the participle ὤν (in concessive sense)
and instead of ἔχων the indicative ἔχω—so McNeile, *Matthew*, 104.
[3] δίδωμι = παραδίδωμι, cf. J. H. Moulton, *Prolegomena*, 115.   [4] *JTS* XXXIX. 45-59.

fresh rules. (3) In *v.* 27, the people pointing to the διδαχὴ καινὴ κατ' ἐξουσίαν may mean that Jesus gives a new doctrine based on רשות [reshuth], or, for that matter, as if it were based on רשות [reshuth]." [1] Dr Daube goes on to illustrate the use of רשות (reshuth) in the Rabbinical texts. It seems to mean the authority which was conveyed by the process of ordination, which was usually effected by the imposition of hands.[2] It was implied that "the person ordained had his full share of that wisdom which, as was believed, ultimately descended from Moses".[3] Only teachers with this authority might issue new *halakhoth.* "There are signs that the earlier of the ordained Tannaites usually dealt with the principal problems only, whilst less important questions might be submitted to their pupils. From a Tannaitic tradition given in *Bab. Sanh.* 5b we know that under R. Judah Hanasi it was found necessary to abrogate this custom: an order was issued that even minor cases, such as questions of purity and impurity, should no longer be decided by a man, אלא אם כן נוטל רשות מרבו, 'unless he had received רשות [reshuth] from his Rabbi'." [4] The meaning of the Marcan passage in question becomes, on this theory, as follows: *Mk. 1. 22:* the crowds were astonished at the teaching of Jesus, for he was teaching not like one of the lowest-grade teachers to whom they were accustomed [5] but as a Rabbi who had been officially authorized. *Mk. 1. 27:* the people were again astonished and remarked on the enunciation of a new rule or teaching backed by official authority. *Mk. 11. 27-33:* the chief priests and scribes and elders, having seen the things done by Jesus in the Temple, ask him what authority he had for doing them, and, an important development of the question, who gave him this authority, i.e., who was the Rabbi who ordained him.

Dr Daube does not suggest that this ἐξουσία (=רשות, reshuth) was all that the Evangelists themselves ascribed to Jesus. "Though we may find that in Mk. 1. 22 and 27 reference is made to רשות [reshuth] *qua* Rabbinic authority, we are far from denying that Jesus' disciples, right from the beginning, considered his ἐξουσία to be of a very different kind." [6] On the question about the ἐξουσία of Jesus (Mk. 11. 27-33) he says: "The reason for the attack is clear: he acts like a Rabbi, like one having רשות [reshuth], without being properly ordained. It is equally clear that, when he refuses to explain himself, ἐξουσία has quite another significance." [7] Dr Daube then goes on to show that, in addition to its technical meaning, "רשות [reshuth] sometimes refers to the domain, the government of God, or even to God himself. . . . Roughly speaking, one may perhaps say the conception of his ἐξουσία was formed in analogy with רשות [reshuth] *qua* Rabbinic authority; only that with his mighty

---

[1] *Op. cit.* 45. [2] This was the case in Palestine, not in Babylonia.
[3] *Op. cit.* 48. [4] *Op. cit.* 49.
[5] "Galilee was much less fortunate than Judaea as regards the general standard of learning: see H. Graetz, *Geschichte der Juden,* 5th ed., vol. iii. pp. 281 sq. The passages John 1. 46; 7. 41, 52 are very significant in this respect. Consequently, when Jesus appeared, preaching as one having רשות [reshuth], this must indeed have been a great surprise to his listeners."—Daube, *op. cit.;* 49 n. 2.
[6] *Op. cit.* 56. [7] *Op. cit.* 56.

works and, in particular, with his Messianic message, he laid claim to a higher title, namely, רשות [reshuth] *qua* sphere of God and supreme power." [1]

The chief objection to this theory is that in these passages the ἐξουσία is connected with the deeds rather than the words of Jesus. In 1.27 the text is differently punctuated by WH, who take κατ᾽ ἐξουσίαν not with διδαχὴ καινή but with καὶ τοῖς πνεύμασι, κτλ. And in 11.28 the opponents of Jesus ask in what authority ταῦτα ποιεῖς, not ταῦτα διδάσκεις, and the reference is apparently to the cleansing of the Temple. The reply which Dr Daube makes to this criticism is, in effect, that teaching and action (especially in the case of exorcisms) were not so widely separated in old Jewish thought as they are in modern minds. Jesus might well have conveyed his teaching by acts as well as by words alone; and "there are many passages in the Talmud suggesting that, throughout the Tannaitic period and for a long time after, great Rabbis were expected to be familiar with the world of the spirits and to master them". [2]

This explanation is probably correct; and it makes all the more interesting the reply of Jesus to his questioners in Mk. 11.27-33, a passage which we must now consider.

Jesus' reply, which is given in substantially the same form by all three Evangelists, is a second question. Was John's baptism of human or divine origin? [3] The immediate effect of this answer was to silence the questioners, and so to avoid the necessity for a direct reply; but it was an answer, and not merely an evasion, and as such it must have been recognized. The point of Jesus' words seems to be twofold: (*a*) he contrasts two sources of authority. There is authority derived from men (ἐξ ἀνθρώπων). Such was the רשות (reshuth) of the Rabbis. It was a real and important form of authority, but it differed from the authority derived from the other source, that is, from God. Men such as Jesus and John had the same authority as the prophets, and it was not dependent upon human intermediaries. There is probably here a tacit admission that Jesus was not an ordained Rabbi. [4] What Jesus does is to transfer the word רשות (reshuth) from its technical meaning to its meaning in theology; as we have seen, these two significations of the word correspond exactly to ἐξουσία ἐξ ἀνθρώπων and ἐξουσία ἐξ οὐρανοῦ. [5] (*b*) Jesus refers to John the Baptist. It is possible that by doing so he meant to affirm that, if his authority was connected with any human source at all, it was connected with John, that is to say, he (Jesus) stood in the prophetic, not the academic, succession. It is more likely, however, that Jesus means simply that his authority came directly from heaven, and possibly also that it came to him at his baptism by John. [6]

It may be noted before we leave this section that Luke (perhaps

[1] *Op. cit.* 57.　　　　[2] *Op. cit.* 58.
[3] "From heaven" is of course a periphrasis from "from God".
[4] Cf. Daube, *op. cit.* 57 n.: "If there should be any doubts, this passage makes it clear that neither Jesus nor John the Baptist had received ordination in the technical sense."
[5] Cf. Gal. 1.1.　　　[6] See also Reitzenstein's comment on Mk. 1.22, referred to below, p. 96.

because he was a Gentile and unfamiliar with the technical terms of the Jewish schools) read Mk. 1. 27 so as to connect the ἐξουσία of Jesus with his exorcisms, and accordingly understood ἐξουσία as a term similar to if not synonymous with δύναμις (see above, pp. 75, 78).

(iv) *'Εξουσία as divine authority.* Here only two passages have to be considered. The first is Mk. 2. 10 (=Mt. 9. 6=Lk. 5. 24). The Son of man has authority to forgive sins. It has often been argued that the thought of forgiveness has been inserted into this pericope, which originally was a simple miracle story. It must be sufficient here to say that the parenthesis in which the subject is raised is characteristically Marcan [1] and that no purpose can be assigned to the present form of the narrative which does not include the association of the healing of the body with the forgiveness of sins, and that the story certainly owes its position at this point in the Marcan narrative to its bearing upon the question of authority and the doctrine of forgiveness. The authority which Jesus claims by his absolution of the paralytic is divine. Str.-B. (on Mt. 9. 6, I. 495) say: "In the earlier period, the freedom from sin of the saved community was usually taken for granted. According to some passages the Messiah contributes to the bringing in of this future ideal, in so far as he destroys the godless out of Israel through the judgement, sets at nought the might of the demonic powers, and protects his righteous people from sin by his government. . . . The notion also appears that Israel will attain forgiveness of sins through the intercession and suffering of the Messiah. . . . But on the other hand no passage is known to us in which the Messiah in his own authority accords to anyone the forgiveness of sins. The forgiveness of sins remains everywhere the exclusive right of God." Thus Mark is quite correct in making the scribes say (2. 7) "Who can forgive sins but God alone?" and in refuting the charge of blasphemy against Jesus. In Mt. 9. 8, on the other hand, the crowds refer to the miracle (ἰδόντες) and to the miraculous power of Jesus when they "glorify God who had given such power (ἐξουσίαν) to men". It is a complete misunderstanding of Mk. to suppose that his "Son of man" is to be interpreted by the later editor's "men"; Mk. does not mean that *any* man had the divine power to forgive sins.

The saying which remains is Mt. 28. 18. This is a claim, reminiscent of sayings in the Fourth Gospel (cf., e.g., Jn. 5. 27; 10. 18; 17. 2), to complete authority which can only be described as divine. We may compare the false claim of Satan (Lk. 4. 6). The saying has deep roots in the Gospel tradition, and appears in another form (without the word ἐξουσία) in Q (Mt. 11. 27=Lk. 10. 22).

THE SYNOPTIC MIRACLE STORIES

About the miracle stories in general we may make the same two observations as with regard to the exorcisms. (i) The great majority

---

[1] Cf. C. H. Turner, *JTS* XXVI. 145-156.

of the miracles are recorded in Mk. The other sections of the Gospel tradition supply comparatively few; for example, in Q there are only two (the centurion's servant, Mt. 8. 5-13=Lk. 7. 1-10; a demoniac, Mt. 12. 22 f.=Lk. 11. 14). It would be mistaken to suppose that this uneven distribution of miracle stories is evidence that there was a period when the Church believed in a Jesus who worked no miracles and was without supernatural authority; there is in Q at least one striking saying about Jesus' miracles (Mt. 11. 2 ff.=Lk. 7. 18 ff.) which is in some respects more important than any Marcan narrative. (ii) Mark often refers briefly in his summaries to miracles worked by Jesus.

We may notice also that it is often difficult to draw a sharp line between exorcisms and other miracles. For example, in the stilling of the storm (Mk. 4. 35-41) Jesus addresses the sea as if it were possessed by a demon; and sickness was often thought to be the result of possession.

(i) *Miracles accompanied by a physical act.* The majority of the Marcan miracles fall into this category; but sometimes they are significantly modified by the editors of the first and third Gospels.
Marcan miracles:

    (a) Peter's mother-in-law. 1. 30 f..
    (b) A leper. 1. 40-45.
    (c) Man with a withered hand. 3. 1-6.
    (d) Many try to touch Jesus. 3. 10.
    (e) Jairus' daughter. 5. 21-24, 35-43.
    (f) Woman with an issue. 5. 25-34.
    (g) A few sick folk at Nazareth. 6. 5.
    (h) The disciples anoint with oil. 6. 13.
    (i) Touching the fringe of his cloak. 6. 56.
    (j) The deaf stammerer. 7. 32-37.
    (k) The blind man of Bethsaida. 8. 22-26.

There is no Q miracle to be mentioned here.

In dealing with the material peculiar to Mt. we must notice first that in the Matthaean form of (d) and (g) the acts associated by Mk. with the cure are omitted and that the later Evangelist omits altogether (h), (j)[1] and (k).[2] It may be observed that (h), (j) and (k) are the miracles in which the amount of manipulation is greatest. The only Matthaean miracle which comes under consideration here is that in 9. 27-31, the healing of two blind men whose eyes Jesus touches. It may be that Matthew was influenced in his manner of telling the story (as has been suggested) by the Marcan narrative of 8. 22-26, the blind man of Bethsaida, though the really distinctive features of the latter story are absent.

Similarly when we examine the special Lucan material, the first test to be made is of Luke's editing of the Marcan narratives. Luke omits the physical contact in (a), merely stating that Jesus "stood over" Peter's

[1] But cf. the general healings which Matthew describes at the corresponding place (Mt. 15. 30 f.) of his Gospel.
[2] But cf. Mt. 9. 27-31, which, according to Streeter, *Four Gospels*, 170, bears traces of Mk. 8. 22-26.

mother-in-law;[1] in his parallel to Mk. 6. 13 (h) he says that the disciples
worked cures but does not mention the use of oil. He omits completely
the passages (i), (j), (k); but these fall within the "great omission"
and their absence is perhaps to be explained on grounds which have nothing
to do with their contents. Luke does not speak of the few sick folk healed
by the imposition of Jesus' hands in (g); again this may be due to Luke's
having used a different source from Mk. for his account of Jesus' preaching at Nazareth; at all events, he was at this point handling Mk. very
freely. There is more miraculous material in the matter peculiar to
Lk. than in that peculiar to Mt., but only a few cases in which physical
means are used for the cure. These are:

α The raising of the widow's son at Nain, 7. 11-17. Here Jesus is said
to have touched the bier on which the young man was lying; it is not
clear whether this action is significant or not.

β The healing of a deformed woman, 13. 10-17.

γ In the narrative of the arrest (Lk. 22. 47-53) Luke inserts the statement that Jesus touched and healed the man whose ear had been cut off
by one of the disciples.

Thus a substantial proportion of the miracle narratives preserved in
the Synoptic tradition involve the idea of healing effected not by the
word of Jesus only, but by the use of some action also, generally on the
part of Jesus, but occasionally on the part of the person healed, action
the chief feature of which was usually the establishing of physical contact
between Jesus and the sick person. Matthew and Luke, if indeed they
were concerned about the matter, only purged away the grosser forms
of miraculous mediation, such as the use of spittle. This physical contact
between physician and patient is characteristic of ancient miracle stories,[2]
but it reinforces strongly what has been said above [3] about the miraculous
δύναμις of Jesus. Mere contact with him infused health into sick persons,
and his authority drove away disease.

(ii) *Sayings in the miracle stories.* There is little to be learned from these
for our purpose. For the most part they are bald imperatives which
bring out powerfully the authority of Jesus but do not in any way define it.
Such commands seem to go back to the earliest stages of the Gospel
tradition, for they are given, in two cases, by Mark, in transliterated
Aramaic (5. 41 ταλιθὰ κούμ; 7. 34 ἐφφαθά). Generally they apply
quite simply to the cure about to be performed. A leper is told, "Be
cleansed" (Mk. 1. 40-45); a man with a withered hand is told to stretch
it out (Mk. 3. 1-6); to the sea Jesus says, "Be quiet, be muzzled"
(Mk. 4. 35-41), and to a fig tree, "May no one eat of thee any
more" (Mk. 11. 12-14). Sometimes the command has less direct reference
to the disease, and a sick person is simply told to go (Mk. 2. 1-12;
10. 46-52). There are the same direct and indirect imperatives in

---

[1] Cf. Lucian, *Philopseudes*, 16: ἐπιστὰς κειμένοις. It was the attitude of the exorcist.
[2] See Bultmann, *GST* 237 f.   [3] Pp. 75 f.

Lk. (5. 1-11; 7. 11-17; 13. 10-17; 17. 11-19). In a miracle narrative peculiar to Mt. (9. 27-31) there is an imperative not immediately connected with the disease in question—κατὰ τὴν πίστιν ὑμῶν γενηθήτω ὑμῖν. This expression (which may have been meant as an echo of Gen. 1. 3, 6, 14—γενηθήτω φῶς, κτλ.) was imported by Matthew into the Q miracle of the centurion's servant (Mt. 8. 5-13; cf. Lk. 7. 1-10 where there is no command of healing). We must not omit here Mk. 2. 10, where the theological significance of the miracles is brought out when Jesus pronounces spiritual absolution over the paralytic.

All these commands simply show that Jesus was one who, as Ignatius (Eph. 15. 1) said, "spoke and it came to pass". He wielded a quite extraordinary spiritual authority. With the miraculous commands we should compare the obedience shown him by men who, at his command, left their work, relatives and possessions to follow him (Mk. 1. 16-20; 2. 13 f.; 3. 13-19; Mt. 4. 18-22; 9. 9; Lk. 5. 1-11 [with a nature miracle]; 5. 27 f.; 6. 12-16).[1] Here too we see plainly the divine but undefined δύναμις of Jesus.

(iii) *Comments of the onlookers at the miracles.* These are not particularly illuminating save in the general impression which they convey. The effect of the miracles upon the crowds who saw them, as indicated by the comments ascribed to them by the Evangelists, may be summarized as follows:

(a) Astonishment. The words ἐξίστασθαι (Mk. 2. 12; 5. 42; 6. 51 f. —in some cases with the Matthaean and Lucan parallels) and θαυμάζειν (Mt. 8. 27; 9. 33; 15. 31; Lk. 8. 25) are quite frequently used. We find also ἐκπλήσσεσθαι (Mk. 7. 37), θαμβεῖσθαι (a Marcan word) and θάμβος (a Lucan word). The tendency of the later Evangelists is to emphasize the astonishment of the beholders; cf. Mk. 11. 21 with Mt. 21. 20.

(b) Fear. This (represented by the words φόβος and φοβεῖσθαι) is found in Mk. 4. 41 (and the Lucan parallel) 5. 15; Mt. 9. 8; Lk. 5. 26; 7. 16; 8. 25. Compare the request of the Gerasenes (Mk. 5. 17 and parallels) that Jesus should depart from their territory. It is, of course, possible to explain this desire as due simply to the wish to lose no more pigs; but, in the context, the fear of Mk. 5. 15 more probably determines its motive.

(c) Glorifying God, rejoicing. The word δοξάζειν is used several times (Mk. 2. 12; Mt. 9. 8; 15. 31; Lk. 5. 26; 7. 16; 17. 15), χαίρειν once (Lk. 13. 17) and εὐχαριστεῖν once (Lk. 17. 16). With these references should go the praise of Jesus in Mk. 7. 37, which is taken over by Matthew (Mt. 15. 31) but connected with another miracle not derived from Mk.

---

[1] Yet he by no means secured universal obedience; his authority was not so manifest as to be compulsive; many were called but few were chosen.

(*d*) Confession of the authority of Jesus. This goes a step further than the last reference given. In an elementary form it appears in Mk. 1. 27 (=Lk. 4. 36).[1] A similar wonder is expressed in Mk. 4. 41 and parallels. Lk. contains two important confessions. In 5. 8 Peter, having seen the miraculous catch of fish, says to Jesus: "Depart from me, for I am a sinful man, O Lord." Clearly this saying means that Jesus had revealed an authority which marked him off from sinful men. In 7. 16 Jesus is recognized as a prophet and the people declare that God has visited his people. Mt. 14. 33 is an interesting case; for in this Gospel, after the miracle of the walking on the water, the disciples confess that Jesus is the Son of God; this is substituted for a very different passage in Mk., which we shall presently consider.

(*e*) Accusation against Jesus. He is accused of casting out demons by Beelzebul (Mk. 3. 21 ff. and parallels; Mt. 9. 34, cf. 10. 25). This too is a confession of the supernatural power of Jesus.[2] In Mk. 3. 6 the Pharisees take counsel with the Herodians to destroy Jesus; but the reason for this is his attitude to the Sabbath, not his miracles as such. Similarly in Mt. 21. 15 the chief priests and scribes, when they see the wonders done by Jesus in the Temple, rebuke him for the Messianic confession made by his followers.

(*f*) Misunderstanding. Those who fail to understand are the disciples (Mk. 6. 51 f., contrast the Matthaean parallel). This passage is of the first importance in any general discussion of the miracles, or of the disciples. It must be taken with 8. 14-21. It is enough here to say that, according to the Marcan theory, there is more in miracles than their outward appearance; they are, to use the Fourth Evangelist's word, $\sigma\eta\mu\epsilon\hat{\iota}\alpha$ of the power of God.[3]

(*g*) Herod's opinion of Jesus. This is a special case; Mk. 6. 14-16 and parallels. By identifying Jesus with the resurrected John, Herod bears witness to the supernatural impression created by his power.

These various reactions to the miracles of Jesus attest in different ways the opinion that he was possessed of unusual (unique would be perhaps too strong a word) spiritual power which manifested itself in his deeds. This impression is both so uniform and so variously expressed that it is difficult to think of it as the creation of the Evangelists, especially in view of outside testimony about Jesus, some of which, while speaking of him in the most uncomplimentary manner, bears witness to a numinous power.[4] These considerations reinforce conclusions that were drawn in our discussion of the word $\delta\acute{\upsilon}\nu\alpha\mu\iota\varsigma$.[5]

(iv) *Sayings about miracles.* The miracles of Jesus made a deeply marked impression upon the Gospel tradition, which presents not only

---

[1] The punctuation of this verse is in doubt ; see above, p. 81.
[2] See below, p. 96.   [3] See below (iv).
[4] Cf. *b. Sanh.* 43a : Jesus was stoned because " he hath practised magic and led astray Israel ".
[5] Cf. p. 77.

miracle stories but also a considerable number of sayings about miracles which are not connected with particular narratives but presuppose their existence. These sayings are of very great importance and may be separated into two classes.

(a) The following passages come under consideration here:

Mk. 3. 23-30, with the parallels, which offer also a Q version of the discourse. This controversial passage has been discussed above [1] in connection with exorcisms: the chief points may be briefly recapitulated. These miracles of Jesus are not due to the power of Beelzebul but to the activity of the finger [2] of God, which proves that the Kingdom of God has come near; Satan is in fact being bound by his stronger adversary the Son of man. In the same context (in Mk. and Mt.) occurs the saying about blasphemy against the Holy Spirit. According to Mk.'s interpretation of this, to attribute the works of Jesus to an evil spirit rather than to the Spirit of God constitutes the blasphemy against the Spirit. The sum of all this is the assertion that the work of Jesus is the personal activity of God [3] and the argument (note the ἄρα in Mt. 12. 28 and Lk. 11. 20) from this assertion that the Messianic salvation is in process of manifestation. There is probably no reason why these chief points should not be detached from their association with the exorcisms and the Beelzebul controversy and applied to the miracles in general. At least, this is borne out by the other sayings which will be considered.

Mt. 11. 2-6 and parallel. John the Baptist sends disciples to inquire whether Jesus is indeed the Coming One (ὁ ἐρχόμενος). The question may be only editorial framework intended to provide a background for the answer of Jesus, which can in any case stand by itself. It seems to contain a direct allusion to Is. 61. 1, interpreted as a Messianic prophecy. John is left to draw the obvious conclusion that Jesus, who fulfils the prophecy by healing the sick, raising the dead and preaching to the poor, is the Coming One. There is no direct reference to the opening words of the prophecy, "The Spirit of the Lord God is upon me", though they may have been in mind; they are quoted clearly enough in Lk. 4. 18 f., where the same use of the Isaianic passage is made. This use of Is. 61 raises the same questions as the Beelzebul controversy, and in so doing takes in a wider field than exorcisms only, and indeed includes the non-miraculous activity of evangelizing the poor. The work of Jesus is inspired by the Spirit of God, is the work of God; the healings and the preaching are *therefore* the signs of the fulfilment of God's salvation (this is shown by the very fact that the OT is quoted).

Mt. 8. 17, an addition to the Marcan context (Mk. 1. 32-34). This verse should be mentioned here because it too is quotation of the OT

---

[1] Pp. 59-63.   [2] Lk.; Spirit, Mt.
[3] Whether described by his "finger" or his "spirit" matters little, since both these terms denote his immediate, immanent power.

(Is. 53. 4), and the fact of quotation again implies the view that the miracles were a visible sign of the fulfilment of God's purpose.

Mt. 13. 16 f. and parallel. This Q saying may also be taken here in connection with those which have just been cited, and which refer to the fulfilment in Jesus of God's purposes and therefore of the prophecies of the OT. It appears in different contexts in Mt. and Lk. Mt. has placed it in his chapter of parables which he has conflated from Mk., Q and some other source or sources peculiar to himself. It stands immediately after the Marcan (Mk. 4. 11 f.) saying about the purpose and understanding of the parables, and, in that context, must mean that the disciples are blessed in contrast with those who do not understand the parables, whose eyes are blinded and whose hearts are made fat. Their blessedness is that it has been given them to know the mysteries of the Kingdom. In Lk. (10. 23 f.), on the other hand, the saying is made to follow the pronouncement of Jesus, "All things have been delivered unto me of my Father: and no one knoweth who the Son is, save the Father; and who the Father is, save the Son, and he to whomsoever the Son willeth to reveal him" (10. 22). That is, the disciples here are blessed because they have received from Jesus his revelation, his παράδοσις, about the Father. Since the Matthaean and Lucan contexts are so different from one another there is no need to suppose that either of them is original; and there is no reason why we should not think that the things "seen and heard" originally included the actions, the miracles, of Jesus, along with his teaching. In any case, the blessedness of the disciples lies in the realization of that which their forebears had longed to see, but which God had not made known in their day. The work of Jesus was the visible and audible fulfilment of God's purpose, of the OT hope.

Mt. 11. 20-24 (=Lk. 10. 13-16). The miracles of Jesus have compelling value as evidence; had they been done in Tyre, or Sidon or Sodom, those cities would have repented; Sodom would have remained to this day; and Tyre and Sidon, because they did not have the advantage of seeing the miracles, will find a judgement more tolerable than that of Chorazin and Bethsaida. Yet, after all, the evidence of the miracles is not compelling; for miracles were wrought in Chorazin, Bethsaida and Capernaum, and those cities disregarded them. Clearly the difference must lie in those who see them; and this difference is not one of advantage in Jewish birth, or of righteousness of life. The Synoptic view of miracles is contained in this section, and we must return to it; [1] at present it may simply be said that the possibility of recognizing the work of God in the miracles of Jesus is always at hand, even though it is not always realized. In this context we may consider also the Marcan saying, *Mk. 7. 27*, and the Q miracle of the healing of the centurion's servant (*Mt. 8. 5-13*; Lk. 7. 1-10; 13. 28-30). In each of these cases a miracle is performed for the benefit of a Gentile, but it also appears,

---

[1] Pp. 92 f.

especially in Mk. 7. 27, that the miracles belong by right to the Jews—
they are the children's bread. The situation is paradoxical. The miracles,
as signs of God's fulfilled salvation, belong to his peculiar people, who,
however, neither understand nor are grateful for them. The Gentiles,
who have no right to expect miracles, yet reveal the faith and apprehension which are so strikingly absent on the part of the Jews.

Mk. 6. 52 (contrast Mt. 14. 33); 8. 14-21 (=Mt. 16. 5-12). This is
difficult material, as Matthew evidently found it to be. Mk. 6. 52 he
completely transformed; the disciples' failure to understand, and their
hardened heart, become in the first Gospel the Christian confession,
"truly thou art the Son of God". In Mk. 8. 14-21 Mt. preserved most
of the Marcan words, but gave a subtle change to their purport, making
it quite clear by an additional verse (16. 12) that by the leaven of the
Pharisees and the Sadducees he meant their teaching,[1] while it is far from
clear what Mk. meant by the leaven of the Pharisees and the leaven of
Herod (8. 15). Of the two accounts, that in Mk. is plainly primary,
that in Mt. secondary. Mt. puts the disciples in a much more favourable
light than Mk.; but he does not make it clear why Jesus should have
referred to the miracles at all. If Jesus was simply warning the disciples
against the teaching of the Pharisees and using the symbol of leaven
(commonly used in Jewish literature of evil influences), why should he
remind them that he had fed five thousand men and four thousand men
with five and seven loaves, and that in each case there had been baskets
full of bread to spare? In Mk. there is no indication that the disciples
did at this point understand what Jesus was saying. Indeed it would be
possible to read his last words (οὔπω συνίετε) not as a question (so WH)
but as a statement. *Vv.* 17 f. class the disciples with whose who, in 4. 11 f.,
are said to be unable to understand the parables of Jesus. They are in
danger of falling into the same obtuse spirit as the Pharisees, who have
just (8. 11-13) been asking for a sign.[2] For our purpose, the important
point to be observed is that, like the parables, the miracles are understandable and ought to be understood, and yet are misunderstood; they
are signs with a potency either for revelation or for hardening the heart.
Even the disciples are in grave danger of completely misapprehending
their meaning.

Lk. 13. 31-33. We need not delay over this obscure saying. The exact
meaning of the repeated "today, tomorrow, and the third (next) day"
is not clear; but there seems to be some allusion to the crucifixion and
resurrection (also in τελειοῦμαι), which would then be co-ordinated, as
the supreme sign, with the subordinate signs of the ministry of Jesus
(cures and exorcisms).[3]

---

[1] In Lk. 12. 1 it is their hypocrisy.   [2] See p. 90.

[3] Perhaps we should mention as relevant to the Messianic significance of the miracles the
association of several of them with the Sabbath day, and the probable allusion to the final
Sabbath rest of the Messianic age; see E. C. Hoskyns, in *Mysterium Christi*, ed. Bell and
Deissmann, 74-78.

The general purport of the sayings about miracles which we have so far considered is that they are acts of divine power wrought through God's representative. As such they are signs of the coming of the New Age of God's salvation, and as such they may be recognized by all who have eyes to see. It is true that many, even the disciples, are blind, but God's power is nevertheless prodigally expended in miracles the significance of which might be grasped by those whose minds are enlightened. Behind the figure of Jesus as a "pneumatic" person (as he is portrayed in the miracle narratives themselves) we see the root of his power—his Messiahship, and his connection with the Kingdom of God.

(b) We must now turn to the second class of sayings.

Mk. 8, 11 f. (=*Mt. 16. 1-4*)[1] and a parallel Q saying, *Mt. 12. 38 f.* =*Lk. 11. 29.* In both forms of this saying the adversaries of Jesus ask from him a sign. In the Marcan version the sign is absolutely refused; in the Q version it is said that no sign will be given except that of the prophet Jonah. It is not clear what was meant by the sign of the prophet Jonah. Matthew certainly understood it to mean the swallowing of Jonah by the great fish, the period which he spent in the fish and his emergence from it, the whole regarded as a type of the death, burial and resurrection of Jesus. Luke does not expressly refer to this experience of Jonah, and it has been held that he regarded the "sign of Jonah" as Jonah's preaching of repentance to the inhabitants of Nineveh.[2] Matthew's interpretation, however, is more likely to be original; and if this is so, Jesus means that the only sign which is to be offered to the people of this generation is his death and resurrection (cf. Lk. 16. 31).[3]

Jesus not merely refuses to give a sign; he suggests that his questioners ought not to have asked for one; it is an evil and adulterous generation that seeks a sign. Of course this does not mean that adultery was a characteristic sin of Jesus' contemporaries, but that they were adulterous in the sense in which Hosea's wife, typifying Israel, was adulterous; they were forsaking their true Lord and God, and seeking illicit unions with things that were no gods. What the people of Hosea's time wanted was corn and wine and oil without the recognition that these things came from God (Hos. 2. 7, 10 f., 14). Similarly the contemporaries of Jesus sought the gratification of signs without the obligation of recognizing the God whose signs they were.[4] They were (at least in the minds of the Evangelists) the same men who had earlier attributed the beneficent works of Jesus to Beelzebul. To ask for a special sign now was to deny the activity of God in all that Jesus had hitherto done, and to suppose the poverty and humiliation of the Son of man to be a less adequate revelation than his wealth and glory. Hence the vigorous refusal of Jesus to work miracles.

---

[1] *Vv.* 2b-3 are not part of the original text.
[2] Yet notice the ἔσται (future) in Lk. 11. 30 ; Jesus was at that time preaching ; it was his death and resurrection that lay in the future.
[3] The suggestion (J. H. Michael, *JTS* XXI. 146-159) that in the text the "sign of Jonah " is a corruption of " sign of John " (the Baptist) is attractive but unconvincing.   [4] Cf. Jn. 6. 26.

Mt. 4. 1-11=Lk. 4. 1-13. The Q temptation narrative has already been discussed.[1] Here we have only to draw attention to the refusal of Jesus to yield to the temptation to work miracles for his own profit or in order to dazzle his people with a show of power. We need not inquire whether the temptation narrative arose as an explanation of the known fact that Jesus did not perform certain miracles which might have been expected of him, or in some other way. It is enough here to say, as is obvious enough, that the response of Jesus to Satan is quite in harmony with his later refusal to produce signs on request, and to point out that such a request for signs is regarded in the Gospel tradition as of diabolical origin.

Several passages suggest that Jesus did not perform miracles when he might have been expected to do so. Thus, according to *Mk. 6. 5* (=*Mt. 13. 58*), Jesus did few miracles in his home town of Nazareth. Neither Evangelist means to suggest that the power of Jesus varied in direct proportion to the degree of confidence in his subjects. It is more nearly another case of a disappointed request for signs with which we have to do. In *Mk. 7. 24-30* Jesus at first refuses to cure the daughter of the Syro-Phoenician woman on the ground that such benefits are for Jews not Gentiles. In *Mk. 14. 32-42* Jesus prays that his approaching death may not take place; nothing happens to avert the crucifixion. *Mt. 26. 53* is an insertion into the Marcan account of the arrest; Jesus might have had the services of more than twelve legions of angels, but did not accept them, in order that the Scriptures might be fulfilled. In *Lk. 9. 9*; *23. 8-12* Herod shows interest in Jesus and desires to see a miracle performed by him; but he is disappointed. In *Mk. 15. 32* the bystanders at the crucifixion challenge Jesus to save himself as he saved others, to come down from the cross to prove that he was indeed the Christ; but he did not.[2]

A few other details may be noted. A miracle, even the most striking, may be ineffectual—*Lk. 16. 31.* If the Jews do not attend to Moses a resurrection will not convince them. The direct and plain testimony of Scripture is more potent than the witness of a miracle which may very easily be misunderstood. The power (not uncommon in the primitive Christian community) to work miracles is not to be boasted of or relied upon as a qualification for salvation. This appears in *Lk. 10. 20*, where the exultant disciples are warned to rejoice not in their power over demons but in their election with God; and in the saying of *Mt. 7. 22* miracle-working is no substitute for doing the will of God.[3] We may notice also the important fact that signs and wonders may be performed by false Christs and false prophets with such verisimilitude as to delude if possible even the elect (*Mk. 13. 22*); and the many injunctions to silence about miracles, which are especially frequent in Mk.

Finally we may mention again passages (*Mt. 11. 20-24*=*Lk. 10. 12-15*; *Mk. 6. 52*; *8. 14-21*) which were referred to above,[4] because though

---

[1] Pp. 51 f.
[3] This Q saying appears in a somewhat different form in Lk. 12. 26.
[2] Cf. the obscure saying of Lk. 4. 23.
[4] Pp. 88 f.

miracles are here set forth as potential revelation, their actual effect had
been to harden men's hearts against the truth.

The two classes of sayings which we have just considered might seem
at first to be contradictory in their teaching. On the one hand, Jesus,
quickly moved by the sight of human suffering, readily performs miracles
which are signs of the power of the Spirit which rests upon him (e.g.
Lk. 4. 18 f.), and hence also signs of the New Age of which his work is
the inauguration (e.g. Mt. 12. 28 and parallel). It is for John—and
others—to take note of what is happening and then to answer for themselves the question whether Jesus is the Coming One. On the other hand,
in the latter group of sayings, Jesus steadfastly refuses to perform miracles
which might, apparently, have ensured the success of his mission. To
ask him to show a sign is a diabolical temptation to be vehemently
resisted. His own disciples betray a complete failure to understand those
signs which they have observed; that is, to the eye-witnesses the miracles
were *not* revelation.

This apparent antinomy runs deep into the substance of the Gospel,
and it will be necessary later [1] to relate it to other themes and to examine
its meaning. Here it will be sufficient to point out how it is developed
in the Synoptic (which means, practically, the Marcan) view of miracles.

In the first place, the miracles were the work of God, performed through
the inspiration of his Spirit, and at the hand of Jesus. This no Evangelist
would have thought of denying in respect of any miracle actually wrought
by Jesus. Other miracles might be done by other spirits than the Holy
Spirit (cf. Mk. 13. 22 and the Beelzebul controversy), but in the miracles
of Jesus the hand of God was at work.

Second, this fact was not perceived and understood, even by the
disciples (according to Mk.). Certainly it was not believed by those
who accused Jesus of acting in the power of Beelzebul, or by those who
demanded further signs from him. It was not apprehended by the
inhabitants of Chorazin, of Bethsaida, of Capernaum, who else would
have repented and recognized the visitation of God. The function of
the miracles corresponds precisely to that assigned to the parables in
Mk. 4. 11 f.: they may reveal; but if they do not, they harden the
hearts of those who are blind to them so that "from him that hath not
is taken away even that which he hath". Hence the indignant refusal
of Jesus to multiply signs to the beholders' damnation; there would be
only one sign—his death and subsequent vindication.

His δύναμις, as we have seen,[2] was regarded both as the power of the
Spirit and also as an anticipation of the unveiling of God's power in the
last days. But it was not, if the expression may be used, the Spirit naked,
unimpeded, stripped of the cloak of human and worldly relativity; nor
again was the ministry of Jesus in any real sense identifiable with the
end of the world. Jesus (so the bearers of the Gospel tradition and the

---

[1] See pp. 119 f., 154-159.   [2] P. 77.

Church preaching believed) was the Messiah, and because he was the Messiah, he was a "pneumatic" person, a man wielding exceptional, uncanny, numinous, miraculous powers; he was manifest as a "pneumatic", as a man having δύναμις, but he was not openly and fully revealed as Messiah, because the temporal and material conditions of this world forbade the complete laying bare of the divine power in him. It is in this paradox, of the fullness of God's power and its inevitable concealment, that we shall find the clue to the problems connected with the doctrine of the Spirit in the Synoptic Gospels.

6

JESUS AS PROPHET

JESUS was held by the people, including some at least of his own followers, to be a prophet. This is explicitly stated in a number of important passages. In Mk. we have 6. 15 (=Lk. 9. 8, no Matthaean parallel) and 8. 28 (=Mt. 16. 14=Lk. 9. 19). The special Lucan material affords three instances: 7. 16, where after the miracle at Nain the people declare that a great prophet has arisen among them, and that God has visited his people; 7. 39, where Simon the Pharisee rejects the view that Jesus was a prophet, a view which must presumably have been taken by others; and 24. 19, a passage whose particular interest lies in the fact that it represents disciples of Jesus holding the opinion that Jesus was a prophet. Two verses in the matter peculiar to Mt. ascribe the same judgement upon Jesus to the people, 21. 11, 46. Jesus is nowhere described as a prophet in Q, and the designation is rare outside the Synoptic Gospels; in the rest of the NT it appears only in Acts 3. 22 f. (cf. 7. 37), where the prophecy of Deut. 18. 15-18 is given a Messianic application,[1] and in Jn. 4. 19; 6. 14; 7. 40; 9. 17 (cf. 7. 52).

Apart from these passages, in which the word προφήτης is actually applied to Jesus, there are many indications in the Synoptic Gospels of similarity between Jesus and the great prophets of the OT. These are fully brought out by Professor C. H. Dodd in his essay, *Jesus as Teacher and Prophet*.[2] There is no need to repeat here what has already been said. Professor Dodd mentions the following points, for the evidence for which reference should be made to his essay.

(i) Jesus spoke with the "note of sovereign authority".

(ii) Much of his teaching has been shown[3] to have been given in poetical form, as was the teaching of the OT prophets.

(iii) "There is a suggestion of other 'pneumatic' traits associated with prophecy, such as vision and audition".[4]

(iv) Like the prophets, Jesus uttered predictions.

(v) He also performed symbolic actions, as at the Last Supper.

(vi) He appealed to the OT prophets in support of his own teaching.

(vii) Like theirs, his eschatology was of a radically ethical nature.

(viii) He announced the Reign of God.

---

[1] It appears that this prophecy was not used messianically at an early date by Jews; it was first taken to apply to the Messiah by the Christians and by the Samaritans. See Jackson and Lake, *Beginnings of Christianity*, I. 404 f. It is now known to have been used at Qumran.
[2] In *Mysterium Christi*, ed. Bell and Deissmann; see especially 56-65, whence the quotations in the following lines are taken.
[3] Notably by C. F. Burney, *The Poetry of Our Lord*.
[4] At this point (*op. cit.* 58) Professor Dodd notes that "like them (*sc.* Isaiah and Jeremiah), Jesus seems to have spoken little of the 'Spirit'".

(ix) He "appears in the Gospels much more as a preacher of 're-pentance' than as a teacher in the ordinary sense. His μετανοεῖτε is an echo of the prophetic שׁוּב [shub]".

(x) "Jesus is said to have received, like the OT prophets, a special calling or designation in a 'pneumatic' experience."

(xi) His possession of a divine revelation involves an intimate communion with, a knowledge of, God.

(xii) "Hence, like the prophets, he is the representative of God; to follow his teaching is to do the will of God; to reject him is to reject God."

(xiii) "Like the OT prophets, the Jesus of the Gospels has a mission to Israel, and his words and deeds are related to the national destiny."

(xiv) "The Hebrew prophets thought of themselves as not merely declaring the Word of God, but as playing a part in the fulfilment of that Word. . . . Jesus frequently speaks as though his own ministry was in fact the critical event in history, and in particular . . . he seems to have expected from his death some momentous consequence."

(xv) "In his personal religion (so far as this is accessible to us in the records) Jesus stands in the succession of the prophets, while he goes beyond them."

To these considerations a few more of a different nature may with some hesitation be added. Certain classes of the sayings of Jesus have been held to have a particularly authoritative nature. Such are, for example, those introduced by the words ἦλθον and ἀπεστάλην. In an article[1] these sayings are discussed by Harnack, who says: "Undoubtedly there is in this 'I am come', whatever it may mean, something *authoritative* and *final*. There is in it the consciousness of a divine mission, and, indeed, it is interchangeable with the expression 'I was sent'."[2] Similarly we may refer to the sayings introduced by the formula ἀμὴν λέγω ὑμῖν.[3] Again we may add the "Ich-Worte," as they are called by Bultmann,[4] which in the same way emphasize the personal authority of Jesus. It is true that Bultmann thinks that these sayings originated in the Hellenistic communities, though a beginning had been made in the Palestinian churches. But he adds:[5] "Here also, it may be supposed, Christian prophets, filled with the Spirit, uttered, in the name of the Exalted Christ, sayings like Rev. 16. 15." The sayings are prophecy, whoever spoke them; and they contribute to the Gospel picture of Jesus as a prophet. The introduction to the saying of Lk. 10. 21, ἠγαλλιάσατο τῷ πνεύματι τῷ ἁγίῳ at once calls to mind the nature of prophetic speech;[6] and, having regard to the content of the sayings of Jesus, Bultmann has a considerable section[7] under the heading,

---

[1] *Zeitschrift für Theologie und Kirche* (1912), 1-30.   [2] *Op. cit.* 28.
[3] Mentioned by Windisch, *op. cit.* 228 n. 2. See also, on "Amen," D. Daube, *JTS* XLV. 27-31.   [4] *GST* 161-175.   [5] *Op. cit.* 176.
[6] See below, p. 102.   [7] *GST* 113-138.

"Prophetische und Apokalyptische Worte," with the sub-headings, "Heilspredigt, Drohworte, Mahnrede, Apokalyptische Weissagung".

We may call attention also to some interesting remarks of Reitzenstein in his *Poimandres*. He discusses [1] the use of ἐξουσία both in *Poimandres* (§§ 26, 32) and in the Gospels (Mk. 1. 22, 27). As he says, in *Poimandres*, though the idea of Power is present, there is also that of Knowledge. Commenting then on Mk. 1. 22, Reitzenstein says: "To 'have authority', ἐξουσίαν ἔχειν, is characteristic of the *prophet*, who unites supernatural power with *immediate perception* of the Godhead. . . . This usage can only have developed in circles in which mysterious knowledge of the Godhead confers supernatural power." But, though evidently any aspirant to prophetic rank claims authority, ἐξουσία, the linguistic connection made by Reitzenstein between prophecy and ἐξουσία is very precarious. It certainly will not stand in the case of the OT, where the prophets have nothing to do with ἐξουσία; and, indeed, the Hellenistic evidence on which he relies is far from satisfactory. He gives one reference, to Dieterich's edition of the Leyden Magical Papyrus, in *Jahrbücher für Phil., Supplem.* XVI. It will be sufficient to write out the relevant part of the passage in question.

v. 4   'Ονείρου Αἴτησις
5   'Α[κ]ριβὴς εἰς πάντα γράψον εἰς βύσσινον ῥάκος
      αἵματι ὀρτυγίου θεὸν ['Ερμ]ῆν
6   ὀρ[θ]ὸν ἰβιοπρόσωπον, ἔπειτα ζ[μύρνῃ] ἐπίγραψον
      καὶ τὸ ὄνομα καὶ ἐπίλεγε καὶ τὸν [λόγ]ο[ν]·
7   ἔρχου μοι, ὦ δέσποτα, ἔχων τὴν ἐξουσίαν,
      ἐπικαλοῦμαί σε τὸν ἐπὶ τῶν [πν]ευ-
8   μάτων τεταγμένον θεὸν θ⟨εῶν⟩ . . .

It will be observed without comment how little this has to do with the picture of Jesus as a prophet, which, in any case, is, in all other respects, founded upon the OT rather than Hellenistic models.

More relevant are the unfavourable pronouncements about Jesus preserved in Mk. 3. 21, 30 (ἐξέστη. . . πνεῦμα ἀκάθαρτον ἔχει). These both attest a sort of prophetic frenzy, a spirit-possession the immediate outward results of which would vary little if the spirit were a demon or the Holy Spirit. We may compare Hosea 9. 7: "the prophet is a fool, the man that hath the spirit is mad". [2]

There can be no doubt that Jesus was in fact regarded as a prophet by many of his contemporaries; the Evangelists, with their developed Christology, cannot have been subject to the temptation to introduce this category into their sources if it was not already there. This fact

---

[1] *Op. cit.* 48 n. 3.
[2] Windisch notices also in this connection the frequent use of εὐθύς; and we may add the fact that Jesus was regarded as *Johannes redivivus*.

strengthens greatly the case that Jesus was a "pneumatic" person, as Otto brings out forcibly.[1] He did confront his generation with abounding spiritual power which was manifest as well in his authoritative words as in his mighty deeds.

But did Jesus speak and think of himself as a prophet? Did he accept the estimate of his contemporaries? In one place at least of the Synoptic Gospels he rejects it. In Mk. 8. 27-29 (=Mt. 16. 13-16=Lk. 9. 18-20) the disciples tell Jesus the common opinion of him: "John the Baptist, others say Elijah, others that you are one of the prophets." But these suggestions are obviously regarded as unsatisfactory. "Who do you say that I am?" Jesus asks: and the reply goes beyond the range of the prophets. But it might well be argued that this passage is not authentic, and further evidence is required to support it.

In spite of the general belief that the age of prophecy was past it is undoubtedly true that a Jew of the first century, well acquainted with the OT, would, if he felt himself called to a special religious mission, more naturally associate himself with the prophets than with any other group of men. Jesus, as we have seen, was commonly held by others to be a prophet; he must have perceived the affinities which did exist between his ministry and those of the prophets. It is therefore the more striking to find that he never plainly speaks of himself as a prophet at all.

Only two exceptions might be urged against this general statement. The first is Mk. 6. 4 (=Mt. 13. 57=Lk. 4. 24). But the saying, "No prophet is without honour except in his fatherland", is too manifestly proverbial in form for us to lay great weight upon it. In using it to explain the frigid reception he found at Nazareth, Jesus no more committed himself to the statement "I am a prophet and therefore without honour", than by his use of the proverb "Physician, heal thyself" he implied that he was ill. Fascher[2] takes the opposite view and holds that Jesus did announce himself as a prophet. This is of course possible; but the facts by no means make it certain. If Jesus had made such an announcement it would have left a more unmistakable imprint on the tradition.

The other possible exception is Lk. 13. 33. Here, too, the expression is in the form of a proverb, but it seems much more probable that here Jesus is made to speak of himself as a prophet, although indirectly. The Q saying (Lk. 13. 34 f.=Mt. 23. 37-39) which follows might as well set Jesus over against the prophets as include him in their number. But even if we have found one exception to the general statement made above, its significance must not be exaggerated. The question remains: If Jesus was commonly regarded as a prophet, why did he never, or hardly ever, speak of himself as such?

The relevance of this question to our subject is not difficult to see. To the Rabbis the Holy Spirit was pre-eminently the Spirit of prophecy. The OT phrases "Holy Spirit", "Spirit of God" are in the Targums

---

[1] *Kingdom of God and Son of Man*, 333-38[1].　　　　　[2] Προφήτης, 173 ff.

consistently paraphrased "(Holy) Spirit of prophecy" [1]; that is, our present question about prophecy is bound up with the primary question of the Spirit, and the fact that Jesus did not claim to be a prophet is a part of his reticence on the general subject of the Holy Spirit.[2]

The question is not sufficiently answered by a reference to the Christological influences which bore upon the Gospel tradition. It is, of course, quite true that the Evangelists held a higher view of Jesus than that he was a prophet, and it is by no means inconceivable that they have eliminated from their sources sayings in which Jesus placed himself among the prophets. Yet it is unlikely that this Christological tendency accounts completely for the present condition of the Gospels. For one is bound to ask why the Evangelists, so thorough in removing traces that Jesus thought of himself as a prophet, should have left so many indications that that was the popular estimate of him. Accordingly, although due allowance must be made for this factor in the situation, it is not an adequate explanation of the facts.

A more obvious, and also more useful, suggestion is that Jesus did not think of himself as a prophet, and therefore did not speak of himself as such. In an (apparently) old Q saying (Mt. 11. 9=Lk. 7. 26) he speaks of John the Baptist as "more than a prophet"; John corresponded to the old prophets in many respects, but because of his position in the eschatological scheme he was greater than any born of woman. If this saying is authentic, it is difficult to suppose that Jesus did not think of himself also as "more than a prophet". John was more than a prophet; if the least in the Kingdom of heaven was greater than John, then, a fortiori, Jesus, who, whatever his exact relation to the Kingdom may have been, was certainly "in" it, was more than a prophet too.[3] Precisely the same point is expressed by Jesus' dissatisfaction with the title Prophet in Mk. 8. 27-29 and parallels. It seems clear, to say the least, that Jesus thought that the description "Prophet" was inadequate.[4]

Need he for that reason have avoided it? We have already reviewed evidence which indicated not merely that many people held him to be a prophet, but also that there were good grounds, in his own character and activity, for that view. Why, then, could he not, provisionally at least, have accepted their opinion with the motive of leading them to see that he was "more than a prophet"?

We have here raised, in a secondary form, one of the fundamental questions of this study, namely the problem why Jesus spoke so little about the Holy Spirit. We have met it before under other forms; for example, why did Jesus expel demons, and compel those whom he cured to secrecy? Why did he perform miracles which he plainly regarded as divine signs, and at the same time refuse signs to those who asked for them? We are

---

[1] Str.-B. II. 127 ff.

[2] Windisch, *op. cit.* 234 : " The Pneuma turns the student of Torah and teacher of Wisdom into a prophet."

[3] Cf. Otto, *Kingdom of God and Son of Man*, 163.

[4] Prophecy may even be due to an evil spirit : 1 Sam. 18. 10.

now asking, Why did Jesus behave as a Spirit-inspired prophet, and refuse to be known as such? The question as a whole will be discussed at a later point.[1] Part of the answer to the present question is that in doing as he did Jesus did not act otherwise than many of the great OT prophets, who, like him, did not speak of themselves as prophets and refrained from the use of the concept Spirit. Part also lies in further considerations of the thought of Jesus about the Kingdom of God and eschatology, which must for the present be deferred.

[1] Pp. 140-162.

7

OTHER PASSAGES

IT will be necessary now to examine some other passages in the
Gospels where the word πνεῦμα is used, but which do not fall into
any of the categories which have so far been considered.

Mt. 12. 18: no parallel; a quotation from Is. 42. 1.

Mt.:   θήσω τὸ πνεῦμά μου ἐπ᾽ αὐτόν.
LXX: ἔδωκα τὸ πνεῦμά μου ἐπ᾽ αὐτόν.
Hebrew: נָתַתִּי רוּחִי עָלָיו (nathatti ruḥi ʻalaiu).

Matthew's future is a possible rendering of the perfect of the Hebrew
text, and his quotation must therefore have been taken from the Hebrew
rather than from the LXX.[1] There is a number of such quotations in
Mt., and it is possible that these constituted á special testimony source
used by the Evangelist, and were not simply added by him to the narrative
out of his own knowledge of the OT.

Bacon [2] suggested that the quotation properly belongs to the baptism
narrative, and that it was transferred to its present position by Matthew.
It is indeed almost certain that Is. 42. 1 is alluded to in the voice from
heaven at the baptism, and this verse also illustrates and explains on the
basis of Scripture the descent of the Spirit. But the chief purpose of the
testimony as it is used here by Matthew is to explain the silence required
by Jesus from those upon whom he performed cures; it is, in fact, a
testimonium for the Messianic secret. Nevertheless, it is possible that, as
in vv. 19, 20, "He shall not strive nor cry out, etc." refers back to v. 16,
"he charged them that they should not make him known", so v. 18,
"I will put my Spirit upon him", refers back to v. 15, "And many
followed him and he healed them all". If this is so, his endowment, as
the Servant, with the Spirit, is given as the explanation of his power to
work miracles; and it may be inferred that the miracles point back,
through Jesus' character as a "pneumatic" person, his possession of the
Spirit, to his peculiar nature as Servant or Messiah of God.

Lk. 4. 18 f.: no parallels; another testimony, from Is. 61. 1. The same
passage is referred to in Mt. 11. 5=Lk. 7. 22 (Q); [3] it was an important
testimonium; [4] and, especially in view of the allusion to it in the Q
material, its importance is not affected by the interesting but here

---

[1] Or from another version; Targ. Jon. has אֲתֵן רוּחָא דְקוּדְשִׁי עֲלוֹהִי (I will put my spirit of
holiness upon him).
[2] *Studies in Matthew*, 474.   [3] See above, p. 87.
[4] See J. R. Harris, *Testimonies*, II. 69 n. 1, where references are given to *Ep. Barn.* 14.9; Irenaeus,
A.P. 53; *adv. Haer.* 3. 18. 1; 3. 19. 3; 4. 37. 1; Eusebius, *Pr. Ev.* 4. 31 [read 21]; *Dem.
Ev.* 3. 1 [1]; 4. 15. 30; 4. 17. 13; 5. 2. 6; etc.; Cyprian [*Testimonia*] 2. 10; Gregory of
Nyssa, 4. 22; Evagrius, 6. 27.

irrelevant question whether the Lucan account of the rejection at Nazareth (in which it is found) is the result of free editing of Mk. or is a separate and complete non-Marcan source to which Luke has given preference. In either case, Luke has put it at the opening of his narrative of the ministry of Jesus because it summarizes the character of the ministry (precisely as the pericope as a whole summarizes its course and outcome). It describes what Jesus, as the bearer of the Spirit of God, will do. The allusion to the text in Q is even more particular, and more closely adapted to the things actually done by Jesus. Just as in Mt. 12. 18, the activity of Jesus (which here includes preaching as well as miracle-working) is made to depend upon his possession of the Spirit, which in turn depends upon his Messiahship; for whatever be the original meaning of Is. 61 it is messianically applied by Luke.

Lk. 4. 14: cf. Mt. 4. 12; Mk. 1. 14, but the words ἐν τῇ δυνάμει τοῦ πνεύματος are Lucan. This verse is summarizing and programmatic.[1] He who has been baptized and has endured the struggle with Satan in the wilderness may properly be described as "in the power of the Spirit"; and so may he who is about to begin a ministry full of works of God's might. Luke seems to mean nothing different from what he has already said about Jesus in 4. 1, namely, that he was πλήρης πνεύματος ἁγίου. Luke (in both Gospel and Acts) uses several different expressions to describe men acting in the power of the Spirit. Πλήρης πνεύματος seems to be his favourite: see Lk. 4. 1; Acts 6. 3; 6. 5; 7. 55; 11. 24; cf. Acts 6. 8. As we have seen above (pp. 76 f.), he several times uses δύναμις and πνεῦμα together. There is no precise parallel to ἐν τῇ δυνάμει τοῦ πνεύματος, but we may compare Lk. 1. 17; 4. 36; 5. 17; 6. 19; 8. 46; Acts 10. 38 in addition to the passages just mentioned. It is important to observe that Luke describes Jesus in the same terms as the apostles, whom he portrays as inspired teachers and miracle-workers.

Lk. 10. 21: cf. Mt. 11. 25: Jesus rejoiced in the Holy Spirit. Mt. has simply, "Jesus answered (ἀποκριθείς) and said".[2] The expression ἀγαλλιᾶσθαι τῷ πνεύματι τῷ ἁγίῳ is strange and apparently without parallel; its strangeness is attested by the fact that many MSS omit the words τῷ ἁγίῳ. But there can be little doubt that Luke wrote them and that he meant them to draw attention to the very important sayings which follow, and which he may have regarded as a species of inspired and even ecstatic prophecy of peculiar significance. The note in *SNT* (Weiss-Bousset) runs: "They seemed to him (Luke) to be words which could only have been spoken out of the most profound excite-

---

[1] Cf. Lk. 4. 1.

[2] In view of the parallel it is interesting to note a passage to which attention is drawn by Str.-B. I. 606; *Midr. Qoh.*, 7. 2 (32b): "In the name of R. Meir it is taught: In general where (in the OT) it is said, He answered and said . . . (as e.g. in Job 4. 1), the person in question spoke in the Holy Spirit."

ment. He explained this in the manner of his time, as follows. Jesus when he spoke was inspired; he speaks here as a prophet, in words which surpass the merely human, and need first of all to be translated back into human speech. We express the same thing in this way: There lies before us an inspired, exuberant hymn, which owes its being to an hour of deepest emotion, and which must be measured by a different scale from the more didactic sayings of Jesus; it must be sympathetically appreciated (*nachempfunden*)." [1]

That the expression τῷ πνεύματι τῷ ἁγίῳ is intended to draw attention to prophetic speech is supported by much Jewish evidence. Str.-B. (II. 127 f.) say: "How self-evident to Rabbinic Judaism was the equivalence of the Holy Spirit with the divine Spirit of prophecy or prediction is especially clear from the fact that the Targums have simply translated the OT 'Spirit of God', or 'Spirit of Yahweh', or 'Holy Spirit' by 'Spirit of Prophecy'. For this reason, without further proof, it should be assumed that the Rabbinic scholars everywhere (except where the context makes it necessary to think of the Spirit inspiring Scripture) understood by the Holy Spirit the Spirit of prophecy, or of prophetic endowment." It might seem, then, that this verse deserved more attention in the section dealing with Jesus as prophet. But it is well to remember that, of all the Evangelists, Luke is the furthest removed from Rabbinical circles and Rabbinical terminology. It is not necessary to assume that one of his Greek phrases, especially one that occurs in what is manifestly an editorial introduction to a group of sayings, is best explained by analogy with Hebrew expressions in Rabbinic literature. It would be unsafe to say more than that here, as in the two passages from his Gospel which we have just considered, Luke is strengthening and heightening his picture of Jesus as an inspired, a "pneumatic", perhaps even an ecstatic, person, without making any direct allusion to OT prophecy.

Mt. 28. 19; no parallels. With some slight variations on the part of a very few MSS, all the witnesses available to us—Greek MSS, VSS and patristic citations—present this verse in the same form. There would be no reason for doubting their authority but that there is one exception to this unanimity. Eusebius frequently, though not always, quotes the verse in the form, "Go ye into all the world and make disciples of all the Gentiles in my name"—thus omitting baptism and the three-fold formula. The textual problem is briefly treated, and references to further discussions given, in Jackson and Lake, *Beginnings of Christianity*, I. 336. (See also F. C. Conybeare, *Hibbert Journal*, i. 56.) The main point is this. It is argued, and not without plausibility, that so neat a Trinitarian formula cannot have arisen at a date so early as the latest possible period for the composition of Mt. (though the same formula occurs twice in the *Didache*, along with the simpler formula which names

[1] 3rd ed., 309.

only Christ). On the other hand, no trace of the shorter (Eusebian) reading, or of anything like it, remains, except in Eusebius. It is very difficult to believe that if this (the short reading) is what Matthew wrote, not one copy of his unaltered MS succeeded in escaping revision. Yet this is precisely what did happen, if Matthew did write the shorter text and revision did take place. If that was so, the revision must have been made at a very early date, almost immediately after the writing of the Gospel. Thus the hypothesis of a revision involves us in precisely the same difficulty as that which it was intended to remove, viz., the difficulty of the early appearance of the Trinitarian formula. It is much better to suppose that the correct text of Mt. is that which has been preserved in all the MSS and VSS.

It is, on the other hand, quite impossible to regard the saying as historical. It first arose after, not before, the apostles customarily baptized in the name of the Lord Jesus only, just as the command to go into all the world and make disciples arose after, not before, the controversy about the admission of Gentiles to the Church. The practice of ascribing to the risen Jesus special teaching committed by him to the apostles, which grew so dangerously in Gnostic circles, began with Matthew and Luke.

The Trinitarian formula does not bear upon the discussion that we have hitherto conducted; that is to say, it is a Trinitarian formula. It does not deal with the inspiration of Jesus, or of anyone else, nor has it any relationship to the eschatological outpouring of the Spirit. It is a theological summary, more advanced than the primitive confession, Jesus is Lord. If Windisch's theory [1] that references to the Spirit were first of all eliminated from the Gospel tradition and then re-introduced be correct, this would be an extreme example of the altered form in which the references to the Spirit were restored. Formerly the Spirit was a power of God; in this aspect it was removed, to magnify the second Person of the Godhead; now it reappears in its own right as third Person in the same Godhead. The present saying does not belong to the period of theological origin and growth which is our proper subject, but to a later period of theological consolidation and fixation. The Holy Spirit has become an object of faith (in a rational sense) as well as an object of experience.[2]

Mk. 3. 28-30 and parallels. If we consider only the Marcan form of this saying, its interpretation is not difficult; at least, 3. 30 makes quite clear how Mark himself intended the words to be taken. They were spoken by Jesus because people were saying (the 3rd person plural here, as in

---

[1] *Op. cit.* 232 f. ; in particular—" The present state of the tradition is accordingly the result of two opposite processes : elimination and introduction, or better, re-introduction of the spiritual (*pneumatischen*) element," 233.

[2] The older formula of baptism in(to) (the name of) Christ contained important references to the relationships denoted (in Pauline terms) by Χριστοῦ, ἐν Χριστῷ, etc. ; but these cannot simply be transferred to the other persons of the Trinity when the fuller formula is adopted. In the case of the shorter formula, interest is concentrated upon the relationship to Christ which is assumed in baptism ; but the intention of the longer formula is to enunciate and safeguard the doctrine of the Trinity.

v. 21, is probably used impersonally) that he was inspired not by the Holy, but by an unclean, Spirit, and Mark's thought clearly is that the sin that can never find forgiveness is that which ascribes the work of Jesus to the power of evil; for example, the assertion that Jesus cast out demons through being in league with Beelzebul. It has been pointed out above that the charge that Jesus acted in the power of Beelzebul could arise from the same facts as the belief that he was inspired by God's Spirit; that is to say, the root of both, if they are historical, must have been the fact that Jesus acted as a "pneumatic" man, a fact which is thereby doubly attested. The decisive question was, whether a man accepted the work of Jesus as due to divine or diabolical inspiration. To take the latter view was in itself to reject God's salvation (for Jesus is thought of as "pneumatic" only because he is first the Messiah—see the discussion of the baptism narrative) and thus to exclude oneself from the sphere of forgiveness.

This interpretation is quite clear and satisfactory; but, very tentatively, a more precise explanation may be attempted. The suggestion which will be made is admittedly precarious, and can be put forward only because there is good reason to believe, on other grounds, that the Synoptic tradition was moulded under very powerful and far-reaching OT influences, especially of the Psalms and the book of Isaiah.

The closest, and perhaps the only, OT parallel to "blasphemy against the Holy Spirit" is Is. 63. 10: "they grieved his holy spirit". The whole of the section (Is. 63. 7-64. 11) in which this verse occurs repays study. It is a prayer for God's salvation offered by the people who are in exile, whose holy and beautiful house is in ruins, and over whom the heathen triumph. The prophet first remembers the mercies of God, the multitude of his loving-kindnesses. He records that "in his love and in his pity he redeemed them; and he bare them, and carried them all the days of old" (63. 9). In view of 63. 11-14 this must refer to the deliverance of the people from Egypt under Moses.[1] In the account of this divine act of salvation 63. 14a is particularly interesting. It is given in different forms in the Hebrew text and in the LXX.

Hebrew: כַּבְּהֵמָה בַּבִּקְעָה תֵרֵד רוּחַ יהוה תְּנִיחֶנּוּ (as the cattle that go down into the valley, the Spirit of the Lord caused them to rest).

LXX: . . . καὶ ὡς κτήνη διὰ πεδίου· κατέβη πνεῦμα παρὰ κυρίου καὶ ὡδήγησεν αὐτούς.

The Massoretes have certainly produced a smoother and more intelligible rendering, and one which preserves the parallelism of the Hebrew verse; probably they give the original text;[2] but the LXX reading is significant because it agrees with the language used in the baptism narratives for the descent of the Spirit. But it is particularly important for us to note the

---

[1] "In 63. 7-14 it is the return under Moses, not that made possible by Cyrus, that is narrated."—Feldmann, *Das Buch Isaias*, II. 259 (*Exegetisches Handbuch zum alten Testament*).

[2] Among recent commentators König (*Das Buch Jesaja*, 1926) and Volz (*Jesaia*, in the *Kommentar zum AT*) prefer the Massoretic text to that of the VSS; Feldmann (*op. cit.*) differs.

sentences "The spirit of the Lord gave them rest" (רוּחַ יהוה תְּנִיחֶנּוּ, 63. 14a) and "Where is he that put his holy spirit in the midst of them?" (אַיֵּה הַשָּׂם בְּקִרְבּוֹ אֶת-רוּחַ קָדְשׁוֹ, 63. 11). The people, however, in spite of the kindness shown to them, rebelled (מָרוּ), whether against God or Moses is not said; probably both are in mind. Thus (63. 10) they grieved the Holy Spirit (וְעִצְּבוּ (weᶜizzᵉbu) is presumably frequentative, in spite of the aorist by which the LXX have represented it).

The Isaiah passage then proceeds as a prayer that God will nevertheless pity his people again in their adversity; that he will rend (Greek ἀνοίγω, cf. Mt. 3. 16; Lk. 3. 21) the heavens and come down to their aid. On this basis we may (as we have said, by way of tentative suggestion only) take up the exegesis of Mk. 3. 28 f. The prayer of the prophet had been answered. God had rent the heavens; he had come down (Is. 63. 20 LXX, 64. 1 MT) in the descent of the Spirit (Is. 63. 14 LXX) upon Jesus, who immediately proceeded, as a Second Moses, with the work of delivering his people. His mighty works had already been made known. The demons recognized their master. But this new work of God was greeted in precisely the same way as the old. The people instead of welcoming it rebelled against it, and grieved (blasphemed) God's Holy Spirit, as Mark says, ὅτι ἔλεγον, πνεῦμα ἀκάθαρτον ἔχει. Since this is God's final, eschatological, deed of salvation, those who utterly reject it can, in the nature of the case, find no salvation. "For if the word spoken through angels proved stedfast, and every transgression and disobedience received a just recompense of reward; how shall we escape if we neglect so great salvation?" (Heb. 2. 2 f.).

The form of the blasphemy saying in Mt. and Lk. is not susceptible of such straightforward interpretation. Mt. 12. 31 corresponds to the Marcan logion and causes no difficulty. But in 12. 32 Mt. has a Q version of the same saying, the parallel being in Lk. 12. 10 (in a different context). In Q a contrast is drawn between speaking a word against the Son of man, which can be forgiven, and speaking (blaspheming, Lk.) against the Holy Spirit, which is not forgiven.

Wellhausen [1] made the very attractive suggestion that the difference between the Marcan and Q forms of the saying arose as follows. The original form was that of Mk. 3. 28 with the expression "son of man" (=Man, generically) in the singular. This was misunderstood as "Son of man" (=Messiah), and this misunderstanding gave rise to the other version of the logion; later the Marcan form was altered to "sons of men" (plural, an unusual expression) to avoid the danger of misapprehension. This, or something like it, may well be true; but in any case we are not absolved from the duty of finding out what Matthew and Luke meant by the saying which they have included in their Gospels; a difficult saying, for in Mk. blasphemy against the Holy Spirit consists in saying a word against the Son of man.

[1] *Einleitung*, 1st ed. 74 f.; 2nd ed. 66 f.

From the time of Origen the Fathers adopt on the whole a uniform explanation of the verse in question. Blasphemy against the Son of man is that which is committed by the heathen. This is, of course, sin, but it may be forgiven, as all sins may be forgiven, in baptism. But in baptism the Holy Spirit is given, and sin takes on a more serious aspect.[1] There was (according to the stricter party in the Church) no second forgiveness, and the argument is used that post-baptismal sins are committed against the Holy Spirit, and are for that reason unforgivable. That is, blasphemy against the Son of man means pre-baptismal sin, remitted in baptism; blasphemy against the Holy Spirit means post-baptismal sin, for which there is no remission. Of course, there is in this no attempt at historical exegesis, and it is encrusted with the theological thought and terminology of much later times; but if we cease to speak of pre- and post-baptismal offences, and speak simply of the blasphemies of those who have and those who have not accepted Christ as Lord, there is much in the patristic interpretation that may be true. Matthew and Luke, if they were like other Christians of their time, must have thought of the Holy Spirit as a characteristically Christian possession, indeed as the absolutely constitutive factor of the life of the Church, and to blaspheme the Spirit must have been tantamount to apostasy; whereas blaspheming the Son of man was the attitude of the outsider who might yet be won to repentance and faith, and be forgiven.

This interpretation is not without support in the NT itself, for there are other books which speak of cases in which forgiveness is impossible. In Hebrews this is explicitly said in 6. 4-6; it is those who have been enlightened, who have tasted the heavenly gift and become partakers of the Holy Spirit (i.e., have been baptized; Theognostus takes up this language, see note below), who have tasted the good Word of God and the powers of the age to come, and then have fallen away, whom it is impossible to bring back to repentance, and thus to forgiveness. They crucify the Son of God for themselves; but unlike those for whom Christ prayed, they know what they do; their sin is not merely against the Redeemer, but against the Spirit in which they have shared in the life of the Church, and this sin it is which, according to the epistle, has no forgiveness. Similar remarks might be made about 10. 26 f.; and the case of Esau is treated (12. 16 f.) in a corresponding manner. Esau was born into the divinely chosen family and enjoyed the rights of the first-born. These he surrendered for a material good, but afterwards, when he wished to recover the blessing, he was unable to do so. Having once removed from the household of faith (a type of the household of the Spirit, the Church) he could not re-enter it.

---

[1] Cf., for example, the fragment of the short work on the sin against the Holy Spirit by Theognostus of Alexandria (Routh, *Rel. Sac.* III. 409 f.). He says (*op. cit*, 410) . . . ὁ μὲν υἱὸς συγκαταβαίνει τοῖς ἀτελέσι, τὸ δὲ πνεῦμα σφράγις (a baptismal metaphor) ἐστι τῶν τελειουμένων· οὕτως οὐ διὰ τὴν ὑπερβολὴν τοῦ πνεύματος πρὸς τὸν υἱὸν ἄφυκτός ἐστι καὶ ἀσύγγνωστος ἡ εἰς τὸ πνεῦμα βλασφημία· ἀλλ' ὅτι ἐπὶ μὲν τοῖς ἀτελέσιν, ἐστὶ συγγνώμη, ἐπὶ δὲ τοῖς γευσαμένοις τῆς οὐρανίου δωρεᾶς καὶ τελειωθεῖσιν, οὐδεμία περιλείπεται συγγνώμης ἀπολογία καὶ παραίτησις.

We find, probably, the same thought in 1 Jn. It is implied (though not stated) in 5. 16 f. that those who commit sin πρὸς θάνατον (as well as those who sin μὴ πρὸς θάνατον) are ἀδελφοί, i.e., Christians; and the most satisfactory explanation of their sin is that it is apostasy.[1] We may compare also Acts 7. 51; 1 Thess. 4. 8; Eph. 4. 30.

Blasphemy against the Holy Spirit seems, then, to be sin committed within the Church, which, because it denies the root and spring of the Church's life, cannot rediscover the forgiveness by which the sinner first entered the community of the forgiven. It would of course be remembered that the apostles, who received the gift of the Spirit at Pentecost, had formerly denied and forsaken, and thus blasphemed, the Son of man.

It is possible that, in some quarters at least, the Q saying may have had a more specific reference than this. In the *Didache*, 11. 7, it is said: πάντα προφήτην λαλοῦντα ἐν πνεύματι οὐ πειράσετε οὐδὲ διακρινεῖτε. πᾶσα γὰρ ἁμαρτία ἀφεθήσεται, αὕτη δὲ ἡ ἁμαρτία οὐκ ἀφεθήσεται. Mt. was probably known to the author of the *Didache*, and this passage is probably to be taken as the Didachist's interpretation of Mt. 12. 32. To many Christians (though not to St Paul) one of the supreme manifestations of the Holy Spirit in the Church was the gift of prophecy, allied to that of tongues. It may be that some such distinction as the following was in the mind of Matthew and Luke (or at least of some of their readers). It was possible (see 1 Cor. 12. 1 ff.) for a man speaking with tongues to say Ἀνάθεμα Ἰησοῦ (cf. 1 Jn. 4. 1-6). This was of course a serious matter, and the gift of distinguishing spirits was a necessary one; but it could be explained as no more than blasphemy against the Son of man; whereas on the other hand a complete denial of all prophecy, such as the author of the *Didache* envisages, would have meant rejection of the life of the Church itself, blasphemy against the Spirit.[2]

Mk. 12. 36 and parallels. The words of the Psalter (Ps. 110. 1) are ascribed to David, who spoke "in the Holy Spirit". Mt. reproduces the thought, only omitting the word "Holy" and slightly recasting the sentence; Lk. has: "David says in the book of Psalms." No other biblical quotation in the Synoptic Gospels is introduced in the same way.[3]

[1] Hoskyns, *Gore's Commentary*, NT, 670: "From the epistle as a whole it may be reasonably deduced that by *sin unto death* the author means apostasy." Cf. 2. 19.

[2] A similar interpretation to that which we have adopted is put forward by Procksch (*TWNT* I. 105). He says: "In the υἱὸς τοῦ ἀνθρώπου God is present but concealed, so that the sin against the Son of man, since it is committed in a state of ignorance, can be forgiven. On the other hand, God reveals himself through Christ in the πνεῦμα ἅγιον of the time after Pentecost, and whoever is convicted by the Holy Spirit, yet nevertheless revolts against his power, and blasphemes (βλασφημεῖ) him, commits an unforgivable sin. The possibility of this sin therefore first arose in the age after Pentecost, after the Holy Spirit had passed from Jesus to the disciples, and had become their inward possession." Procksch refers to Baer, *Der Heilige Geist in den Lukas-Schriften*, 75 f.; Baer in turn refers to Hofmann, *Der Schriftbeweis* (1860), 342 f. He might have gone further back, to Calvin. "The reason why *blasphemy against the Spirit* exceeds other sins is not that the Spirit is higher than Christ, but that those who rebel, after that the power of God has been revealed, cannot be excused on the plea of ignorance. Besides, it must be observed that what is here said about *blasphemy* does not refer merely to the essence of *the Spirit*, but to the grace which He has bestowed upon us."—*Commentary on a Harmony of the Evangelists Matthew, Mark and Luke*, II. 74 (Calvin Translation Society, 1845).

[3] But cf. Acts 28. 25; 2 Tim. 3. 16; 2 Pet. 1. 21.

When such quotations, as distinct from allusions, are introduced, there is often direct reference to the written book, e.g., in the common use of γέγραπται (or—three times in Lk.—γεγραμμένον) and in the use of ἀναγινώσκειν. Similarly we have the phrase Μωϋσῆς ἔγραψεν, and perhaps we should include ἡ προφητεία . . . ἡ λέγουσα. There is little difference between this direct reference to the written OT and the Matthaean ἐρρέθη (Lk. once has εἴρηται). Occasionally there is more obvious allusion to the speech of the inspired man, in the quotation forms ἐπροφήτευσεν . . . λέγων; Μωϋσῆς εἶπεν, ἐνετείλατο; perhaps also in ἡ προφητεία . . . ἡ λέγουσα, and Δαυεὶδ λέγει ἐν βίβλῳ ψαλμῶν. In all of these forms, however, there is no express reference to the inspiration of the speaker or writer, or to the fact that the saying attributed to him is regarded as not his own but God's. Such reference is found particularly in Mt. It is implied in the various phrases which use the preposition διὰ with τοῦ προφήτου, or the name of a prophet, or both. In two places (Mt. 1. 22 f.; 2. 15) the divine origin of the proof text is made quite clear by the addition of ὑπὸ Κυρίου; and in Mt. 15. 4; 19. 5, and 22. 32 biblical citations are ascribed directly to God without mention of a human prophet.

The Gospels, then, rarely refer to the divine authority of the Scriptures they quote, and in the present passage only is that authority connected with the Holy Spirit. It is, of course, implied that David was inspired when he pronounced the Psalm in question; but the statement arises from the fact that the Psalm was contained in a book the whole of which was believed to be inspired; Jesus said that David spoke in the Holy Spirit, not because he knew anything about David but because David's Psalm was contained in the OT. The fact that, in this connection, the word πνεῦμα occurs only once (twice counting the Matthaean parallel) in the Synoptic Gospels, is, for reasons which we shall see, a further datum in the general silence of these Gospels about the Spirit. In respect of the OT at least the Synoptists might have been expected to speak often of the Spirit. To bring out this fact it will be necessary to refer briefly to the treatment of the OT in Judaism, to the concept of inspired Scripture in Greek thought, and to Philo.

Judaism and the OT. In Judaism, prophecy and Scripture are not occasionally but customarily linked with the work of the Holy Spirit. It is impossible to do better than quote the words of Moore:[1] "God's promise (Deut. 18. 15 ff.) to raise up prophets in Israel and put his words in their mouth to deliver to the people is fulfilled by putting the Holy Spirit in the mouths of the prophets after Moses.[2] The Holy Spirit is the Spirit of prophecy; all the prophets spoke by the Holy Spirit. The

---

[1] *Judaism*, I. 237.

[2] Zech. 7.12. Sifré on Deut. 18. 18 (§ 176); cf. also Is. 40. 13, " Who put the Holy Spirit in the mouth of all the prophets ". The phrase " the Holy Spirit " is very rare in the OT (Is. 63. 10 f.; Ps. 51. 13), and never in connection with prophecy. It is common in Rabbinical literature of inspiration and the inspiration of Scripture. On the various uses of the phrase see the classified collection in Bacher, *Terminologie*, II. 202-206; on its meaning, *ibid.*, I. 169 f.

Holy Spirit is so specifically prophetic inspiration that when Haggai, Zechariah, and Malachi, the last prophets, died, the Holy Spirit departed from Israel."[1] Moore goes on to show[2] what a short step it was from this to the view that the whole of Scripture was the product of the Spirit, and points out that it was particularly emphasized that the disputed works were given by the Spirit. Thus *Cant. R.* on Cant. 1. 1: "The Holy Spirit came upon him, and he spoke three books, Proverbs, Ecclesiastes, and the Song of Songs." We may note also the frequent use in Rabbinic literature of the phrase "(Holy) Spirit of prophecy"; see Str.-B. II. 129 *et al.*

Inspired Literature in Greek Thought. It is evident that there was nothing in Greek thought or literature which occupied the place which was held in Judaism and primitive Christianity by the OT. The Greeks could never be called the people of a book. With inspiration, including prophetic inspiration, they were not unfamiliar, but there was no inspired corpus of literature universally regarded as having decisive and binding authority. This statement, however, may be modified by two considerations.

(i) There were some inspired books. The story of the Sibylline books is too well known to require repetition. The utterances of the Sibyl in her divine frenzy were valuable as a written collection as well as when they were first spoken. They supplied a means of divination in later times. The high estimation in which they were held is attested by the numerous spurious oracles; and the Jewish and Christian "Sibyls" are for us particularly important.

(ii) An important and widespread feature of Greek religious and philosophical practice at the period of the beginnings of Christianity was the method of allegory, applied in exegesis of the old Hellenic traditions, especially as recorded in Homer. This method was practised notably by the Stoics and Neo-Pythagoreans; it was particularly convenient in a day when the prevailing philosophical tendency was syncretistic.[3] The impulses which directed men's thoughts towards allegory were, chiefly, two. (*a*) There was, among thinkers, a "failure of nerve"; they sought further support for their opinions in addition to what could be supplied by the free movement of their own minds. There was authority, so it was felt, in antiquity; if one's beliefs could be found in, for example, Homer, they secured the backing of immemorial tradition. And the way to find any desired belief in the unsuspecting Homer was the way of allegorical exegesis. (*b*) There was much in Homer, and the other poets, which was shocking to more developed taste and morality: it was unthinkable that Homer should merely have been telling improper stories; therefore Homer must have been doing something else. In fact,

[1] *Tosefta Soṭah* 13. 2 ; *Sanh.* 11a. Subsequent revelations were given by a *bath qol.*
[2] *Op. cit.* 238.
[3] Bréhier, *Les Idées philosophiques et religieuses de Philon d'Alexandrie*, 37.

so far from being obscene, he was concealing philosophical truth behind a camouflage which would deceive all but the initiated.

When the motives of allegorical interpretation are thus described it is clear that its trend was to ascribe a measure of authority to Homer and the other sources used. It has indeed often been said that Homer became the Bible of the Greeks. In this, as in most epigrams, truth and falsehood mingle. Homer was never a Bible to the Greeks as the OT is to Judaism and Christianity. He was a purveyor of the myths; at best a very early Stoic, or Neo-Pythagorean, or whatever it might be. Yet the fact that his lapses had to be explained away, and that it was worth a good deal of artificial manipulation to have him on one's side, indicates that his authority was rather more than that of mere antiquity and tradition.

The poets themselves are not accorded the same authority as the NT ascribes to the writers of the OT. For the most part, little is said about them. The most striking discussion of their inspiration is in Plato's *Ion*.[1] In this dialogue the work and usefulness of the rhapsode are discussed. It is sometimes difficult to distinguish between current opinions and those held by Plato himself; for our purpose we need not do so. The view is put forward that the poets were inspired and that their inspiration is passed on to the rhapsode and by him to his audience, just as a piece of lodestone "not only attracts iron rings themselves, but also imparts power to the rings so that they in their turn are able to do the very same thing as the stone, that is, to attract other rings" (533d). In the same context occur words which summarize the opinion of the poets which is contained in the dialogue: πάντες γὰρ οἵ τε τῶν ἐπῶν ποιηταὶ οἱ ἀγαθοὶ οὐκ ἐκ τέχνης ἀλλ' ἔνθεοι ὄντες καὶ κατεχόμενοι πάντα ταῦτα τὰ καλὰ λέγουσι ποιήματα (533e). They are further compared with the Corybantes (*ibid.*). The poets were inspired ecstatics, who said beautiful things but did not know what they were saying—which did not commend them to Socrates as wise men (*Apol.* 22e).[2]

But the poets are not often described in this way. Decharme[3] says of the Stoics: "Ils enrôlèrent Homère et Hésiode dans leurs rangs"; that is, they did not regard them as inspired so much as early (and therefore very wise) philosophers, who fortunately agreed with them (the Stoics). This view, which prevailed, removes any idea of authority and inspiration comparable with the Jewish and Christian ideas of the authority and inspiration of the OT.

There is a further point to be observed in this connection. That which is allegorized is commonly not the words of a particular poet, but the myths which lay behind the great mass of Greek literature and were the common stock of all Greek writers. A representative source of Greek allegorical interpretation is Cornutus' Περὶ θεῶν. We may note how

---

[1] Cf. *Apol.* 22c, *Meno* 99c, d.
[2] Plato does not in this connection use the word πνεῦμα, but this fact has no particular significance. The words ἔνθεος, ἐνθουσιάζω, are common; they are not in the NT.
[3] *Critiques des Traditions religieuses chez les Grecs*, 352. The chapter, "L'Exégèse stoïcienne," 305-353, is important; also 270-303.

"the poets" are treated there. An interesting observation may be made simply upon the form of this work. Cornutus, who is bent on allegorizing anything he can lay hands on, does not actually quote verse nearly as often as does Plutarch, who objects to the allegorical method, in *de Audiendis Poetis*. For Cornutus the poets themselves have little significance; they are simply the bearers of the myths which he allegorizes. Thus *c.* 17[1]: ἔοικε γὰρ ὁ ποιητὴς μυθοῦ [τε]παλαιοῦ παραφέρειν τοῦτο ἀπόσπασμα; cf. *c.* 30[2]: ὁ παρὰ τῷ ποιητῇ δὲ μῦθος . . . In the introduction to a particular reference we have πάλιν τοίνυν πρῶτον μὲν ἐμύθευσαν (a characteristic word) τὸ χάος γενέσθαι, καθάπερ ὁ Ἡσίοδος ἱστορεῖ. . . . (*c.* 17; p. 28, ll. 2-4). Cf. Sallustius, III.[3]

With the origin of these myths we need no more concern ourselves than did the allegorists. They more than anything else were the allegorists' Bible; they were a datum of tradition. It is unnecessary to point out that there is nothing here in any true sense parallel to the primitive Christian reverence for the OT; the Church and Judaism here form a block over against Hellenism.

Philo. Philo is important as a double link. He stands between Judaism and Hellenism in his attitude to his authorities, and between Platonism and Judaism-Christianity in his notion of inspiration and in his terminology.

(i) Philo was always consciously a Jew, and never departed from his loyalty to the traditions, the exclusiveness, and the Bible of Judaism. Yet he was familiar with Greek allegory, and Greek authors, and alluded to and used them,[4] and his use of the books of Moses resembles in some respects the use which we have seen was made of Homer—Moses is made to agree with the eclectic philosophy of Philo. At least one important difference, however, remains; Philo never removed altogether by means of his allegories the underlying ground of history and law, which he always took seriously.

(ii) He speaks of Moses as inspired, but not as an ecstatic who did not know what he was saying; in this connection he uses frequently the term πνεῦμα. According to *de Vit. Moys.* 1. 175 Moses' inspiration by the Spirit was not occasional but customary. In *de Vit. Moys.* 2. 40 the inspiring spirit is said to be enshrined in the Pentateuch, in both its Hebrew and Greek forms. In *de Decal.* 175 also Moses is the bearer of God's Spirit. There is an important discussion of what πνεῦμα θεοῦ (Gen. 6. 3) means in *de Gigant.* 22-26. It is used in one sense for the third of the elements (as in Gen. 1. 2); in another for the pure knowledge in which every wise man naturally shares (Exod. 31. 2 f.). This Spirit Moses had in pre-eminent degree; this is the wise, the divine Spirit (τὸ σοφόν, τὸ θεῖον). It is not peculiar to Moses, however; we have just seen that it belongs to every wise man; Balaam (*de Vit. Moys.* 1. 277)

---

[1] P. 26, ll. 16 f., Ed. Lang (Teubner).   [2] P. 62, l. 16.
[3] Ed. Nock, pp. 2, 4.   [4] Cf. Bréhier, *op. cit.* 38 f.

received the προφητικὸν πνεῦμα; and Philo himself (de Somn. 2. 252) heard the voice of the πνεῦμα ἀόρατον.

What we see in Philo is the assimilation of Jewish thought and terminology to the sort of Greek thought which was ultimately to issue in Neo-Platonism. He can write easily (much more easily than the Christians) about the Spirit because he is enough of a Stoic to think of it as the immanent reason which pervades all being, and which belongs especially to the (Stoic) sage, who lives in accordance with nature and reason; and at the same time his Platonism is of a sufficiently mystical brand for the word πνεῦμα to suggest to him the experience of ecstatic illumination, of union with deity and supernatural knowledge.[1]

The position, then, which we have discovered, may be briefly stated thus. The Gospels, since they frequently quote the OT and since they were in touch with Palestinian Judaism at least in their subject matter, might be expected (if, as is probable though not certain, we may infer the state of Judaism in Palestine before A.D. 70 from somewhat later Rabbinic sources) to speak often of the Holy Spirit of prophecy. In fact, they do so on but one occasion. This silence is not to be explained by the influence of Hellenism, for, as we have seen, the mental and spiritual atmosphere of Hellenism is, in this respect at least, widely different from that of the Gospels. It is, on the other hand, significant that the Rabbis, who spoke so frequently of the Holy Spirit in connection with the prophets, made no claim to similar inspiration themselves. For them revelation from God was no longer direct but mediated by indirect audition (the *bath qol*). There was no check on their statements about the prophets in the form of present experience. In the Church the situation was different. The Christians were quite familiar with prophecy, believed to be due to the immediate inspiration of the Spirit. Perhaps for this very reason they were reluctant to speak about the OT prophets and their relationship to God; not because they disparaged them, but because they understood them, and themselves knew what it was to be a prophet. They knew that the authority of prophecy lay not in an overwhelming spiritual experience in which the mind was paralysed but in an obedient apprehension of the purposes of God in history.

Philo, at first, appears to be nearer to NT thought about the Spirit as inspirer of the men of old; but he proves to differ from it on two radical points. For him the Spirit is to be thought of in terms of a cosmic, pervasive principle; and it produces an ecstasy in which it is not necessary, if indeed it be possible, for the human mind to work independently.

We have now completed our survey of the material in the Synoptic Gospels which relates Jesus and the Spirit of God;[2] we must next draw some conclusions from it before proceeding further in our study.

---

[1] Cf. the Platonic passages mentioned above, p. 110.

[2] For completeness we may mention, though there is no need to discuss, the variant readings in Lk. 9. 55 and 11. 2.

8

JESUS AND THE SPIRIT

A

WE have now learned, from observation of the NT and approximately contemporary sources, a number of traits of the "spiritual" or "pneumatic" man, and it may be well to summarize them, and to say as precisely as the rather nebulous facts permit what is to be understood by the term. An extensive description of the phenomena involved is given by Otto in Book Four ("The Kingdom of God and the Charisma") of his *The Kingdom of God and the Son of Man*. He speaks of the "charismatic type" as characteristic of all religions, ancient and modern. It will be worth while to quote at length an important passage in which he is speaking particularly of St Paul.

"Both the nature and the inner connection of the charismatic gifts may be recognized in Paul. The points to consider are:

The gifts do not in any way involve omnipotence or omniscience.

They are not magic powers such as a goētēs (sorcerer) thought he possessed.

They are mysterious heightenings of talents and capacities, which have at least their analogues in the general life of the soul.

They are not magic invasions into the life of nature; they do no violence to natural power nor are they magically increased natural powers. They work no nature miracles as portenta, miracula, prodigia, such as the standing still of the sun or the collapse of the walls of Jericho.

But they are:

Capacity for spiritual and psychic experiences of a distinctive kind.

Heightened talents such as kubernēsis (guidance) and diakrisis (discernment).

Operations of the soul and of psychic powers upon other souls, phenomena which indeed far surpass the limits of normal psychic operation, but are nevertheless rooted in the general mystery of the psychic processes of the will.

They form an approximately closed circle of possibilities which have a perceptible relationship of kind among themselves. They are regarded as of a miraculous character, and yet the charismatic knows himself to be different from the real miracle-worker and rejects miracle in the sense of a miracle of display, i.e., a nature miracle, as portentum or prodigium."
(*Op. cit.* 340 f.)

Later in the same section of his work Otto analyses the charismatic

E

gifts as follows: the gift of healing and exorcism; preaching with (super-natural) authority; the gift of the distinguishing of spirits; the gift of prophesying (foretelling); the gift of forgiveness of sins; the gift of being charmed against injuries (*op. cit.* 346-367). By a "pneumatic" or "spiritual" person, then, we mean one possessing, or appearing to possess, some or all of these gifts; one who seems different, even though undefinably different, from his fellows, because there is about him an aura of uncanny, "numinous" power. He does and says things which other men do not say and do; and, while he lives the life of a human being, he is manifestly also an inhabitant of another, unseen world, in which he possesses some effective authority.

In the course of our examination of the evidence which has passed before us, it has been impossible to escape the marked correspondence between Jesus and the "charismatic type". This is not to say that the Evangelists had no other description of Jesus. Apart from any faith in the divine aspect of his nature, he is portrayed in their pages (in the words of friends and foes) in a variety of rôles. But unmistakably he belongs to the category of "spiritual" persons. The grounds upon which this statement rests have already been set out at length and in detail; but we may here briefly recapitulate them as follows:

(i) The world of the NT was a world of spirits and demons. This fact appears clearly both in the NT and in the Jewish and pagan literature of similar date. The Gospels themselves take into account legions of demons (Mk. 5. 9 and parallel) and of angels (Mt. 26. 53). Paul knew of angels and principalities, powers of height and depth, which would if they could separate men from God's love (Rom. 8. 38 f.). The author of Ephesians knew of a struggle not against flesh and blood but against principalities and powers, against the world rulers of this darkness and the spiritual powers of evil in heavenly places (Eph. 6. 12). No less clearly does 1 *Enoch*, for example, refer to the spirits who shall "destroy until the day of the consummation" (16. 1); and we have seen sufficient evidence elsewhere of the widespread belief in demons which characterized the ancient world.

Jesus is represented in the Gospels as familiar with this spirit world, and as capable of holding direct intercourse with demons and angels.

(ii) Jesus not merely was acquainted with this world of spirits; he was its Lord, and in him the demons recognized their master. It is clearly the belief of the Evangelists that there was no demon whom Jesus was not able to expel. The same impression is conveyed by the miracle stories, for, though rationalization may sometimes point us to what actually happened, it does not help us to see what the Evangelists believed about Jesus. For them, the miracles were manifestations of the divine power (Lk. 5. 17) which rested upon Jesus, and, as it were, flowed out from him in health-giving contact with the sick. Jesus acts, not as a doctor who treats disease, but as a "pneumatic" man who commands it.

(iii) As a miracle-worker, Jesus resembles in one particular some of the OT prophets; and, as we have seen,[1] there are other striking resemblances too. Jesus made predictions about his own fate and that of Jerusalem which were the result of "divination, not ratiocination" (Otto, *op. cit.* 357, where the phrase is used of the prophets).

(iv) Other instances of the "charismatic gifts" mentioned by Otto may be observed. The Temptation is recorded (in Q) as a series of visionary experiences. The most natural, though not the only possible, interpretation of Lk. 10. 18 is that Jesus saw a vision of the fall of Satan. On several occasions Jesus is said to have known men's thoughts before they were uttered (e.g., Mk. 2. 8).[2] He was attacked by a mob but passed unharmed through the midst of his assailants (Lk. 4. 30). The "pneumatic" *milieu* of the life of Jesus is emphasized by other events not immediately connected with himself. Thus when Peter makes his Messianic confession at Caesarea Philippi Jesus replies (Mt. 16. 17): "Blessed art thou, Simon Bar Jonah, for flesh and blood hath not revealed it to thee but my Father who is in heaven." The revelation bestowed upon Peter is, however, dependent upon his relationship with Jesus. Perhaps the Transfiguration should be mentioned at this point. The scene is set forth in the Gospel tradition as a sort of anticipation or representation of the parousia,[3] but it is very difficult to decide what historical event (if any) lies behind the narrative as it now stands. It is clear enough, however, that, unless the whole scene was created by theological motives, it must have originated in some sort of vision, seen indeed by the disciples (not by Jesus), yet dependent upon him.

(v) It is important to note here in what sense the baptism narrative is to be understood. It has already been pointed out that this event is not given by the Evangelists as a *Berufungsvision*; it is not simply the call of a prophet or the endowment of a miracle-worker with supernatural power. It is essentially the solemn appointment of the Messiah to his office, the installation of the Son of God, and it stands in the Gospel tradition as an indication of how the ministry, in the form given to it by that tradition, was to be understood. This is a most important pointer for our understanding of the various "pneumatic" phenomena which we have noted. In this fundamental instance, the baptism, details which as they stand refer to inspiration by the Spirit are in fact subordinated to the intention of the writers to set forth Jesus as the Messiah; consequently, it is to be expected that, in the later instances, we shall err if we lay great stress on the "pneumatic" features of the narratives, and do not subordinate them to the expressed intention of the Evangelists. It cannot be too forcibly emphasized that the primitive

---

[1] Pp. 94-99.

[2] It is not suggested that the only meaning of these incidents, or even their primary meaning, is that Jesus was a visionary. Here too there is an OT background (e.g. Ps. 93. 11; Lam. 3. 60 f. (LXX)). But if the events took place as they are recorded, the *impression* given must have been of supernatural (" pneumatic ") knowledge.

[3] See G. H. Boobyer, *St Mark and the Transfiguration Story*.

116 JESUS AND THE SPIRIT

Church pressed into use a variety of categories to describe Jesus, and that sometimes a particular view of him (e.g., a belief in him as a Messiah endowed with prophetic and miraculous spirit) may have produced unhistorical narratives in the Gospels.

(vi) These considerations must be viewed in the light of the broader knowledge, or rather faith, which the Evangelists possessed. For them all, the events between the baptism and the crucifixion did not exhaust either the significance or the activity of Jesus. Calvary was not an end but a beginning. They lived in a charismatic environment, in a Church which was quite confident that it possessed the Spirit of God, but which never dreamed that its possession was founded upon its own right or merit. The Spirit was come because of Jesus the Lord of the Church, who was now ascended into heaven; "he hath poured forth this which ye see and hear" (Acts 2. 33). When they wrote the earlier parts of their Gospels the Evangelists knew that they were to tell the story of the empty tomb and the resurrection appearances.[1] It is not a part of our task to discuss the historicity of the empty tomb or to compare the different accounts of the resurrection body of Jesus. But the narratives in question have the *form* of visions, and the appearance, for example, of angels [2] suggests that the events were at least thought to be related to the world of spirits. The "appearance" which contains the most grossly material details (Lk. 24. 36-52) opens with a mysterious appearance of Jesus (αὐτὸς ἔστη ἐν μέσῳ αὐτῶν 24. 36) and concludes with an equally mysterious disappearance (διέστη ἀπ᾽ αὐτῶν 24. 51).

Moreover, the resurrection narratives point forward to the later spiritual experience of the Church. In Mt. the disciples are given a solemn charge to evangelize the world and are promised the spiritual presence of Christ himself (28. 19 f.). Luke postpones the great event of the descent of the Spirit until his second volume, but quite distinctly refers to it (24. 49). We do not possess an authentic ending for Mk., but the "longer ending" explicitly describes the "pneumatic" traits to be expected in the Church (in language probably based on Acts—see Mk. 16. 17-20).

We have so far observed a number of "pneumatic" traits in the Synoptic portrait of Jesus, and noted two chief indications to help us to understand them. These are (a) that similar phenomena undoubtedly occurred in the primitive Church and were there accounted for as instances of the fulfilment of prophecy, properly to be looked for in the last days; and (b) that the baptism narrative carefully defines Jesus' inspiration in terms of his Messiahship and of his being Son of God. These considerations are of first-rate importance in showing how the Evangelists intended their material to be understood; but they do not

---

[1] This includes Mark. Dr W. L. Knox, answering some recent criticism, has shown (*HTR* XXXV. 13-23) that Mark did not intend to stop at 16. 8, whether in fact he succeeded in writing more or not.   [2] Mk.'s " young man " is certainly intended as some such being.

aid us in answering the question whether the "pneumatic" features of
the Gospels make a historically accurate picture of what took .place in
the life of Jesus, or were created by a particular form of faith in Jesus
as Messiah.

B

There is no doubt that these "pneumatic" traits are to be found in
the Synoptic Gospels; but it is also true that they are not found unless
they are looked for. They are not set out by the Evangelists as they have
been set out in the last few pages. The word πνεῦμα itself occurs but
rarely in the Synoptic Gospels, and this is an index of the attitude of the
Evangelists which we have already observed on several occasions with
regard to deeds of Jesus which were, or which might have been, ascribed
to the Spirit. Jesus keeps his exorcisms and cures' secret, he never
refers to his baptism (Mk. 10. 38 f. and Lk. 12. 50 have an entirely
different connotation from that of Mk. 1. 9-11), he lays no stress
on his visions, and he hardly ever speaks of himself as a prophet. The
"pneumatic" features of his character and of the narrative are mentioned
occasionally and incidentally. Yet it would be wrong to say that they
were suppressed. If those who handed on and at the same time moulded
the Gospel tradition had intended to get rid of all traces of spiritual
phenomena from the matter with which they were dealing, they would
no doubt have done so more successfully than appears to have been the
case. For the traces are there in the Gospels to be found. Nor do the
data correspond with the theory propounded by Windisch in the work
already mentioned,[1] namely, that uses of the word πνεῦμα and indications of "pneumatic" events were first of all removed from the Gospels
on dogmatic considerations, and were later reintroduced because they
occupied so important a place in the life of the Church itself.

The fact plainly is that the Evangelists were not particularly interested
in general references to the Spirit, either to emphasize them or to suppress
them. It is this fact that we have to account for.

The writers of the Gospels were not interested in "pneumatic" men
as such. They had no reason to be. Such men were too common to
attract attention. In a few pages of the Acts we read of Simon Magus
and of Elymas, who were pagans; of the woman ventriloquist at Philippi;
of the seven sons of Sceva, who were Jews; and of a multitude of
Christians, all of whom had spiritual gifts and dealt in ecstatic
phenomena. To describe another such person would have attracted,
and would have deserved, no attention in the day when every Corinthian
believer thought of himself as πνευματικός. When Philostratus wrote
the life of Apollonius of Tyana he was wise enough to make him a
philosopher as well as a thaumaturge; and when Lucian wanted to
poke fun at the oriental cults (including Christianity) he portrayed their
representative as a "pneumatic" pure and simple. The Evangelists (and

---

[1] *Jesus und der Geist*, in *Studies in Early Christianity*, ed. S. J. Case.

their predecessors) had accordingly no temptation to multiply the references to spiritual phenomena in their material. To do so would have brought but little fresh glory to their subject even in the eyes of the non-Christian world, and still less among those who had found in him Κύριος, Σωτήρ and Θεός.

For, as the most recent study of the Gospels has shown, the Evangelists, no less than the other NT writers, were concerned with the divine and exalted aspect of the nature of Jesus of Nazareth. Opinions differ on the question whether the writers of the Gospels found this interest in their material or themselves introduced it; but it is hardly open to doubt that the Gospels as they now stand were written under the influence of a "high" Christology and in the interests of a thoroughly dogmatic Church *kerygma*.

In particular, Jesus is set forth as the promised Messiah of Judaism. It is true that the title Χριστός is not found frequently in the Synoptic Gospels; indeed, it does not appear at all in Q. But there are important substitutes for the title. It is not too much to say that Mk. is built upon a framework of declarations of the Messiahship. The first verse of the Gospel proclaims the office of Jesus in a headline. Men may be slow-witted, but the demons, supernatural beings, recognize him at once (1. 34; they use other titles, e.g., "the holy one of God", 1. 24; "the son of the most high God", 5. 7). The turning-point of the Gospel is Peter's confession at Caesarea Philippi (8. 29), and its climax (as far as the revelation of Jesus' person is concerned) is his own avowal of Messiahship before the High Priest (14. 61 f.).[1] The Q material, as we have said, does not contain the word Χριστός, but such a passage as Mt. 11. 2-6 (=Lk. 7. 18-23), where Jesus, in terms of the (Messianically applied) proof text Is. 61. 1 f., asserted clearly enough that he was what John meant by the "Coming One", is quite as significant as if it said Χριστός five times over.

To the Messiahship of Jesus many witnesses point. We have already seen that the demons, the disciples, and Jesus himself directly asserted it. John the Baptist, when he is identified with Elijah, implies the following Messiah. OT Scripture is continually quoted or alluded to; a clear indication that the Messianic hope was (in the opinion of the narrators) being fulfilled.

Jesus was the Messiah; and such he was in the period of his ministry. It is not sufficient to speak of him as at that time no more than *Messias designatus* [2] or a *futuristic* Messiah.[3] Jesus was not restricted to the notions of Messiahship which his contemporaries and forebears held, nor was he bound rigorously to fulfil any arbitrary eschatological time-table;

---

[1] Héring (*Le Royaume de Dieu et sa Venue*, 111-120) argues that Jesus did not claim Messiahship before the High Priest.

[2] As does, for example, Michaelis, in his interesting small book, *Reich Gottes und Geist Gottes*.

[3] Cf. Schweitzer, *Mystery of the Kingdom of God*, Ch. VIII. "Not yet was he the Messiah" (185). "In the midst of the Messianic expectation of his people stood Jesus as the Messiah that is to be. . . . This futuristic consciousness of Messiahship . . ." (189). Cf. Héring, *op. cit.*

Messiahship was a form which he used—inevitably, in view of the OT—to express his consciousness of mission, but Jesus controlled his tools and was not mastered by them.[1] To apply the title Messiah to one who was living the ordinary life of men was no *tour de force*; it was a title applied in the OT much more frequently to human kings and priests than to a supernatural being, and much more frequently to men of the present than to a man of the future. It is not so with the designation Son of man. Elsewhere (notably in Daniel and in 1 *Enoch*) the title Son of man calls to mind a figure of glory, who dwells in heaven or appears thence on the clouds. It was no less than a revolution in thought to say δεῖ τὸν υἱὸν τοῦ ἀνθρώπου πολλὰ παθεῖν (Mk. 8. 31). It is not impossible that the suffering of the Son of man-Messiah was read back into the teaching of Jesus by the Church in the light of Calvary; but it is more probable that the creative moulding of the older tradition was the work of Jesus himself. Otherwise, why should the title Son of man have been used at all? To introduce an astounding paradox is not the simplest way of explaining a difficulty.

Jesus was the Messiah; and if we are to qualify that title by an adjective it must be to call him, not *Messias designatus* or *Messias futurus*, but *Messias passurus*, and *Messias absconditus*. As we have seen, the whole of the life of Jesus was constrained in the direction of suffering; that was his vocation. Moreover, his Messiahship was concealed. Wrede's explanation of the Messianic secret was mistaken, but his demonstration of its existence has not been shaken,[2] and it is strikingly reaffirmed, from an opposite quarter and with a different interpretation, by Schweitzer.[3] At first the secret is kept from everyone; then it is revealed to the Twelve; but only in the trial before the High Priest does Jesus make an open avowal of his claim. These twin facts, of the inevitable suffering and the closely guarded secret of the Messiah, are of the highest importance in the present argument.

The Evangelists, we have said, had no occasion to be interested in, or impressed by, "pneumatic" men as such. They did, however, believe in Jesus as the Messiah, and it was for this reason that they included those "spiritual" elements which we have detected in the Gospels. For, as we have pointed out in each instance, the "pneumatic" traits in the character of Jesus point to his Messiahship, and therein, for the Evangelists, lay their value. They had evidential value. Yet the evidence was not good evidence, and for that reason it was sparingly used. The more strongly "pneumatic" elements in, for example, the miracles of Jesus were stressed, the more those miracles were thereby assimilated to the deeds of the common thaumaturge, and correspondingly the less closely were they related to the Messianic salvation. The Messiah was necessarily

---

[1] It is Schweitzer's great mistake, perhaps his only serious mistake, to suppose that Jesus was dominated by an eschatological time-table; it is true that eschatology determines both the dogma and the history of the Gospels, but it is an eschatology of which Jesus himself always remained master. [2] See Wrede, *Das Messiasgeheimnis in den Evangelien.*
[3] *Mystery of the Kingdom of God*, Ch. VIII.

(granted that he was to appear in the conditions of ordinary human life) a "pneumatic"; but the converse of this statement was by no means true; not every "pneumatic" was the Messiah. Here is the explanation of the strangely mixed attitude which we have already noted on the part of the Evangelists. Because Jesus is Messiah, "pneumatic" details are bound to arise; but they are bound to arise, as it were, as by-products, of only secondary significance.

The few uses of the word πνεῦμα in the Synoptic Gospels which have no direct connection with "pneumatic" phenomena attest the same situation. We have already shown that the agency of the Spirit in the birth of Jesus indicates his status in God's new creation; the baptism we have seen to be not so much a moment of inspiration as the initiation of the Messiah into his office. In each case, the word πνεῦμα as the Evangelists use it points to their central interest in the Messianic dignity of Jesus; but a freer use of the term might have concealed his office behind a superficial view of his inspiration.

One further point must be made here, though it will have to be taken up more fully later. Jesus was the Messiah; *as such* he was the bearer of the Spirit. But he kept his Messiahship secret, and knew himself to be a Messiah destined for suffering and death; hence it might be expected that the Spirit which rested upon him would not be openly and entirely manifest. And so it was. The miracles were not unmistakable portents; it was not beyond doubt that it was by the finger of God that Jesus cast out demons. There was no spiritual power in the preaching or teaching of Jesus to compel universal assent. Jesus himself hardly ever spoke of the Spirit; he could not have done so (in the only way in which he could truthfully have related the Spirit to himself) without declaring the Messiahship which it was his purpose to keep secret.

C

The evidence for the expectation that the Messiah, when he came, would be equipped with the Spirit of God is not extensive.[1] To a great extent the reason for this is that the Messiah himself was thought of (not, of course, universally) as a heavenly figure who could not naturally be said to possess the Spirit; a Messiah such as Jesus was not expected by anyone. There is, however, quite good evidence for the hope that, in the last days, the Spirit would be generally given to all men, or rather, to all Israel. This hope can be found in several passages in the OT itself, notably in Joel 3. 1 ff.; Ezek. 36. 27; 37. 14; 39. 29; Is. 44. 3; Zech. 12. 10; Num. 11. 29.[2] We may compare *Test. Jud.* 24. 2 f., *Zadokite Fragments* 2. 10.

[1] The passages are considered on pp. 42-44.
[2] This passage was interpreted eschatologically. See *Midr. Ps.* 14. 6 (57b) (quoted Str.-B. II. 134 *et al.*) : " Twice do you find it written in the book of Psalms, ' O that the salvation of Israel were come out of Zion ! ' once in the first book (Ps. 14. 7) and once in the second book (Ps. 53. 7). Why ? R. Levi (c. 300) said : With reference to the teacher and with reference to the scholar. . . . The teacher is God who said : O that there were such an heart in them, that they would fear me ! Deut. 5. 26 ; the scholar is Moses who said : Would God that all the

There is no doubt that the Church thought that these prophecies were fulfilled in itself. No writer in the NT would have disputed the use made of the Joel passage in Acts 2. Paul and John, with the other theologians of the NT, do not fall behind the popular historian in their claim that the Church was the home of the Spirit of God. What justification was there for this confidence, for this bold appropriation of the OT by the community which professed to have Jesus for its Lord? That there is a marked change of tone and emphasis between the teaching of Jesus and (e.g.) that of Paul must be observed by any careful reader of the NT. It is much to the credit of the Synoptic Gospels as historical sources that this contrast has been preserved. There is certainly a deep and significant unity which underlies the differences; Paul and Jesus alike speak of God and man, of sin and grace, of reconciliation and redemption. But it remains true that a Galilean Jew would have found the teaching of Jesus familiar because he spoke in apocalyptic terms of the Kingdom of God and the Son of man, of imminent judgement and eschatological salvation; while a Corinthian mystagogue would have understood Paul because he spoke of a divine Lord who had instituted a cult meal and a ceremonial initiation which secured to the neophyte a spiritual salvation mediated by God's Spirit in the environment of the present world. There is here a real difference in stress which must not be neglected in the present concern of theologians to demonstrate the unity of the NT; a difference which can be summarized in the statistical fact that whereas Jesus in the Synoptic Gospels (counting all instances, whether authentic or not) speaks of the Spirit seven times, Paul mentions him about ninety times.[1]

Was this difference due merely to an outburst of religious feeling? Was it based upon the teaching of Jesus himself? Or is neither of these alternatives true? That is to say, was it based upon a drawing out of what was implicit not so much in the teaching as in the fact that Jesus had appeared, throwing all eschatological expectations into confusion? An examination of the data with regard to the Church and the Spirit will lead us to a discussion of the problem of the relationship between the NT doctrine of the Spirit and the eschatological teaching of the Gospels.

Lord's people were prophets! Num. 11. 29. But the words of the teacher and of the scholar have not come to fulfilment in this world ; but the words of both will come to fulfilment in the future. The words of the teacher : I will give you a new heart, Ezek. 36. 26 ; and the words of the scholar : I will pour out my spirit upon all flesh, Joel 3. 1." The use of the last two prophecies shows that Str.-B. are right in explaining the "future" referred to by the words, " der messianischen Zeit ".

[1] The figure is necessarily inexact because it is impossible in some cases to be certain whether Paul is speaking of the divine or human spirit. Eph. and the Pastorals are excluded from the count.

Note. Though I still believe the argument of this chapter, which stands here as in the first impression, to be substantially sound, I should now write differently about Messiahship in the gospels.

PART TWO

9

THE SPIRIT AND THE CHURCH

THE data may be set out as follows:

(a) *The Prophets of Lk. 1 f.: John the Baptist*

In the Lucan infancy narratives one character after another is filled with the Spirit and prophesies. The following instances come under consideration:

1. 41: Elisabeth, when she meets Mary, feels the babe leap in her womb, is filled with the Holy Spirit, and pronounces prophetic words.[1]

1. 67: Zachariah is filled with Holy Spirit, and prophesies about his son John (the *Benedictus*).

2. 25-27: Simeon was a righteous and pious man; the Holy Spirit was upon him; the Holy Spirit had advised him that he should not die before the coming of the Lord's Christ; when the parents of Jesus brought him into the Temple Simeon was (in a special sense, presumably) in the Spirit and blessed God and spoke the *Nunc Dimittis*, and the prophecy of 2. 34 f.

2. 36-38: nothing is said of the Holy Spirit in connection with Anna, but she was a prophetess.

In addition, these statements are made about John the Baptist:

1. 15, 17: he will not drink wine or strong drink; he will be filled with Holy Spirit; he will go before the Lord in the Spirit and power of Elijah.

1. 76: he shall be called a prophet of the Highest and prepare the ways of the Lord.

We may compare Mt. 11. 9 f. (=Lk. 7. 26 f.) and Lk. 7. 28 (*v.l.*): John is a prophet and more than a prophet because he fulfils Mal. 3. 1; and Mt. 11. 12-14 (=Lk. 16. 16), which is of doubtful meaning but seems at least to link John with the prophets.[2]

In these chapters of Lk. we meet a *pre-Christian* Church, equipped with the Holy Spirit and with prophets. The verses which we have quoted, in respect of what they imply with regard to inspiration as well as in their contents, correspond to a few OT passages. It is well known that the songs themselves—magnificent as they are—are in structure little more than collections of phrases from the OT; similarly, there are OT passages

---

[1] Including possibly the *Magnificat*; see Creed, *ad loc.*, with his references.
[2] Other passages connecting John with the prophets (and in particular with Elijah) are Mk. 1. 6 and parallels; 11. 32 and parallels; Mt. 17. 13.

where prophecy is ascribed to the action of the Spirit.[1] The correspondence, however, with Rabbinical thought about prophecy is more striking, for in the later Jewish literature the connection between prophecy and the Holy Spirit is regular, and so frequent that Str.-B. write (II. 127 f.): "For this reason it should be assumed without further proof that the Rabbinic scholars everywhere (except where the context makes it necessary to think of the Spirit inspiring Scripture) understood by the Holy Spirit the Spirit of prophecy, or of prophetic endowment." Some of the Rabbis themselves also experienced the work of the Spirit, but they were not prophets in any strict sense of the term. They have supernatural knowledge, but they do not utter inspired speech. This is true in all the cases mentioned by Str.-B. [2] and by Dr Abelson.[3] The line of the prophets ended with Haggai, Zechariah and Malachi, and with the first Temple.[4] From that time the Holy Spirit was rather an ethical than a prophetic gift.[5] As Dr Abelson [6] says, "It is a divine endowment akin to prophecy which anyone may attain provided he lives the life which leads up to this high state of moral, religious, and intellectual perfection".

Most definitely of all, however, do the psalms and singers of Lk. 1 f. recall what we know, from the rest of the NT, about the worship of the primitive Church. Dr Oesterley [7] assumes that 1 Cor. 14. 26 is sufficient to "show that in the Gentile churches the liturgical use of psalms was customary from the beginning; and this can only have been adopted from the Jewish Church". But (as is shown by other passages quoted by Dr Oesterley, Eph. 5. 19; Col. 3. 16, as well as by the context in 1 Cor. 14, which deals with spontaneous worship inspired by the Spirit) the "psalms" in question were not the Psalms of David, taken over from the Synagogue, but fresh Christian compositions; that is, compositions such as the songs of Lk. 1 f. We should notice also Acts 2. 47; 4. 24 ff.; but the reference to 1 Cor. 14 is particularly important, because it could have been, and no doubt was, said of these singers that they were filled with the Holy Spirit, precisely as Zachariah (the father of the Baptist) was said to be filled with Holy Spirit.[8]

The successor to this older generation of prophets, Zachariah and Simeon, is John. The angel announces to Zachariah that John will be a prophet ("he will go before him in the spirit and power of Elijah "),

[1] E.g. Num. 11. 25, 29; 24. 2; 1 Sam. 10. 6, 10; Ezek. 2. 2; Joel 3. 1 f. Not all of these imply prophetic *speech*.
[2] *Op. cit.* II. 133q.　　[3] *The Immanence of God in Rabbinical Literature*, 259.
[4] "Five things which existed in the first Temple were lacking in the second. These were (a) Fire from on High, (b) Anointing Oil, (c) the Ark, (d) Holy Spirit, (e) the Urim and Thummim " (*Song of Songs Rabba* 8, and in different forms elsewhere, e.g., *T.b. Yoma* 21b, *Numbers Rabba* 15. 10). "With the death of Haggai, Zechariah, and Malachi the Holy Spirit ceased in Israel " (*T.b. Sukkah* 48a, *Sanh.* 11a, *Song of Songs Rabba* 8. 9 f.).
[5] *Mishnah Sotah* 9. 15: R. Phineas b. Jair says: "Heedfulness leads to cleanliness, and cleanliness leads to purity, and purity leads to abstinence, and abstinence leads to holiness, and holiness leads to humility, and humility leads to the shunning of sin, and the shunning of sin leads to saintliness, and saintliness leads to the Holy Spirit, and the Holy Spirit leads to the resurrection of the dead."
[6] *Op. cit.* 260.　　[7] *The Jewish Background of the Christian Liturgy*, 148.
[8] The expression " to be filled ($\pi\iota\mu\pi\lambda\eta\mu\iota$) with Holy Spirit " is common in Acts: 2. 4.; 4. 8, 31; 9. 17; 13. 9.

that he will be a Nazirite ("he shall not drink wine or strong drink"), and that he will be filled with Holy Spirit from birth.

We have already given some account of the prophetic work of John the Baptist.[1] It will be sufficient here to lay stress on the fact that by Luke (or by his source) this office of prophesying is intimately connected with the Holy Spirit. John's mother and father have the Spirit (Lk. 1. 41; 1. 67); it is promised that John himself will be filled with the Spirit (Lk. 1. 15; cf. 1. 80, where πνεύματι may refer to the Spirit of God). John, we may briefly say, was a prophet, that is, he preached in the same way (and in great measure to the same effect) as the great OT prophets;[2] and Luke did not hesitate to ascribe his prophesying to the Spirit.

Luke's free use of the term πνεῦμα, and his description of John as a prophet, raise a problem because they are unique in the Gospels. Nowhere else in the Synoptic Gospels is it said that anyone but Jesus received the Holy Spirit. Elsewhere these Gospels justify the Johannine pronouncement, οὔπω ἦν πνεῦμα ὅτι Ἰησοῦς οὔπω ἐδοξάσθη (Jn. 7. 39). But the explanation of the difficulty is not hard to find, and is much simpler than the elaborate connection which Leisegang[3] tries to establish between manticism and the birth of a divine child. Dibelius puts us well on the way in his remark about legends:[4] "Legends put halos round men, and set in a transfiguring light the very things with which religious men deal. Hence everything belonging to the very fact of holy men may become significant in a Legend. Paradigms have to do with the message as such, and Tales with miracle. But Legends sometimes lack concentration, and their interests are manifold, because *nothing proper to the fact of a man of God must be excluded*" (my italics). Now Luke, who certainly worked carefully over the sources of his infancy narratives, was familiar with two groups of holy men: those of the OT, and the new generation, their successors in the Church. All of them, in particular the latter, were men of the Spirit, and Luke was giving Zachariah and the others no more than their due in declaring that they too were filled with the Spirit. Besides, Luke knew well that though there had been a new and supreme gift of the Spirit after the death and resurrection of Jesus, it was impossible to deny the work of the Spirit under the old Covenant, and to that Covenant the characters of Lk. 1 f. (except John, Jesus and perhaps Mary) belong; they are still looking for the consolation of Israel.

John himself stood in some connection with the New Age. He was more than a prophet. The least in the Kingdom of Heaven was greater than he, but at least he stood on the border-line of the Kingdom, and might be expected to have tasted of the powers of the age to come (Mt. 11. 12-14; Lk. 16. 16).

---

[1] See pp. 26-34.
[2] He is, of course, especially connected (here, as elsewhere in the Gospels) with Elijah (Lk. 1. 17). Many of the parallels given (pp. 94-99) between Jesus and the prophets could be applied here.
[3] *Op. cit.* 14-72; see above, pp. 12 f.   [4] *From Tradition to Gospel*, 132.

Lk. 1 f. really shows us an island of the OT, surrounded by the New, although Luke has drawn on (ultimately) Christian sources for the words which he puts into the mouths of his characters, and has probably been influenced by Christian experiences of and beliefs about the Spirit in his description of them. Zachariah and his fellows are classed by Luke with Elijah himself; in the Gospel narrative they wear his mantle and it is a double portion of his spirit that they have received.

(b) *He shall baptize you with the Holy Spirit*

This saying of John the Baptist has been preserved in two forms. They are:

Mk. 1. 8: He shall baptize you in ($\epsilon\nu$) Holy Spirit.

Mt. 3. 11 = Lk. 3. 16: He shall baptize you in ($\epsilon\nu$) Holy Spirit and fire.

The shorter, Marcan, form must doubtless have been understood by the Evangelist and his readers as a reference to the gift of the Spirit to the Church. This is clearly shown by Lk. 24. 49; Acts 1. 5; 11. 16; 19. 1-7; the last passage in particular indicates that the distinguishing feature of Christian baptism was its power of conferring the Spirit, which was not possessed by the Johannine rite. It is an attractive conjecture, though of course no more than a conjecture, that if we possessed the end of Mark's Gospel we should find there a fulfilment of the prophecy recorded in the first chapter. Be that as it may, we have here a perfectly clear statement that Jesus, who was himself about to receive the Holy Spirit when he was baptized by John, would in turn bestow the same gift upon his followers. Mark gives no indication that this event took place before the resurrection, and he must therefore have understood it to have belonged to the subsequent period. Whether he used the word "baptize" metaphorically (as in Mk. 10. 38) or thought specifically of the rite of Christian baptism, which was believed to confer the gift of the Spirit, is a difficult question which it is not necessary for us to answer.

Matthew and Luke add to the Marcan saying "and fire"; these words were no doubt derived from the common source from which they drew also a further passage of John's preaching (Mt. 3. 7-10 = Lk. 3. 7-9). Acts 2. 3 is a sufficient indication that, for Luke at least, the addition conveyed no fresh thought; the fire was the fire of the Spirit. This Leisegang[1] takes to have been the original meaning of the fire baptism. Fire has connections with the baptism of Jesus;[2] in a good deal of Greek thought $\pi\nu\epsilon\hat{\upsilon}\mu\alpha$ and $\pi\hat{\upsilon}\rho$ are closely related; and so, too, fire is bound up with the experience of ecstasy, in, e.g., Philo, *de Vit. Moys.* 1. 70, and the Mithras Liturgy.[3] Leisegang says (p. 76): "Baptism with fire is nothing else than baptism with the Spirit, which would, in Hellenistic circles

---

[1] *Op. cit.* 72-80.

[2] Justin, *Dial c. Tryph.* 88: κατελθόντος τοῦ Ἰησοῦ ἐπὶ τὸ ὕδωρ καὶ πῦρ ἀνήφθη ἐν τῷ Ἰορδάνῃ There is a similar tradition in the Old Latin MSS a g¹, and in Ephraem Syrus. See Burkitt, *Evangelion da-Mepharreshe,* ii. 114 f.

[3] See Dieterich, *Mithrasliturgie,* 2, 12 ; 8, 16-24 ; 10, 13 f. (ταῦτα πάντα λέγε μετὰ πυρὸς καὶ πνεύματος).

of early Christianity, in reference to the Greek cultus of Dionysus, to magic and the mysteries, be thought of as bound up with an appearance of fire." Thus he is able to find another Synoptic reference to the Spirit grounded in Hellenistic religion. But this view is to be rejected.[1] The Q context suggests very strongly that the fire should be understood as the fire of judgement.[2] There is no difficulty in the objection raised by Leisegang, that baptism is essentially a means of creating new believers, and judgement fire is not such a means. The whole Johannine discourse has in mind not the life of a settled community with an initiation ceremony, but the imminent arrival of the Messianic age, which would involve both the pouring out of the Spirit upon the faithful (the "wheat" of Mt. 3. 12=Lk. 3. 17) and the judgement of the ungodly (the "chaff", of the same verses).

Wellhausen[3] and Bultmann[4] are of the opinion that the original form of the saying was "He will baptize you with fire", and that this simple eschatological doom saying was corrupted to its present forms by the Christian experience of the Spirit. It seems even more plausible to conjecture that the earliest form of the logion was, "He will baptize you with πνεύματι καὶ πυρί", πνεύματι being taken to mean, not "spirit" but "wind". In this case we have a parallel with the immediately following verse: "He will baptize (i.e. judge) you with wind and fire; the wind will sweep through the threshing floor to carry away the chaff, which will then be burned." Wind and fire are the instruments of judgement.

Very slight support for this view may be found in the few witnesses of Lk. 3. 16 that omit the word ἁγίῳ. They are the MSS 63, 64, and Tertullian (de Bapt. 10), Augustine (de Cons. Ev. 2. 26), and Clement of Alexandria (Eclog. 25).[5]

The forms in which the saying appeared in Mk. (? and in the Q source) were due to the influence of the Christian experience; we cannot see here a prophecy of the gift of the Spirit to the Church. The contrast between the very rare use of πνεῦμα in the Gospels with its frequency in the rest of the NT is accentuated; for the present occurrence is due to a "reading back" from the later period.

(c) God will give the Holy Spirit

Lk. 11. 13: We need use very few words on this text. Hardly any

---

[1] With Bultmann, GST 116 n. 1.

[2] Cf. Mt. 3. 10, 12 ; Lk. 3. 9, 17 ; and cf. Bultmann, loc. cit.: "The fire of judgement is a concept met with in Mt. 3. 12 just as, for example, in Mal. 3. 2 f., and baptism as the image of an annihilation is met with in Mk. 10. 38 f. ; Lk. 12.50." "Fire" is not part of the original text of Mk. 1. 8, but as it stands there, in certain MSS, it *need* not mean judgement.

[3] Commentary on Mt. 3. 11 f.   [4] GST 116 n. 1.

[5] This passage is worth quoting for the sake of an interpretation given there. The verse is quoted ; then πυρὶ δὲ οὐδένα ἐβάπτισεν. Ἔνιοι δέ, ὥς φησιν Ἡρακλέων, πυρὶ τὰ ὦτα τῶν σφραγιζομένων κατεσημήνατο (sic MPG IX. 709 with the note, "Pluraliter legendum videtur κατεσημήναντο ut feratur ad ἐνίοι.") οὕτως ἀκούσαντες τὸ ἀποστολικόν· τὸ γὰρ πτύον ἐν τῇ χειρὶ αὐτοῦ, τοῦ διακαθᾶραι . τὴν ἅλω· καὶ συνάξει τὸν σῖτον εἰς τὴν ἀποθήκην· τὸ δὲ ἄχυρον κατακαύσει πυρὶ ἀσβέστῳ. Πρόσκειται οὖν τῷ Διὰ πυρός, τὸ Διὰ πνεύματος. ἐπειδὴ τὸ σῖτον ἀπὸ τοῦ ἀχύρου διακρίνει τουτέστιν ἀπὸ τοῦ ὑλικοῦ ἐνδύματος διὰ πνεύματος καὶ τὸ ἄχυρον χωρίζεται διὰ τοῦ πνεύματος λικμώμενον· οὕτως τὸ πνεῦμα διαχωριστικὴν ἔχει δύναμιν ἐνεργειῶν ὑλικῶν.

scholars could now be found to dispute the very great probability that the Matthaean form of the saying (Mt. 7. 11, " . . . will give good things to those who ask him") is original in comparison with the Lucan. Luke's special interest in the Holy Spirit has led him to substitute the supremely good thing (in his estimation) for the more general statement of his source. Here, even more clearly than in the last instance, we see the influence of Christian experience upon the Gospel tradition, and the absence of the Holy Spirit from the accounts of the life of Jesus stands out with still greater distinctness.[1]

(d) *The Mission Charges.* Mk. 3. 15; 6. 7-13; Mt. 10. 1-42; Lk. 9. 1-5; 10. 1-16. These passages have been briefly referred to above, pp. 56, 65.

The question of the historicity of a mission of apostles [2] is now inevitably raised. It is difficult to find any satisfactory reason for thinking that this event, which is attested by Mk., by Q and by L, did not take place. Wellhausen thinks of the narrative in Mk. as the account of an experiment: "It [the passage in question] contains no historical tradition. The Apostolate here is already founded by Jesus, without, however, playing any part; the Twelve—the expression is synonymous with apostles, and in Mk. always has its special meaning—only make an experiment, and are thereafter as dependent and passive as before, although the experiment succeeds. The truth is that Jesus undertook no practice journeys with his Seminar (*hat keine Übungsreisen mit seinem Seminar veranstaltet*)." [3] But the event is certainly not set forth by Mk. as an experiment, and still less was it so regarded by the Q source. Rather it appears as a very significant stage in the development of the story of Jesus. It is simply not true that the disciples afterwards appear merely passive; it is true that they do not play a very glorious rôle, and that they continue to display their failure to understand both the person and the message of Jesus; but after the mission of the Twelve (in Mk.) occur the feeding miracles, in which the disciples play an active though secondary part; they question Jesus (Mk. 7. 17; 9. 11, 28; 10. 26, 28; 13. 3 f.; cf. 11. 21); they make (through Peter) the Messianic confession at Caesarea Philippi, and also presume to rebuke Jesus when he prophesies his suffering; their own sufferings are foretold, and they are represented at the Transfiguration; they try (unsuccessfully) to cast out a demon; they reprove an exorcist, not of their company, who uses the name of Jesus; they check those who were bringing children to Jesus; the sons of Zebedee beg for the best seats at the Messianic banquet, and the ten are displeased; all participate in the Triumphal Entry into Jerusalem;

---

[1] At this point we may mention also the Marcionite reading in the Lucan version of the Lord's Prayer (Lk. 11. 2): ἐλθέτω τὸ ἅγιον πνεῦμά σου [ἐφ᾽ ἡμᾶς] καὶ καθαρισάτω ἡμᾶς. Here too we have the introduction of a reference to the Spirit into a Synoptic saying which did not originally contain it.

[2] There is no need to discuss the numbers " twelve " and " seventy-[two] ". Luke's account of the sending of the " seventy- [two] " is plainly a doublet of his mission charge to the " twelve "; for the former he has used Q material, for the latter, Mk.

[3] *Das Evangelium Marci* (1st ed.), 46.

(according to Matthew's interpretation of Mk.) they complain of the waste of the nard poured over Jesus' head; they are all present at the Last Supper, and three of them in Gethsemane; one of them betrays Jesus and another denies him. Especially when we consider the single-mindedness with which Mark follows the career of Jesus, this appears indeed a strikingly active passiveness. In fact, the sending out of the Twelve would be more readily comprehensible after some of these events than before them all.

Again, there seems to be no good reason why Bultmann [1] should say, "originally the speaker here is the Risen, exalted one (cf. Mt. 28. 19 f.; Lk. 24. 47 ff.), that is, we have a community formation". No critic would assert that the Matthaean and Lucan passages mentioned are authentic utterances of the risen Christ, and they can hardly therefore be used in the way in which Bultmann uses them. It is quite another question whether the whole of the mission charge is historical; it seems quite probable that community rules for missionaries have been introduced into it. But this probability in no way affects the assertion (attested, we may repeat, by no fewer than three Gospel sources) that Jesus did send out his disciples on a healing and preaching tour.

The question is whether this mission involved the possession by the disciples of the Holy Spirit. According to Mt. 10. 20 it did; but this verse occurs in a passage of doubtful historicity,[2] in which, moreover, the reference to the Spirit is probably secondary.[3] We may for the present neglect this passage and consider the rest of the evidence.

In Mk. 3. 15 the disciples are promised ἐξουσία to cast out demons; the same ἐξουσία, presumably, as that which Jesus had. In Mk. 6. 7 they receive, specifically for the mission, ἐξουσία over unclean spirits. Nothing is said in this Gospel about preaching until after the mission, 6. 12; the preaching was of repentance. Mt.'s long discourse, 10. 1-42, embraces the relevant Q material (and some that is not relevant) in addition to the Marcan charge. Mt. repeats the gift of authority over demons and adds to it the power to cure other diseases. The disciples are to preach the Kingdom of God (κηρύσσειν τὴν βασιλείαν τοῦ θεοῦ, Lk. 9. 2), i.e., to announce its imminence (ἤγγικεν (ἐφ' ὑμᾶς) ἡ βασιλεία τῶν οὐρανῶν (τοῦ θεοῦ), Mt. 10. 7 (Lk. 10. 9)). In virtue of the message they bear they can confer "peace" upon a house that receives them, and deny it where they are rejected.[4] In all this, however, there is nothing that need imply the gift of the Holy Spirit. It is implied by Lk. 10. 17; Mk. 9. 38 and parallels that the exorcisms would be in the name of Jesus.[5] The exorcisms of the disciples are brought into much closer connection with those of Jesus by a comparatively incidental

---

[1] GST 156.
[2] Mt. 10. 18 deals with the appearance of disciples before governors and kings, for testimony to them and the Gentiles, a possibility which certainly did not exist during the ministry of Jesus.   [3] See below, pp. 130-132.
[4] If we are justified in seeing in the εἰρήνη of Mt. 10. 13, Lk. 10. 5 f. more than the common Semitic greeting.   [5] See above, p. 56.

Matthaean saying, Mt. 10. 25. This verse is reminiscent of Mk. 3. 22 and parallels, where Jesus is alleged to cast out demons in the power of Beelzebul. Our passage is an indication of the meaning of the name Beelzebul, which is probably, as the play upon words suggests, בַּעַל זְבוּל (ba'al zᵉbul), οἰκοδεσπότης. This is important, because it points at once to the existence of a household governed by the οἰκοδεσπότης, which is not a synagogue of Satan but a true household of God. As Schlatter [1] rightly says, "Since Jesus forms, with his disciples, an οἶκος the new community is visible. In the place of the οἶκος 'Ισραήλ stands the οἶκος 'Ιησοῦ and now this house is God's house." It is strange that Schlatter, rejecting the opinion that Beelzebul is בַּעַל זְבוּל (ba'al zᵉbul), adopts Riehm's [2] suggestion that the origin of the word is בַּעַל דְּבָב (בַּעַל דְּבָבָא), ba'al dᵉbab (bᵉ'el dᵉbaba').

Yet it would be wrong to suppose that this saying of Jesus about his house (if it be authentic, a question which cannot certainly be settled—it might well be held to reflect the controversies of the Palestinian communities) postulates the existence of a Spirit-filled community. Even if the slander against the disciples which is in question had been occasioned by their exorcisms, this would still not be the case. We have seen above [3] that in the Beelzebul controversy, though the opposition of Jesus' Jewish adversaries may well have begun simply as a charge of witchcraft (cf. *Sanh.* 43a, 107b, *Soṭa* 47a), the argument, as given by the Evangelists, turns towards the relation of the work of Jesus to the Messianic age; this (to the Evangelists if not to Jesus himself) was the significant point rather than the original accusation. The disciples, in their turn, by their exorcisms taken with their preaching (of repentance, according to Mk., which recalls John's preaching; of the Kingdom of God (heaven), according to Q, which recalls that of Jesus himself) made a similar claim. The importance of their work, including their miraculous work, lay in its relation to the Messianic age. By making this claim, they laid themselves open to an accusation similar to that which had been brought against their master. It is unnecessary to consider whether these sayings as they are given by the Evangelists are historically accurate; if in their present form they do not imply endowment with the Spirit it is very unlikely that they did so in any earlier form.

There is no occasion, then, to find in the mission charge any indication that the Spirit had been given, or was then given, to the apostles.[4] They were heralds [5] rather than prophets, and their healing ministry was probably carried out "in the name of Jesus", a formula which no doubt carried with it not a little of the numinous but which in no way rested upon a personal endowment of the Holy Spirit. It is noteworthy that, when the disciples asked Jesus (Mk. 9. 28 f. and parallel) why

---

[1] *Der Evangelist Matthäus, ad loc.*
[2] See McNeile, *Matthew*, 143. The reference is presumably to Riehm's *Handwörterbuch des biblischen Altertums*, 195 f.   [3] Pp. 62 f.
[4] Except in Mt. 10. 20, on which see below, pp. 130-132.
[5] κηρύσσειν, Mt. 10. 7; Lk. 9. 2.

they had not been able to expel a demon, his reply was, not that if they had possessed the Spirit they would have been able to perform the cure, but that the key to success was prayer (in Mt. 17. 19 f., faith).

(e) *The Gift of the Spirit in Time of Persecution*

Jesus promised that divine assistance would be given to his followers when they were put on trial before human authorities. The tradition to this effect is so well attested that it is hardly possible to doubt its authenticity. In Mk. we have 13. 11, in the Apocalyptic discourse. There is one parallel in Mt., in 10. 19 f., that is, in the mission charge to the disciples. Two Lucan passages come under consideration. In 12. 11 f. there is a saying similar in form to that of Mt. 10. 19 f. It occurs in a collection of teaching, the several parts of which are loosely connected, in some instances merely by common words or phrases. From the saying about confessing or denying the Son of man (*vv.* 8 f.) Luke passes to that which contrasts speech against the Son of man with blasphemy against the Spirit (*v.* 10); thence (the term Holy Spirit being the connecting link) he proceeds to the promise of assistance in time of trial (*vv.* 11 f.); next, with no apparent connection at all, he gives the incident of the man who asked Jesus to effect a partition of his inheritance. In 21. 14 f. Luke has a parallel to Mk. 13. 11, which does not, however, speak of the Holy Spirit: "I will give you (says Jesus) mouth and wisdom."

It is not necessary (nor would it be easy) to assign the Matthaean and Lucan forms of the promise to their sources. Two questions arise:

(1) The saying, in different contexts, is applied to different times. Which (if any) is original?

(2) Which form of the saying is the earliest?

(1) According to Mk., the saying was uttered by Jesus in the last week of his life, and refers to the period after his death. It stands in Mt.'s mission charge (Mt. 10), where, however, it is united with matter that does not very appropriately fit a restricted journey in Palestine (Mt. 10. 18; contrast 10. 23). Lk., as we have seen, has the saying once in an arbitrarily collected and placed catena of logia which gives us no clue to the original time of reference of the promise; and again, in modified form, in the same place as Mk.

Dr Schweitzer accepts both the unity of the Matthaean discourse and the place given to it by the Evangelist in the life of Jesus.[1] The sufferings there predicted are the pre-Messianic woes, and the gift of the Spirit that is promised is that of the Messianic age. It is unfortunate that Dr Schweitzer has not given equal consideration to the alternative setting of the saying with which we are concerned, the Apocalyptic

---

[1] *The Mystery of the Kingdom of God*, 91 : " In the commission to the Twelve Jesus imparts instruction about the woes of the approaching Kingdom. In the descriptive portions of it there may be much perhaps that betrays the colouring of a later time. By this concession, however, the character of the speech as a whole is not prejudiced."

discourse of Mk. 13. Is it possible to find room there also for predictions of sufferings for the disciples, after Jesus has (according to Schweitzer) come to the belief that the Messianic affliction would be absorbed in the cross? Is it possible to find room for any such predictions, which presuppose the continued life of the Church as a community in the world?[1] No help can be derived from the setting of the saying in Lk. 12; and this fact empties the Matthaean placing of much of its significance. The composite nature of the Matthaean discourse is roundly denied by Dr Schweitzer,[2] but no amount of theological justification can alter the fact that Mt. 10 contains Marcan, Q and M material, and that the Q material is scattered in various parts of Lk. We are driven to the conclusion that the promise of divine assistance to disciples on trial had no fixed place in the tradition; it very probably goes back to an authentic utterance of Jesus, but we cannot be sure upon what occasion it was spoken, nor whether it refers to the time before or after his death, if indeed he expected any time to elapse between his death and the parousia. The saying may, of course, have suffered some modification and expansion in the course of the tradition.

(2) Did Jesus promise the Holy Spirit as helper to his persecuted followers? Or did he (as Lk. 21. 14 f. alleges) promise himself to give them aid? One general consideration points to the latter alternative. It has been pointed out above (p. 63) that many scholars argue, in the case of Mt. 12. 28=Lk. 11.20, that Luke's "finger of God" is original rather than Matthew's "Spirit of God" because Luke, who in general shows so great an interest in the work of the Holy Spirit, would not have omitted a reference to the Spirit which he had found in a source. Precisely the same argument may be applied here. Is it conceivable that Luke has removed the reference to the Holy Spirit from a saying which originally contained it? It is at least very improbable.

Other considerations support the contention that Lk. 21. 14 f. preserves the oldest form of the logion with which we are concerned. It contains idioms which have a distinctly Semitic colouring, although Burney[3] says that the Semitic rhythm of the parallel passage in Mk. has been destroyed. With v. 14, θέτε ἐν ταῖς καρδίαις ὑμῶν, we may compare Haggai 2. 15 וְעַתָּה שִׂימוּ־נָא לְבַבְכֶם (weʻattah simu-naʼ lebabkem), which is translated by the LXX, καὶ νῦν θέσθε εἰς τὰς καρδίας ὑμῶν. Schlatter[4] adduces also Sifre Deut. 34, תֵּן הַדְּבָרִים הָאֵלֶּה עַל לְבָבְךָ (ten haddebarim ha'elleh 'al lebabka), but here the parallel is not so close. Of the next verse Easton[5] says "στόμα, 'mouth', in this sense ('power of speech') is probably Hebraistic", but refers to Klostermann, who, however, cites as his only non-Jewish parallel Nepos, Alcibiades, 1. 2: "tanta erat commendatio oris atque orationis, ut nemo ei [dicendo]

---

[1] If, that is, Jesus expected his death to be followed by a divine vindication in which, for him, resurrection, ascension and parousia were not differentiated.
[2] Quest of the Historical Jesus, 361.
[3] Poetry of our Lord, 119.
[4] Der Evangelist Lukas, 417.
[5] Commentary, ad loc.

posset resistere". We can, on the other hand, cite numerous OT parallels: Exod. 4. 11 f., 16; Judg. 9. 38; 1 Kings 13. 21; Job 16. 5; Ps. 17. 3; Prov. 11. 9, 11; Is. 34. 16; 40. 5; 58. 14; Jer. 1. 9; Ezek. 3. 27; 24. 27; 29. 21; Mic. 4. 4. The gift of Wisdom is of course not peculiarly Semitic, but the following parallels may be noted: Exod. 28. 3; 31. 3, 6; 35. 31, 35; 36. 1, 2; 1 Kings 5. 9, 26; 2 Chron. 1. 10, 12; Job. 38. 37; Prov. 2. 6; Is. 11. 2; Dan. 2. 23. The phraseology is taken up again by Luke in Acts 6. 10.

There is thus good reason to think that Lk. 21. 14 f. contains the earliest form of the saying.[1] If this be so, another reference to the occasional possession by a group of disciples of the Spirit disappears. That the later form of the saying should have arisen in the Church is very natural and understandable. The persecution which the Christians had to undergo was sometimes represented as part of their warfare against demonic powers [2] and for their struggle they were equipped with the Holy Spirit, a point repeatedly brought out in the Acts.[3] But this was what the Church later experienced, not what it had been led to expect.

In saying this we have so far agreed with Leisegang; [4] the present form of Mk. 13. 11; Mt. 10. 19 f.; Lk. 12. 11 f. is due to Church interpretation and application. But the rest of Leisegang's discussion is so far wide of the point that it must be let alone; there is no suggestion of *glossolalia* in any of the passages we have dealt with, nor (which is perhaps more important) is there such suggestion in the accounts given in Acts of apostolic defences. The non-biblical references given by Leisegang are by no means all relevant.[5]

(f) *Sayings in the Resurrection Narratives*

Such sayings are relevant in only a secondary degree to the problem with which we are dealing, for as soon as the resurrection is reached each Evangelist stands on the same side of the Divine event which upset every eschatological *schema* as Paul and the other NT theologians. Consequently these sayings cannot be freely used in a comparison of the teaching of the Synoptic Gospels, and of the teaching of Jesus as therein set forth, with the thoughts and beliefs current in the later, Spirit-filled Church. In any case, the sayings in question are few and not very important.

Mt. 28. 19. We have already shown [6] that this saying, though a genuine part of the text of Mt., is late in origin, and, further, is not

---

[1] We may perhaps go further than this and account for the later form in the following tentative suggestion. In the Syriac VSS (Sinaitic, Curetonian and Peshitto) Lk. 21. 14b runs: 'ethyalphin leʰmappaq ruḥa'. It is very probable that the Aramaic form of the saying, before it was translated into Greek, was similar. Now mappaq ruḥa' is a quite regular expression for *excuse, apology, defence*. But it is not impossible that a translator, not very familiar with Aramaic, should detach ruḥa' from mappaq and join it to the next sentence, with the necessary change of person, thus creating the new saying.

[2] Cf. Weinel, *Die Wirkungen des Geistes und der Geister*, 18-20.

[3] A fact which makes all the more striking Luke's preservation of the saying without πνεῦμα in 21. 14 f.

[4] *Op. cit.* V.

[5] Büchsel, *Geist Gottes*, Ch. IX, also disagrees with Leisegang.

[6] Pp. 102 f.

specifically related to the gift of the Spirit to men, but rather exists as a theological formula, a defence of the doctrine of the Trinity.

Mk. 16. 17 f., 20. This passage also is late. The word Spirit is not mentioned, but the signs which are to accompany the Christians are those which are commonly ascribed to the activity of the Spirit. No more is implied here than is stated explicitly in the next passage.

Lk. 24. 49. Luke refers, of course, to the events of Pentecost which he is about to describe in his second volume. Luke had his own quite clear views of the origin of the Church. The disciples were not permitted to begin their work until the event of Pentecost: they were then equipped with the power of the Spirit, and the gift of the Spirit was repeated at each baptism (or imposition of hands). Interested as Luke manifestly was in the doctrine and work of the Spirit, he does not (except in chapters 1 and 2) speak of him as possessed by persons other than Jesus until after Pentecost. For him the divine vindication of the life and death of Jesus is fully differentiated into three distinct events: the Resurrection, and Pentecost, both past; and the Parousia, which was still to come. For Matthew,[1] apparently, Resurrection and Pentecost were one; the disciples were commissioned and sent forth with the assurance of a divine presence from the mountain in Galilee where the risen Jesus appeared to them; and their work was to continue until the end of the age. Unfortunately we have no means of knowing how the earliest Evangelist ended (or intended to end) his Gospel; and if we could find out exactly what Jesus expected to happen after his death our eschatological problems would be solved. But all the history, thought and experience of the Church gather to cloud this belief of Jesus from our view. We shall return, however, to this point later.

(g) *Passages where a Spirit-filled Community is implied*

Mt. 12. 32=Lk. 12. 10. We have already [2] discussed this difficult saying, and we have seen reason to believe that it reflects a period later than that of the ministry of Jesus. In words we have quoted above from Procksch,[3] "Thus the possibility of this sin first arose in the age after Pentecost"; that is, the possibility of the sin implies a community which has received the gift of the Holy Spirit, a community for which Christ and the Spirit were distinguishable persons (or powers). The Marcan form of the blasphemy saying (Mk. 3. 28 f.) shows that this was not so in the time of Jesus himself, and perhaps was not so even while the earliest formulation of the Gospel tradition was being made. There is no indication in the Marcan passage of the existence of a community, but such a community, a post-Pentecost community, is implied by Mt. and Lk. Again we are left with the impression of an unexpected event, a change of plan, which has distorted our view of everything, events and teaching, before the death of Jesus. Mt. 12. 32 implies the existence of a Spirit-filled

---

[1] And for the Fourth Evangelist.　　　[2] Pp. 105-107.　　　[3] *TWNT* I. 105.

Church (especially if it is to be understood in the light of the *Didache* 11. 7), but, in fact, it is the Church which implies its own existence, and the subtle change given to the Marcan saying bears witness to the strange happenings which intervened between the crucifixion and the beginnings of Church History.

Mk. 9. 38 ff.; Lk. 9. 49 f. See above, ·p. 66. This story reveals a time when Christian exorcists used the name of Jesus and were divided among themselves; when a leading group within the Church considered that it had the monopoly of spiritual power, and objected to the successful expulsion of demons by others. This time must have been after the crucifixion, and there is nothing to suggest that the saying itself (in its present setting) was of earlier origin. The words in Mk. 9. 40 appear elsewhere in the tradition and may be an original logion of Jesus; but it is now impossible to establish their context.

Mt. 5. 3. According to Leisegang,[1] $\tau\hat{\omega}$ $\pi\nu\epsilon\acute{\nu}\mu\alpha\tau\iota$ in the first Beatitude refers to the Holy Spirit: "Blessed are those who are poorly endowed with the Holy Spirit." Leisegang quite rightly remarks that this astonishing pronouncement is contrary to the general desire which is expressed alike in Hellenistic piety and in all other Christian literature. There the desire is to be rich in the Spirit (see 1 Pet. 4. 14; *Ep. Barn.* 19. 2; cf. Rom. 14. 17). It is for this reason that Luke omits the words $\tau\hat{\omega}$ $\pi\nu\epsilon\acute{\nu}\mu\alpha\tau\iota$. This fact, along with the sharper contrast given in Lk. between the "Now" and the "Then" of the Beatitudes, and his Maledictions, places the Lucan parallel in the class of the Stoic diatribe. The poverty of the wise man was a popular theme in Hellenistic (but not in Jewish) thought. In Mt. the Beatitudes are quite general and apply to all men; in Lk. they are addressed specifically to the disciples, who are thought of as wandering philosophers, of the sort well known in the Graeco-Roman world of the first century. They proved their genuineness as philosophers and prophets by their poverty (see Philo, *Quod Det. Pot. Ins.* 34; Simon in Acts 8. 18-24; *Didache*, 11. 8; Hermas, *Mand.* XI. 1. 7 f.; cf. 1 Jn. 4. 1 ff.; 1 Pet. 4. 14; 1 Tim. 4. 1 ff.). The contrast between the Lucan Beatitudes and Maledictions is based upon that between Prophets and False Prophets—in a Hellenistic sense.

It is difficult to know how to reply to such fantastic exegesis. Bultmann[2] does so by means of an exclamation mark. Leisegang is, of course, quite correct in saying that a blessing upon those who possess the Spirit of God in small measure is entirely unprecedented in the NT. The obvious conclusion to draw from this is that the saying in question, if it is patient of any other interpretation, simply does not mean what Leisegang says that it means. It is, of course, by no means difficult to find an alternative explanation. The poor man of the Psalms is well known as an object of the divine blessing; to him (seen in new light because of the coming of Jesus) the Lucan Beatitude refers. The

---

[1] *Op. cit.* VI.; 134-140.   [2] *GST* 117 n. 1.

Matthaean form is an attempt to show that the blessing is not simply a crude approval of absence of money, but assurance of divine aid to the man who, being stripped of this world's goods, has a spiritual trust in God.

Mt. 5. 3, then, is not, *pace* Leisegang, relevant to this study.

(h) *Jesus and the Church*

The results so far of our search in the Synoptic Gospels for evidence that Jesus looked forward to the existence of a Community endowed with the gift of the Spirit have been negative. We have found no sayings of Jesus which unmistakably pointed to such a gift of the Spirit, and the passages which come nearest to doing so are demonstrably late, and reflect the events which took place after the crucifixion. Before leaving this section it will be necessary to deal more generally, though of necessity very briefly, with the question of the relationship of Jesus to the Church.

Two books [1] have recently been published which conveniently summarize a great deal of modern work upon the subject, and which also put forward different views of the time at which the Ecclesia may be said to have begun.

Dr Flew sets out to show that the teaching and action of Jesus prove that he had in mind the existence of a community, organized and permanent in so far as a "Community of the Interval" could be. "If 'Church' means a new religious community, with a new way of life, a fresh and startling message, and an unparalleled consciousness of inheriting the divine promises made to Israel of old, then Jesus did most certainly . . . take action with such a community in view" (p. 25). In order to establish this position Dr Flew first discusses the teaching of Jesus about the Kingdom of God. He concludes: "So far we have discovered that the sayings and parables of Jesus with regard to the *Basileia* have not furnished us with more than a few slight indications that He had a community in view" (p. 40). The difficulty raised in this connection by the eschatological teaching of the Gospels is stated and answered by Dr Flew as follows: "Is it possible that the very conception of the *Basileia* which Jesus preached precludes the conception of any kind of new community, because He thought that the end of human history was at hand? The answer to this difficulty lies in the fact that, according to our sources, Jesus anticipated a certain sequence of events in history, and that therefore He allowed for a future in time and on this earth in which His followers would have to live and work. Further He expressly declared that He did not know how long this interval would endure" (p. 41). Dr Flew rejects (p. 45) Professor Dodd's "attempt . . . to identify the references of Jesus to the day of the Son of man with the resurrection, as expressing a timeless fact." [2] It is in his third chapter that Dr Flew

[1] R. N. Flew, *Jesus and His Church* (1938); G. Johnston, *The Doctrine of the Church in the NT* (1943).
[2] He does not, however, deal with the suggestion that Jesus himself did not, in his hope of a divine vindication after his death, differentiate between a resurrection and a second coming, both thought of as taking place in time.

treats in detail the "idea of the community which (Jesus) had in view". He assembles "under five main headings the evidence that He had in view a community of a new kind". These are (i) the conception of a new Israel; (ii) the ethical teaching of Jesus which presupposed a new community, equipped with power—the gift of the Holy Spirit—to fulfil its demands; (iii) the conception of Messiahship and the consequent allegiance; (iv) the "Word of God" or "Gospel" as constituting the new community; (v) the mission of the new community. Thus, before considering the promise to Peter (Mt. 16. 17-19), which is admittedly of disputable authenticity, Dr Flew is able to come to the conclusion (p. 122), "A community which can thus be described is surely the *ecclesia*, Israel as God intended Israel to be", and such a community must be held to have existed during the ministry of Jesus.

Dr Johnston sets forth his views about the relationship between Jesus and the Church in pp. 46-58 of his book. Jesus is to be regarded as the founder of the Church, since he is the Saviour. Dr Johnston quotes: "The Redeemer is Redeemer only as the creator of a new, delivered, justified people."[1] But the question still remains at what stage in the career of Jesus the Church can be said to have begun. Dr Johnston enumerates the four periods which have been suggested: "(1) The call of the first disciples; (2) the confession of Peter as representative of the Twelve; (3) The Last Supper, which established a New Covenant, to be sealed by Christ's death; (4) The union of the disciples in the Resurrection faith, that is, either at Easter itself with the appearances to Peter, the other apostles, or the five hundred brethren; or at the Pentecostal gift of the promised Spirit".[2] He has something to say on behalf of each of these views with regard to the date of the inception of the Church. Of Dr Flew's five-fold argument[3] he makes a very important criticism: "The weakness of this is its failure fully to do justice to the necessity of Jesus' death for the constitution of the new Israel. Messiahship, it is true, involves a community; so does the ethical teaching by its very definition: yet the 'Messianic' dignity won recognition for what it was only through the glorious exaltation which followed the final humiliation."[4] The word ἐκκλησία should be more strictly defined. It is a technical term for the Christian society. "In Matthew it is an anachronism; Mark and the Fourth Evangelist must have known it, but omit it; while Luke in his two-volume history carefully introduces it only after Pentecost."[5] The title Church, Ecclesia, ought to be reserved for the post-resurrection community. Dr Johnston concludes:[6] "They [the "little flock", the Remnant, the disciples] are the Messianic community prefigured, not fulfilled. . . . The disciples are potentially the Church. They are and they are not yet the ἐκκλησία. This may be called an adoptionist ecclesiology: they become the Church *through the*

<hr>

[1] G. Gloege, *Reich Gottes und Kirche im NT*, 218; quoted by Johnston, *op. cit.* 46.
[2] *Op. cit.* 46 f.
[3] Flew, *Jesus and His Church*, 48-122; summarized above.
[4] *Op. cit.* 50.   [5] *Op. cit.* 51.   [6] *Op. cit.* 56.

baptism of the Spirit. Without the Cross and Resurrection there is no Church.
Hence, whatever answer may be given to the historical question, there
cannot be the slightest doubt that the relationship of Jesus to the Church is
that of God-sent founder: Jesus in life, dying, and rising again. *This* Jesus
is the *Retter*, Redeemer, who gathers the redeemed into a community."

A few observations may be made on the basis of the views which have
now been summarized.

(*a*) Great weight should be given to Dr Johnston's contention that the
existence of the Church presupposes the death of Christ. The Church
is the redeemed society. It is not, and was never by Christians thought to
be, a community whose members try to lead a good life, according to the
ethical standard of the Sermon on the Mount, or any other standard.
The distinguishing feature of the Church is not that its members are
ethically better than other people (though this is a fact that follows—
or ought to follow) but that they have been saved by God through Christ.
This is implied in the title Israel, for Israel is the people whom God delivered from slavery, whom he took up in its weakness and cleansed from
its filthiness (Ezek. 16. 1-14).[1] The New Israel, the Ecclesia, was the
fruit of a fresh act of redemption, and that act, though it may have been
initiated during the ministry of Jesus, was consummated only by his
death. This is the meaning (or part of the meaning) of Mk. 10. 45 and
parallels. The λύτρον was the means whereby the "many" were constituted a liberated and redeemed community, and the λύτρον was the
life of the Son of man. Until his life had been given, the many, though
some of them were gathered together in the entourage of Jesus and lived
in fellowship with one another, were an aggregation of individuals, and
not Israel. The death of Christ is fundamental to the existence of the
Church in proportion as it is fundamental to the Christian salvation.
Accordingly, and quite apart from any other evidence, it seems un-
desirable to say that the foundation of the Church took place before the
death and resurrection of Jesus.

(*b*) In the sense of being redeemer, Jesus founded the Church, and in
this Dr Flew and Dr Johnston are agreed. The Church has no being
except as the redeemed society, and therefore it does not exist apart from
the redeemer.[2] But this statement (which is historical as well as theological) does not settle the question whether Jesus contemplated the
continued existence of a community in this world. That he left any
rules for the organization of such a community seems in the highest
degree improbable,[3] but it is of course quite possible that he thought of

---

[1] Cf. Deut. 33. 29 : " Happy art thou, O Israel : Who is like unto thee, a people saved by
the Lord ? "   [2] Cf. Eph. 5. 25-27.
[3] Inge, *Quarterly Review* (1918), 33 (quoted by C. A. A. Scott in *The Spirit*, ed. Streeter, 135) :
" The first disciples believed that they had their Master's authority for expecting the end of
the existing world-order in their own lifetime. Whether they understood Him or not, clearly
they could not have held this opinion if they had received instructions for the constitution of a
Church."

an enduring organism without planning for it a definite organization.[1] Did he envisage such a Church? We have not yet seen evidence for thinking that he did, for there is nothing in Dr Flew's five-fold argument which makes us think of a community living on in the earthly conditions of space and time rather than of a glorified Church in heaven with God, after the complete and final consummation of the Kingdom. The "New Israel" could quite possibly be the kingdom of the saints of the Most High at the end of time;[2] the "absolute" ethical teaching of Jesus would be entirely appropriate to such an Israel, in the day when heaven and earth had vanished and with them the Law of Moses.[3] The presence of the Messiah and allegiance to him are on any showing as appropriate to heaven as earth; the "Word of God", the "Gospel", the mission of the disciples belong to the period before the crucifixion. The whole question here turns upon the further problem of what Jesus expected to follow his death. (See below, (d).)

(c) If in fact the Church properly so called belongs to the period after the close of the ministry of Jesus, we are compelled to look further for the decisive foundation of it, a foundation resting entirely upon God's redemptive act in Christ, yet distinct from the activity of Jesus before his death.

A comparison of the primitive Church with the community of disciples is instructive here.[4] There are two notable differences between the two groups (or rather between the two stages in the history of the one group). There is a difference (i) in understanding. The disciples of Jesus, especially as they are represented in Mk. (who "hates the Twelve") completely fail to understand his person and his mission (Mk. 8. 21, 33; 9. 32, 34; 10. 37), and the logical conclusion of the story, as far as they are concerned, is their denial and desertion. The later community presents a quite different appearance. Not only do these men who recently were scattered like sheep display the utmost boldness in confessing their Lord (now under the additional obloquy of crucifixion); they also reveal a remarkable penetration of understanding, both of his Messiahship and of his sufferings and death. Even if Paul himself be left out of account, his contemporaries, as far as we can trace their thought, show an entirely new and creative insight into the meaning of Scripture and the purpose of God in the history of Israel.

The Church shows a difference also (ii) in power. We have already mentioned the new courage which the apostles and their followers displayed in bearing witness to the resurrection. Their testimony was not without effect. There is no evidence of great success on the part of the Twelve in the mission they are recorded to have made in Israel during the ministry of Jesus; but we do not need the, no doubt extravagant,

[1] Cf. Flew, *op. cit.* 25.
[2] Cf. the heavenly Jerusalem of Gal. 4. 26 ; Heb. 12. 22 ; Rev. 3. 12 ; 21. 2 ; *Test. Dan* 5. 12.
[3] See Mt. 5. 18 compared with Mk. 13. 31.
[4] And at the same time confirms our view that the founding of the Church should not be placed before the crucifixion.

figures of Acts to assure us of the rapid growth of the Church in its first days.

It is quite clear from these differences that something of quite unique significance happened to the disciples of Jesus; not only an external event, such as the death of Jesus, but something within themselves. The narrative of Pentecost in Acts 2 may in itself and in detail be historically quite untrustworthy; yet it represents what must have happened, an event apart from which the history of the primitive Church becomes incredible. The difference between the company of Jesus (οἱ περὶ αὐτὸν σὺν τοῖς δώδεκα, Mk. 4. 10) and the Church was the gift of the Holy Spirit, the baptism of the community with divine power and inspiration. To this event corresponds the fact that there is no indication that the earlier group possessed spiritual gifts of any sort,[1] while the later could never adequately express its continual sense of indebtedness to and guidance by the Holy Spirit.

(d) If some such event as this was the "foundation" of the Church; and if Jesus intended the Church; we must suppose that he foretold the event, and that he prophesied the gift of the Spirit, or at least that he had the event and the gift in mind even if he did not speak of them. There is no evidence that this was so. It is useless to point to Mk. 13. 11 and parallels. Apart from the fact that we have already seen reason to accept the view that the original saying represented by this verse did not speak of the Holy Spirit, the passage speaks only of an exceptional and occasional spiritual aid in particular circumstances—which is very far from what the Church believed about the Spirit. The question why references to the Spirit are so few in the Synoptic Gospels is now raised in its final and most acute form.

---

[1] Except perhaps that of exorcism.

10

WHY DO THE GOSPELS SAY SO LITTLE ABOUT THE SPIRIT?

WE have just emphasized again the paucity of references to the Spirit of God in the Synoptic Gospels. We have several times referred to the problem which is raised by this fact, and a discussion of the question can no longer be postponed. Why is so little said about the Spirit in the life of the founder of a religion one of whose most characteristic beliefs was that its adherents were in a unique sense the possessors of the Spirit? If every Corinthian Christian could claim some spiritual gift, why is it so rarely said that such gifts were shared by Jesus and his immediate followers? If the apostles, in Acts, were directed at every step by the promptings of the Spirit, why was not their Lord also led in this way? We shall find that consideration of this question leads us deeply into the further problem of the relationship between the primitive Christian belief in and experience of the Spirit and the eschatological proclamation of Jesus. This new question may be put in this way. A characteristic (perhaps the most characteristic) element in the teaching of Jesus, who said little about the Spirit, was the assertion, "The Kingdom of God is near" (cf. Mk. 1. 15; Mt. 4. 17; Mt. 12. 28; Lk. 11. 20; and many other passages where the same is implied). A characteristic element in the Church's preaching, in which the Kingdom of God appears but rarely, was the offer of personal experience of the Spirit (Acts 2. 38; Rom. 8. 9; Gal. 3. 2; Jn. 14. 26; 1 Pet. 4. 14; and many other passages). In what sense, then, can it be said that the preaching of the Church rests upon, or was derived from, that of Jesus?

In the first place, we must examine some solutions of our problem which have already been offered.

(1) Dr E. F. Scott [1] draws attention to the growth in pre-Christian Judaism of belief in demons, angels and other spiritual beings which arose (under foreign influence) as the old tribal God of the Hebrews became more and more exalted in holiness, and as his sphere of jurisdiction expanded to cover all nations. It was felt that there lay so great a gulf between God in heaven and man upon earth that one or more intermediate beings were necessary to span it. Dr Scott says that this hierarchy of spiritual intermediaries was uncongenial to Jesus, who brought to men the possibility of direct intercourse with the Father. In comparison with such immediate communion, "an idea like that of the Spirit removed God to a distance, or put an abstract power in place of him".[2] Dr Flew rightly criticizes this explanation: "This would argue Jesus less skilled in spiritual discernment than Paul, or than hundreds

---

[1] *The Spirit in the NT*, 77-80.   [2] *Op. cit.* 79.

of obscurer saints." [1] Moreover, Jesus seems (according to the Evangelists) to have accepted without hesitation the current belief in demons (e.g. Mk. 3. 15; Lk. 13. 32), spirits (e.g. Mk. 5. 8; Lk. 10. 20; Mt. 12. 43 ff.) and angels (e.g. Mk. 8. 38; 12. 25), which was for the most part a development in Jewish thought subsequent to the close of the OT period, and thus to have sided with the Pharisees against the Sadducees; it is unlikely that he would have believed in these minor beings and yet disliked speech about the Spirit of God, which has a secure place in the OT, simply because the Spirit stood between God and man.

(2) Dr Vincent Taylor [2] bases an argument upon the methods of Form-criticism. It is now agreed by most scholars that the Gospel tradition took its present form under the influence of the conditions which obtained in the Christian communities in which the traditional material was handed down. We know from many sources that these communities were confident that they possessed the Spirit; their members, especially their leaders, were conscious that they were living from day to day under his guidance. Consequently there was no need to repeat and keep in mind sayings of Jesus about the Spirit. No one disputed the presence of the Spirit, and there was therefore no need to prove it by words of Jesus. This argument is not entirely satisfactory.

(a) It assumes that controversy was the most important—almost the only—formulating factor in the early Church's handling of the tradition. Because there was no controversy on the subject there are few references to the Spirit in the Gospels. But, on general grounds, it is at least possible to suppose that the reverse might have taken place; that an Evangelist in selecting his material might have chosen what was agreed and omitted controversial subjects. [3] In addition, there were other than polemical motives that governed the selection of the Gospel material. Dr Dibelius, for example, stresses the importance of preaching; Dr Bultmann emphasizes the teaching work of the communities, especially their task of ethical instruction (though he also makes much of the polemical motive); Dr Bertram points to the importance of the Christian cultus, especially upon the formation of the passion narrative; and many other motives of less widespread application might be named. We may ask whether it would not, for example, have been natural for an early Christian preacher, preaching as did Peter on the day of Pentecost and making a like offer (Acts 2. 33, 38), to round off his argument with a word of the Lord himself? "He hath poured forth this which ye both see and hear"; what preacher would not have added, if he could have done so, "as he himself promised"? Baptism, no less than the Eucharist, was a fundamental Christian rite, closely associated with the gift of the Spirit; dominical sayings on this head would surely have been preserved. [4]

---

[1] Op. cit. 69.　　[2] The Holy Spirit (the Headingley Lectures, 1937), 53-55.
[3] Cf. Lk. 1. 1, if τὰ πεπληροφορημένα are " the things most certainly believed ".
[4] It was no doubt in this context that the saying of John, " He shall baptize you with the Holy Spirit (and fire)," Mk. 1. 8 and parallels, was handed down.

(b) There was controversy on the subject of the Spirit. Some passages in Acts (18. 24-28; 19. 1-7) indicate differences between Johannine and Christian groups on the question of baptism; others (e.g. Acts 2. 38 compared with 8. 14-17) that there was disagreement on the question whether the Spirit was given by baptism alone, or by the imposition of hands.

Since, then, there seem to have been quite sufficient reasons in the life of the primitive Church for the preservation of sayings about the Spirit, it cannot be said that we have yet found an adequate explanation of their absence from the Gospels.[1]

(3) Dr Flew [2] has another explanation: "There are few sayings about the Spirit, because Jesus saw that a richer and profounder understanding of the Spirit was needed than any which his disciples with their lack of insight could glean from the Old Testament; and this reinterpretation of the Spirit's work could only be lived out in His own ministry. So it was with the idea of the Messiahship. He refused the titles which came from popular misconceptions of His mission; 'no conception of it, current among His contemporaries, answered to His own. It is highly doubtful if He ever used the term Christ of Himself.' [3] This explanation of the problem of the 'Messianic Secret' suggests a parallel solution of the problem of the silence as to the Spirit. . . . The whole conception of the Spirit in the Old Testament must needs be baptized into the death of Christ. Calvary was the only gateway to Pentecost."

This explanation is very important, chiefly for two reasons: it brings together the doctrine of the Spirit and the death of Christ, and it brings into consideration the Messianic secret. It is not, however, beyond criticism. In the first place, it does not really explain why Jesus did not teach his disciples about the Holy Spirit. From the time when, at Caesarea Philippi, the secret of his Messiahship was revealed to the Twelve, "he began to teach them that the Son of man must suffer much" (Mk. 8. 31). Not only did Jesus repeatedly prophesy his own death (Mk. 8. 31; 9. 12, 31; 10. 33 f.), and interpret it (Mk. 10. 42-45; 12. 1-12, and in the Last Supper); he also told the disciples plainly that their allegiance to such a Messiah as himself would involve suffering for them too (Mk. 8. 34; 10. 29-31; 10. 35-40). If, then, Jesus could begin to educate the disciples in his own conception of Messiahship, why should he not also have taught them the true meaning of the Holy Spirit? Dr Flew says: [4] "How easy it was even for His chosen followers to seize upon the lower elements in the Old Testament conception of the Spirit of God is proved by the Acts of the Apostles. At first the stress is on the ecstatic, the abnormal, the transitory." Surely, it might be urged, this misapprehension of the mission of the Spirit could have been avoided if Jesus had given his followers even as little instruction on this subject as

---

[1] Dr Taylor has given me leave to say that he has seen, and appreciates the force of, these two arguments, and is convinced that there is much more to be said.
[2] *Jesus and His Church*, 70 f.   [3] V. Taylor, *Jesus and His Sacrifice*, 20.   [4] *Op. cit.* 70.

he gave them with regard to his death. The facts that Jesus did not teach his followers about the coming gift of the Spirit and their mis-understanding of that gift when it was made certainly do fit together; but this does not explain why in the first place no such teaching was imparted. In fact, the problem is intensified rather than solved.

In the second place, the explanation given of the Messianic secret is not sufficient. For though at the time dealt with in the Gospels the Holy Spirit had not been given and that subject could be avoided without difficulty, Jesus himself was present and men were, for good or ill, formu-lating their thoughts about him. Many of them thought of him in Messianic terms, whether as the Messiah or as a prophet proclaiming the imminent arrival of the Messiah; there can be no other explanation of the enthusiastic crowds which followed him in Galilee and acclaimed him in Jerusalem. The whole ministry of Jesus is set by the Evangelists in a Messianic framework. Moreover, it was only from the multitudes that the secret of the Messiahship was kept (at least after Mk. 8. 29). To the disciples Jesus expounded the doctrine of the suffering Messiah, or Son of man. It is true that they did not understand his exposition at the time, but after the crucifixion it must have been remembered, for not even the resurrection could have persuaded them that Jesus was the Messiah if he had never previously suggested the fact to them. But there was, apparently, no corresponding teaching about the Holy Spirit, given in preparation for the Church's inspiration. Such teaching was not given even to those who might have been expected to receive it, the inner circle of the disciples.[1]

Accordingly, the problem why there is hardly any teaching about the Spirit, and indeed very few references of any sort to the Spirit, in the Synoptic Gospels, remains unsolved. Before we attack it directly, two preliminary considerations may be set forth.

(1) General observation of the Synoptic Gospels shows that they commonly set out theological teaching not in theological terms but in symbolic narrative or parable. There is no need to give detailed illustra-tion of this self-evident fact. It is now quite widely recognized that even if, for example, Paul's doctrine of justification by faith is not to be found expressed in scientific terminology in the teaching of Jesus, it is no less clearly present in such parables as the Pharisee and the Publican, the Prodigal Son, and the Unprofitable Servants. In the Synoptic Gospels there is little that will serve as a precise parallel to the treatment of the law in Rom. 1-3, 7; but one controversy story after another, with the Sermon on the Mount, and many another point, delineate the same attitude. It is in line with this principle that we have already found numerous traces of the fact that Jesus was a "pneumatic" man quite apart from references to the word πνεῦμα. This pictorial quality of the

---

[1] We must leave out of account, in this study of the Synoptic Gospels, the possibility that the Fourth Gospel preserves in the farewell discourses genuine teaching of Jesus. This seems, however, improbable. See the note on p. 121.

Synoptic Gospels must be constantly borne in mind as we deal with the problem before us; but this quality is not a sufficient explanation of the problem, for we have already seen [1] instances where not uses of the word πνεῦμα but "pneumatic" features of the story have been suppressed.

(2) One group of metaphors in particular calls for mention here. Dr H. Wheeler Robinson has shown [2] that in primitive Semitic thought "psychical and ethical functions are considered to be just as appropriate to the bodily organs as the physiological".[3] This belief that the bodily organs have psychological functions can be well illustrated from the OT for Hebrew thought. For example, Dr Robinson quotes Ps. 63. 2:

> My *néphesh* [soul] thirsteth for thee,
> My "flesh" longeth for thee.

"where the 'flesh' is functioning psychically just as much as is the *néphesh*".[4] "This attribution of psychical functions to parts of the body which to us seem to be purely physiological is not confined to the central organs. It operates also in regard to the peripheral organs, such as eye and ear and mouth and hand." [5] This means, of course, that in many places where we should expect to read of the spirit or mind of man we find instead a reference to some part of his body.

Since Hebrew thought about God was anthropomorphic we are not surprised to find this sort of language used also about God; that is, we sometimes read not of his Spirit, but of (for example) his hand or arm. This occurs very frequently in the OT; it is not suggested that this is so in the Synoptic Gospels, but the point is worth noting, if only because of one signal instance. Comparison of Lk. 11. 20 with Mt. 12. 28 shows that the phrases "finger of God" and "spirit of God" could be exact equivalents. Lk. 1. 66 could certainly have been rewritten with reference to the "spirit" instead of the "hand" of the Lord, and we must allow for the possibility that in other passages, where a modern writer, with a developed doctrine of the Holy Spirit, would have spoken of the "Spirit", the same thought has been quite differently expressed.[6]

We have mentioned earlier the fact that the *bath qol* or heavenly voice had come to be regarded as a substitute for the Holy Spirit. In the baptism narratives we have both voice and Spirit; but in the Transfiguration the voice only.

It will be necessary next, in our attempt to answer the question why the references in the Synoptic Gospels to the Holy Spirit are so few, to make some examination of the references to the Spirit in the OT. Since,

---

[1] See pp. 68, 90-93, 98 f.   [2] *Hebrew Psychology*, 353-382, in *The People and the Book*, ed. A. S. Peake.   [3] *Op. cit.* 353.   [4] *Op. cit.* 366.   [5] *Op. cit.* 364 f.

[6] See an important note on "Christ as the Hand of God" in J. R. Harris, *Origin of the Prologue to St John's Gospel*, 43-52. Cf. also *3 Enoch* 48, with Odeberg's comment : "The *Right Hand* or *Right Arm of the Lord* represents the actualization of the Kingdom of God on earth, the deliverance of Israel. That the Right Hand is laid behind the Lord is a symbol of cessation in his activity for this purpose. The deliverance of the Right Hand, hence, becomes synonymous with the deliverance of Israel. . . . It was God's Right Hand that stretched out the heavens and the earth, and so it must be his Right Hand that will bring about the final establishment of the Kingdom on earth." (H. Odeberg, *3 Enoch*, 139.)

in the Gospels, the result of the gift of the Spirit is most frequently inspired speech, we shall consider this aspect of the Spirit's work, and it will be necessary to examine also the OT teaching about prophecy and the prophets.[1]

(i) *OT passages where Spirit (רוח (ruah)—πνεῦμα) inspires prophetic speech and activity.* These passages are few and not evenly distributed.

(a) *In the Law and Historical Books*

Num. 24. 2. The Spirit inspires Balaam's *Mashal.* It is generally supposed that the prophetic speeches attributed to Balaam are of great age, and are indeed among the oldest parts of the OT, and the words of Balaam themselves certainly imply inspiration, and even ecstasy. Thus 24. 4,

> He saith, which heareth the words of God,
> Which seeth the vision of the Almighty,
> Falling down, and having his eyes open,

clearly indicates trance or rapture of some sort, and so does Balaam's refusal to promise an oracle according to order. But it will be observed that the oracles themselves do not contain the word Spirit; this is found only in the narrative framework, which of course need be, and probably is, no older than the redaction of the JE document.

Num. 11. 17, 25, 29; another piece of JE. *Vv.* 26-29 in particular show the connection between Spirit and prophecy, though "prophecy" here does not necessarily mean "speech"; this is evidently a characteristic feature of this document.

1 Sam. 10. 5-13; 16. 13; 19. 20-24; cf. 2 Sam. 23. 2; 1 Kings 22. 24; 2 Kings 2: 9, 15 f. There is important information here about early ideas both of the Spirit and of prophesying. Inspiration, which is an occasional phenomenon, means possession (cf. 1 Sam. 10. 6: "The Spirit of the Lord will come mightily upon thee, and thou shalt prophesy with them, and shalt be turned into another man"). This prophesying involves a sort of trance, sometimes, apparently induced by music; the prophets for the most part appear together in groups—the sons of the prophets; the words spoken by the inspired prophet are not, it seems, as important as the fact that he is inspired and acts in a frenzy.

1 Chron. 12. 18; 2 Chron. 15. 1; 20. 14; 24. 20. In these much later books it is noteworthy that far more attention is given to the content of the inspired message and less to the manner in which it is delivered.

Nehem. 9. 20, 30. These are obviously late comments on the history of Israel.

(b) *In the Writing Prophets*

Hosea 9. 7. This is a notoriously difficult verse. Is the person described

---

[1] This is by no means a systematic and complete study of the OT doctrine, but observations upon it made with a particular end in view.

as "the prophet . . . the man that hath the Spirit" [1] a true prophet of the Lord, or is he a false prophet (as in Hosea 4. 5)? It is not necessary for us to settle this question. What is important is to observe the background of the prophecy, which is that of the book of Hosea as a whole, namely the agriculture of Canaan, and agricultural religion, that is, fertility cultus. 9. 1 f. shows that the supplies of corn and wine are in question, and the sort of religion adopted by unfaithful Israel. If *v.* 7 refers to the prophet of the Lord, it is the complaint against the national religion of those who had adopted the Canaanite religion; if, on the other hand (as I am disposed to think, in view of other passages which will shortly be taken into account), it refers to false prophets, we have Hosea associating both the terms נָבִיא (nabi') and רוּחַ (ruah) with the indigenous religion against which all the faithful in Israel resolutely set their faces. Of course, Hosea would probably not have denied that he too had the Spirit.

Mic. 3. 8. Here, too, genuine prophecy is contrasted with inspiration due to another source. Seer (חֹזֶה, hozeh) and diviner (קֹסֵם, qosem) no doubt claimed to have the Spirit, as Micah did (cf. 2. 11), and probably acted in a very similar manner. Micah points out where the difference lies. It is in part *ethical* ("The prophets . . . make my people to err . . . and whoso putteth not into their mouths, they even prepare war against him", 3. 5), and in part lies in the *content* of their messages (compare 3. 5 "They bite with their teeth and cry, Peace" with 3. 12, "Therefore shall Zion for your sake be plowed as a field, and Jerusalem shall become heaps, and the mountain of the house as the high places of a forest"). The difference is *not* in inspiration, in רוּחַ (ruah); though possibly there is a special emphasis in 3. 8: "I truly am full of power by the Spirit of *the Lord*", hence the ethical content of the prophetic message—"to declare unto Jacob his transgression, and unto Israel his sin". [2]

Jeremiah never attributes his prophetic inspiration to the Spirit. The word רוּחַ (ruah) occurs a number of times in the book, but almost always with a purely physical meaning. It is once translated "Spirit" in the English VSS, in Jer. 51. 11; but this has nothing to do with prophecy, and is not in a passage attributable to Jeremiah himself. It is once associated with false prophets (5. 13), but here it means only wind, emptiness.

The word רוּחַ (ruah) occurs over 50 times in the book of *Isaiah*, but only twice, in late parts of the book, does it refer to prophetic inspiration—59. 21 and 61. 1.

Ezekiel uses the word frequently in connection with his own office. In 11. 5 Spirit is directly said to be the cause of his speech; cf. also 2. 2;

---

[1] הַנָּבִיא . . . אִישׁ הָרוּחַ (hannabi' . . . 'ish haruah).

[2] The words " by the Spirit of the Lord " (אֶת־רוּחַ יהוה, 'eth-ruah '*adonai*) do not properly belong to the structure of the sentence, and it is not improbable that they do not belong to the original text of the verse. However, even if they are a gloss they do not lose their significance. The gloss was early (it is in the LXX), and shows what the source of the ethical prophetic power was thought to be.

3. 12, 14, 24; 11. 1, 24; 37. 1; 43. 5. In 13. 3 it is said of the false prophets that they "follow their own spirit".

In two late books the Spirit is spoken of as the cause of prophecy. In *Zech. 7. 12* the writer looks back and speaks of "the words which the Lord of Hosts had sent by his Spirit by the hand of the former prophets"; *Joel* (*3. 1 f.*), speaking of the future, says: "I will pour out my Spirit upon all flesh; and your sons and your daughters shall prophesy." It will be observed that neither of these prophets claims to have the Spirit himself.

We may add here another reference to those taken from the prophetic books, *Job 32. 8.* The Spirit of God in Elihu is that which gives him understanding, and the understanding leads to speech.

From these data we may observe (*a*) that although the Spirit is frequently mentioned in connection with the early (sons of the) prophets,[1] the writing prophets very rarely describe their inspiration as the result of the presence of divine רוּחַ (ruah); Jeremiah, First and Second Isaiah and Amos never do so, nor is the idea present in the Psalms; and (*b*) in some cases where spirit-inspired speech is thought of there is some connection with or suggestion of "false" prophets, or the indigenous religion of pre-Hebraic Canaan. The use of the word prophet (נָבִיא, nabi') illustrates these statements.

(ii) *Nabi' in the OT.*

The etymology of the word is very obscure. Robertson Smith[2] looked with some favour upon the view that the name was of Canaanite origin rather than a native Semitic form. Lods[3] says: "The very word *nabi'* does not seem to be of Hebrew origin." These pronouncements are of very great importance, although we must beware of laying too great weight upon an uncertain etymology. But this should not lead us to neglect the certain relationship, or at least resemblance, which existed between the early Hebrew *n^ebi'im* and what is known of primitive Palestinian religion, for which there is non-biblical as well as biblical evidence. "A collective inspiration expressing itself in dances and shouts, although not wholly unknown to the nomad Semites, was nevertheless uncommon among them, while this type of religious experience was fostered by the cults of Phoenicia, Syria and Asia Minor, whence the phenomena of orgiastic prophecy may have spread to Syria and Palestine. Hence there is every reason to suppose that the earliest bands of *n^ebi'im* may have arisen among the Israelites as the result of contact with and imitation of the Canaanites. The sacred madness of these ecstatics impressed the newcomers as a higher manifestation of the divine power, hence Jahweh must show himself the equal of the Baals."[4] Lods refers to 1 Kings 18. 19; Heliodorus, *Aethiopica*, 4. 16; Golenischeff Pap.,

---

[1] And with the judges, e.g. Samson, Gideon.
[3] *Israel (ET)*, 445.
[2] *Prophets of Israel* (1919), 390.
[4] Lods, *op. cit.* 444 f.

Revue de Theol. (Montaubon), xxi. 22-23; Celsus (in Origen, *c. Cels.* 7. 9); *de Dea Syria*, 43, 50; Apuleius, *Metamorph.* 8. 24-29; Florus, 3. 29 (2. 7).

The activities of the Israelite *nᵉbi'im* (*bᵉne hannᵉbi'im*) are too well known to require description here [1]. This title seems to have supplanted the earlier term רֹאֶה (ro'eh) (1 Sam. 9. 9).[2] They were ecstatics, their prophesying was accompanied by dancing and music, and was possibly fomented by intoxicating drinks. They seem sometimes to have been gathered into communities, sometimes in association with the national armies.

The earliest of the so-called prophets, Amos, was at pains to distinguish himself from the *nᵉbi'im* (Amos 7. 14). Their fanatical patriotism,[3] together, it may be, with the non-moral (or even immoral) background of agricultural religion, blinded them to the ethical facts which, to Amos, cried aloud for denunciation. This separation is important. We have already shown how rarely the OT speaks of speech inspired by the Spirit of God. Examination of the use of the word נָבִיא (nabi') yields the following results.

Amos: we have seen that in 7. 14 Amos disclaims the title *nabi'*, though he can find no other name for what he is to do. In 2. 11 f. and 3. 7 f. the word is used in a good sense.

Hosea: some of the passages relating to the prophets are singularly obscure (4. 5; 9. 7, 8), but in 6. 5; 12. 11 the prophets are prophets of the Lord, and in 12. 14 the prophet by whom the Lord brought Israel up out of Egypt is Moses.

Isaiah I (i.e., Is. 1-39): the word *nabi'* is found 7 times; three of these are in chapters 37, 38, 39, which are taken from 2 Kings and therefore need not be considered. For the remaining four instances we find: in 3. 2 nothing evil is said of the prophet but he is in not very good company—with the diviner; 9. 14 is generally considered to be a gloss, though Skinner [4] contends that the strophe is not complete without it. In any case, the prophet is a false one.[5] In 28. 7 the prophets are false prophets; in 29. 10 the words *prophets* and *seers* are glosses—but even the glossed text speaks of prophets with closed eyes.

Micah: the three uses of the word are uniformly bad (3. 5, 6, 11).

Nahum: does not use the word.

Habakkuk: the word is used twice, in 1. 1 and 3. 1, passages that are obviously editorial and do not represent words of Habakkuk himself.

Zephaniah: one reference only, 3. 4: "Her prophets are light and treacherous persons."

---

[1] See W. R. Smith, *Prophets of Israel*, Chs. I and II ; Lods, *Israel (ET)*, 442-448 ; Guillaume, *Prophecy and Divination*, Lectures I-IV ; *et al.*
[2] Did the Canaanite drive out the old Semitic term ?
[3] Perhaps induced by their connection with military operations.
[4] Cambridge Bible, *Isaiah I–XXXIX*, 80.   [5] This verse also helps to interpret 3. 2.

Jeremiah: the usage of the word נָבִיא (nabi') may be roughly analysed as follows, taking Peake's [1] analysis of the text, passages assigned by him to Jeremiah and Baruch being accounted genuine. The results are:

"Prophet" used in a good sense: genuine, 29; not genuine, 10.

"Prophet" used in a bad sense: genuine, 39; not genuine, 10.

Doubtful cases: genuine, 6; not genuine, 0.

The majority of the "genuine" uses of "prophet" (in a good sense) are in Baruch's phrase, "Jeremiah the prophet", so that it may be said that on Jeremiah's own lips the word נָבִיא (nabi') had nearly always a bad connotation.[2]

Isaiah II (i.e., Is. 40-55): does not use the word.

Ezekiel: the result of analysis is as follows:

"Prophet" used in a good sense: 5.

"Prophet" used in a bad sense: 11.

"Prophet" used in a neutral sense: 1.

Haggai: in 1. 1, 3, 12; 2. 1, 10 we find the words "Haggai the prophet", where prophet has a good connotation, but the passages are editorial.

Zechariah 1-8: the word *nabi'* has always a good sense (1. 1, 4, 5, 6, 7; 7. 3, 7, 12; 8. 9). It refers either to Zechariah or to the prophets of old.

Malachi: once, 3.23, of Elijah, i.e., in a good sense.

Isaiah III (i.e., Is. 56-66): the word is not used.

Joel: the word is not used, but it is noteworthy that the corresponding verb occurs in a good sense in 3. 1.

Jonah: the word is not used.

Obadiah: the word is not used.

Zechariah 9-14: in 13. 2, 4, 5 (the only instances in which the word is used) it has a bad sense, quite akin to that of Amos 7. 14.

Daniel: in 9. 2, 6, 10 the word *nabi'* denotes the prophets of old time. It is used curiously in 9. 24 but certainly in a good sense.

From these facts, together with the old narratives which bring out the opposition between the prophets of the Lord and those of the Baals and the Asherah (see, e.g., 1 Kings 18. 19), inferences of some importance may be made.[3] Prophecy in its primitive forms was probably not of Israelite origin. This is shown not only by the unwillingness of many of the prophets to call themselves by the name *nabi'*, but also by the continued existence of prophets of other cults. Where the name and practice of prophecy first arose is a very difficult question which, fortun-

---

[1] Century Bible, *Jeremiah.*

[2] Attention may be drawn especially to 2. 8 ; 23. 13 f., where the prophets prophesy by Baal. [3] See the quotation from Lods' *Israel,* 444 f., above.

ately, it is not necessary for us to attempt to answer.[1] Israel, probably quite soon after the settlement in Canaan, took over the practice of prophetism, and, apparently, two orders of prophets existed side by side. The earliest notices of Hebrew prophets in the OT are those most closely akin to the descriptions of the foreign prophets. Both groups lived in bands, they were ecstatics, they practised wild actions as well as inspired speech.[2] Later, however, new prophets arose who, though they retained many of the charcteristics of the older n^{e}bi'im, differed from them so radically in their message that they did all they could to separate themselves from them. Amos and Hosea made a rather tentative use of it, but after their time even the word nabi' seems to have been suspect, until it came back into use at a much later period, when Hebrew religion had been so thoroughly ethicized that there was no longer any reason to fear a reversion to the old ways.

The parallel between the phenomena we have just observed in connection with the word nabi' and the use (or disuse) of the word ruah is clear. The prophets in many respects resembled the older n^{e}bi'im; yet they distinguished themselves from them; they revealed all the phenomena of inspiration, yet they avoided the use of the term Spirit. "From the fact that Amos repudiated all connection with the degenerate professional prophets of his own day it by no means follows that he did not regard himself as standing in the succession of inspired men through whom Yahweh had formerly made his presence known in the life of Israel; nor is there any reason to assume that he looked on the manner of his inspiration as essentially different from theirs: `the verb which he uses to denote his own prophetic activity (hinnabe' 7. 15) is that which was commonly applied to the N^{e}bi'im. . . . The fact that the great prophets far surpassed their predecessors in their apprehension of religious truth is no reason for denying the reality of the ecstatic element in their experience, or for explaining it away as a mere rhetorical accommodation to traditional modes of expression."[3] Hebrew prophecy never lost this "double polarity"; there remained the same tendency to vision, ecstasy, and equally the same reserve in speaking of it, and resting upon it. The

---

[1] See Alfred Jepsen, Nabi, soziologische Studien zur alttestamentlichen Literatur und Religionsgeschichte. On 246 f. he summarizes as follows : " By understanding the nature of prophecy (Nabitum), however, we have not yet solved the problem of its origin. It can hardly have been a phenomenon proper to all races of originally Semitic speech, since the Israelites did not know it in their pre-Canaanite period, and there is no reason why it should have disappeared precisely among them. So perhaps we should see in prophecy (Nabitum) a peculiarity of the pre-Israelite, Semitic inhabitants of the land. It would also be possible to think of a resurgence of older, pre-Semitic phenomena ; something similar (the re-emergence of pre-Greek notions in the Classical period) is supposed to have happened in Greece. It is further possible that it was tribes from Asia Minor or North Syria (Subaraean), invading with the Hyksos, that brought these mediators of revelation to Palestine. Finally it is conceivable that an ecstatic mystical movement, such as meets us later in Phrygia, Thrace and Greece, came with Aryan groups to Syria, and was there adapted to the Semitic notion of God, by the substitution, for natural union with God in ecstasy, of possession by God and Spirit."

[2] It is significant that in 1 Kings 22. 1-28 Micaiah says that the spirit (a lying spirit, but yet a spirit from the Lord) has spoken by the false prophets (who are officially prophets of the Lord but are sharply contrasted with Micaiah) but does not say that he speaks by the spirit.

[3] Skinner, Prophecy and Religion, 4 n. Cf. ibid. 220, " Visions and auditions, mysterious inward promptings to speech and action, are still a part of the prophet's experience."

writers of Deuteronomy could think of no distinction between true and
false prophets of the Lord save that only the prophecies of the former
came true (Deut. 18. 22). This cuts both ways. It means that the true
prophets were distinguishable neither because they were more sober nor
because they were more frenzied than their rivals. The only vindication
of truth was history, or, more properly, God in history.[1]

We have suggested that the existence (and perhaps the name) of the
nᵉbi'im is of non-Jewish origin. Volz [2] makes a similar suggestion with
regard to *ruaḥ*. Originally, he thinks, *ruaḥ* and the Lord stood over against
one another; "mit Jahwe hat dieser Ruḥ-dämon ursprünglich nichts
zu tun".[3] In this *ruaḥ* is distinguished from the hand of the Lord, which
of necessity is closely connected with his person. This separation of *ruaḥ*
from God prevails in later Judaism. In Rabbinic usage הרוּחַ [haruaḥ] is
Demon; in Jos. *Ant.* 6. 8. 2 (166) Saul's sickness is ascribed to δαιμόνια.
In explanation of the disuse of "Spirit" by the great pre-exilic prophets
Volz says: [4] "It can therefore be said that the prophets did not need
ruaḥ because they had Yahweh, and they rejected it because it was foreign
to them and their Yahweh. Significantly, when speaking about themselves, instead of *ruaḥ* they occasionally use the term 'the Hand of Yahweh'
to describe the mysterious, spiritual, intercourse that Yahweh has with
them; the expression denotes the being drawn (*Hineingezogenwerden*) into
Yahweh, the being bound (*Gebundenheit*) to him, and here, as in the
legends of Elijah and Elisha, proves to be more spiritual and more closely
connected with Yahweh than *ruaḥ*." Ezekiel's more frequent use of the
word Spirit (Volz thinks) is due to his greater interest in cultus and in
the Messianic hope.

The same reserve about ecstatic experience can be seen, according to
Volz, in later Judaism, and in this he seems to be right. It is true that
Rabbinic writers very frequently attribute the work of the prophets to
the inspiration of the Holy Spirit; but they do not say that the Spirit
was still operative in their own day, but rather the contrary; the Spirit
had been withdrawn.[5]

So far we may agree with Volz's observations, though the conjecture
that *ruaḥ* was originally a demonic being distinct from the Lord is—a
conjecture. His conclusions with regard to the Synoptic Gospels are more
dubious. He says: [6] "I hold the relatively rare use of Pneuma in Mt.
and Mk., in describing Jesus, to be not simply due to chance. The two
evangelists do indeed describe Jesus as a spiritual (*pneumatischen*) man of
God, just as the legends had described Moses, Elijah and others. The
miracle narratives are the popular expression of the belief that in him men
were looking upon a messenger from the supernatural sphere, and they

---

[1] And, at a later time, God's already revealed will. "To the Torah and to the testimony!
Surely it is thus that men should speak" (Is. 8. 20, accepting an emendation of the corrupt
latter part of this verse). And cf. Deut. 13. 2-4.　　　[2] *Der Geist Gottes*, 1910.
[3] *Op. cit.* 5.　　　[4] *Op. cit.* 68.
[5] Volz quotes (*op. cit.* 143), b. *Sanh.* 11a; *Soṭa* 48b; *Qoḥel. R.* 12. 7 (106a); for the substitution of the *bath qol* for the Holy Spirit (*op. cit.* 186), b. *Sanh.* 11a; b. *Soṭa* 48b; j. *Soṭa* 23d.
[6] *Op. cit.* 197.

attest the fact that Jesus had many striking traits, and did much that was wonderful. But more important to the Gospels than these miracles is the inward fact that in Jesus one had appeared who possessed the full reality of God and of the holiness of perfect love." The larger number of occurrences of the word Spirit in Lk. is due to Hellenistic influence: "It must rather be supposed that a strong Greek influence from Asia Minor had been at work".[1] Volz does not here allow sufficiently for the Messianic interests and beliefs of the primitive Church. Nor does he sufficiently stress the fact that the prophets both of the OT and of the NT had visions and ecstatic experiences though they did not lay great weight upon them. Paul and John (i.e., the author of 1 Jn.) had to lay down tests of prophets. "No man speaking in the Spirit of God saith, Jesus is anathema; and no man can say, Jesus is Lord, but in the Holy Spirit" (1 Cor. 12. 3). "Hereby know ye the Spirit of God: every Spirit which confesseth that Jesus Christ is come in the flesh is of God: and every spirit which confesseth not Jesus is not of God" (1 Jn. 4. 2 f.).[2] Paul was very reluctant to come to his "visions and revelations of the Lord" (2 Cor. 12. 1); but he had them, and he spoke with tongues "more than you all" (1 Cor. 14. 18).

The explanations that have been offered of the prophetic reticence with regard to the name *nabi'* and the word *ruah* cannot be applied directly to solve the problem why so little is said in the Synoptic Gospels about the Spirit. The conditions were entirely different. Traces of the old cults no doubt still persisted then, as they do, indeed, today,[3] but Jesus moved within the closed circle of Judaism, which was not broken by any prophets of the Baals, or disturbed by the frenzied dances and wild pronouncements of Canaanite dervishes. He must, however, have inherited the same "polarity" in his attitude to the Spirit and to inspiration which we have observed in the case of the prophets. The Gospels, as we have seen,[4] exhibit a tension between the belief that spiritual phenomena are valid signs of the Kingdom of God and the Messiahship of Jesus, and the conviction that such signs must not be sought for, and that the true believer does not need to lay stress on them.

How is this tension related to the theological convictions about the Messiah and the Kingdom of God by which the work of the Evangelists was formulated, and which, according to them, determined the ministry of Jesus himself? This is the problem towards which the whole of our study has pointed, and to the solution of which we have already observed several pointers. These must now be combined, and we must give such answer as we can. The problem was last raised [5] in the discussion of the question concerning Jesus' prophecies about the Church, and it is imperative that it should be considered in terms of the deeper problem of the

---

[1] *Op. cit.* 198.
[2] This test given by Paul and John is in fact the same historical test as that imposed in Deuteronomy; for the OT prophets the decisive history is in the future, for the NT it is in the past.
[3] See S. I. Curtiss, *Primitive Semitic Religion Today.*
[4] Pp. 68, 86-93, 97-99, 117-120.
[5] P. 139.

relationship between the eschatological gospel of Jesus and the spiritual gospel of Paul and the Church.[1]

I. THE SPIRIT IS THOUGHT OF IN ESCHATOLOGICAL TERMS

(a) The references to the Spirit in the Synoptic Gospels are, as we have seen, few; but they show a persistent OT background from which they are rarely divorced. OT terminology governs most of the passages we have considered. The opening scene of the ministry of Jesus, his baptism, has as an essential feature the descent of the Spirit; and the whole is regarded as the fulfilment of Scripture, as the voice from heaven shows.[2] Other passages show dependence upon Is. 42. 1; 61. 1 as fundamental sources, while the belief that the Messiah would be equipped with the Spirit appears in (or was deduced from) Is. 11. 2 (cf. 28. 6) as well, and was fairly widespread in later Judaism.[3] Similarly, the expectation of a general possession of the Spirit in the last days is fairly widely attested;[4] thus the notion of a Spirit-bearing community also had the nature of fulfilment.

(b) As has just been said, in the OT itself the Spirit was the subject of prophecy, and was described in passages which it was easy for later readers to interpret eschatologically, that is, as apocalyptic. The Spirit is by no means unknown among judges, kings and prophets; but the expectation arose that it would in a pre-eminent degree be given in the last days.

(c) The framework of the ministry of Jesus is supplied by events which both are described in the language of eschatology and involve the action of the Spirit. At the beginning comes the birth of Jesus (according to Mt. and Lk.), or the baptism (according to Mk.). In both of these events the work of the Spirit is central, and we have seen reason to believe[5] that its significance lies in the inauguration of God's new act of creation, the dawning of the Messianic Age. As the turning-point between the ministry of Jesus and the life of the Church stands the event assigned by Luke to the day of Pentecost, the decisive endowment of the believers with the gift of the Holy Spirit. This event and this gift were eschatologically conceived. In Acts itself the experience of Pentecost is plainly related as the fulfilment of the prophecy of Joel 3. 1 ff.; it thus becomes the immediate precursor of the great and notable day of the Lord. For Paul also, the gift of the Spirit meant both the realization of eschatology and a reaffirmation of it; so much is implied by his use of the term ἀρραβών; the present possession of the Spirit means that part of the future bliss is already attained, and equally that part still remains in the future, still unpossessed.

[1] Pp. 121, 140.
[2] The Western variant in Lk. shows the complete assimilation of the saying to the OT (Ps. 2. 7), and the manner in which the incident was understood is thereby clearly revealed.
[3] See 1 *Enoch* 49. 3 ; 62. 2 ; *Test. Lev.* 18. 7 : *Test. Jud.* 24. 2 ; *Pss. Sol.* 17. 37 ; 18. 7.
[4] Joel 3. 1 f.; Num. 11. 29 and other Scripture references formed the basis of many passages in later Jewish literature.   [5] 17-24, 45.

II. JESUS AND THE KINGDOM OF GOD

The Spirit, then, is rightly understood only when it is apprehended as a factor in the eschatological framework of the Gospels. It will be necessary, therefore, to delineate that framework and to draw out very briefly the eschatological teaching of the Gospels, and especially to examine the use made of the terms Messiah and Kingdom of God.

(a) First of all, it must be pointed out that Jesus used these words in a manner that was at once original and creative. On his lips they took on a new and deeper meaning than they had previously borne. The term Messiah, indeed, he rarely used, if he used it at all. On the two occasions (at Caesarea Philippi and before the High Priest) when he seems to have accepted it, it was immediately glossed by the title he evidently preferred, "Son of man". "Son of man", however, is itself not an expression whose significance can be exhausted by combining Dan. 7 with the *Similitudes of Enoch*, or by any other simple method. Here too we can trace the activity of a creative mind. In Daniel, the Son of man represents the people of the saints of the Most High; in the mouth of Jesus the Son of man is a person.[1] In *Enoch*, the Son of man is a figure of glory, to whom suffering is an entirely foreign experience. Suffering and death have a prominent place in Jesus' Son of man sayings. Jesus in speaking about himself, though he used traditional language, was not governed by it. The same observation is true about his use of the phrase Kingdom of God. It is not difficult to find in Rabbinical and Apocalyptic books parallels to many of the "Kingdom" sayings of Jesus; but he is certainly original in the connection that he makes between the Kingdom and himself, and in his treatment of it as something already existing.

Since Jesus used his terminology in so unprecedented a manner it will be necessary for us not so much to pay attention to its background as to consider what Jesus himself said about the Messiah and the Kingdom, so far as that may be perceived through the refracting medium of the tradition; for there can be little doubt that many of his sayings were not understood and consequently suffered distortion in the course of their transmission.

(b) Jesus believed himself to be the Messiah (even though a Messiah of a kind no one had ever expected); and the Evangelists held the same view. Yet he refused to make known his status.[2] The time was not yet (in the period of his ministry) come for him to be made manifest universally. Moreover, there lay upon him the obligation not only of secrecy but also of suffering. There was no escape from the way of the cross. The prophecies of the passion are the dominant notes in the

---

[1] For criticism of Dr T. W. Manson's interpretation of the title as having a collective force, see Flew, *op. cit.* 75 ; Johnston, *op. cit.* 55 n. 5.
[2] See above, pp. 118-120.

earliest Gospel,[1] and although they have probably been filled out in detail it seems very unlikely that they were entirely community products. They are the most original part of the creative treatment of the Messianic hope to which we have referred, and they bear the mark of one creative mind. Jesus fulfils his Messianic vocation by suffering; in fact, suffering is his vocation. But suffering was not to be the end. Each of the three great prophecies of the passion in Mk.[2] is accompanied by a prediction of the resurrection. It is very doubtful whether these, as they stand, are authentic. They conform closely to the Church's Easter faith and Easter experience; and one must ask why, if Jesus spoke so explicitly of a resurrection, his disciples did not wait after his death for the event which they must needs have expected. They did not wait; the crucifixion proved a shock which not only smote the shepherd but scattered the sheep. How was it that the suffering of Jesus, which he predicted, proved to be the death-blow to the disciples' faith? Part of the answer to this question is no doubt that although Jesus had predicted his passion his followers had neither wholly understood nor believed him (Mk. 8. 32 *et al.*). But this is only part of the answer, for however little they had understood and believed him, his words must have rung in their ears when the crucifixion actually took place. Their demoralization is accounted for if they were disappointed. Rightly or wrongly, they seem to have understood Jesus to foretell a divine vindication of himself which was to supervene directly upon his suffering. And if we ask what form their hope took, the most probable answer is that they hoped for a manifestation in glory of the Messiah immediately after his humiliation. What they were not prepared for was an interval of two or three days, followed by resurrection appearances.

We may suppose, then, that Jesus foretold his suffering and death, and that these would be followed by a divine act of vindication, in which he did not differentiate between a resurrection and a parousia. It was enough to say that the Messiah who had first appeared in weakness and incognito would be universally recognized in his glory. Jesus never speaks explicitly of an interval between his resurrection and his return, nor does he prophesy an intermediate period during which he is in glory with God. The specific prophecies of resurrection "after three days" (Mk.) or "on the third day" (Mt., Lk.) are probably based on sayings referring to Hosea 6. 2, where the prophet speaks of a general restoration rather than of a resurrection as such. If Mk. 13. 32 is genuine, Jesus himself refused to date the time of his vindication; but his followers probably expected it to take place immediately after his death.

[1] Mk. 8. 31; 9. 12; 9. 31; 10. 33; 12. 8, and other passages. Cf. Burkitt, *Christian Beginnings*, 29: "What I seem to read from the documents, what is emphasized in Mark as uppermost in the mind of Jesus, is not the choice of this or that epithet or title as the most appropriate, but the irresistible sense of vocation. And this took shape in a conviction that the God of Israel, who had called Him Son in a special sense not shared by others, had marked Him out thereby as the instrument of bringing in (or at least hastening) the End of the present state of things by His becoming in some way a sacrifice or ransom for the elect. In Mk. 10. 45 this is condensed into a single saying, but it is implied everywhere." [2] 8. 31; 9. 31; 10. 33.

The Gospels do not attempt to explain why it was necessary that this process should be carried out: why it was necessary that Christ should suffer and then enter his glory. It was the will of God; and as such, Mark supposed, it must have been written somewhere in the OT, though he himself did not know where.[1] Matthew and Luke, however, were able to supply the evidence, and soon the assertion that "Christ died for our sins according to the Scriptures" (1 Cor. 15. 3) was well documented.

(c) The teaching of Jesus about the Kingdom of God runs parallel to his doctrine of the Messiah. This is what we should expect, both by analogy and also for the more cogent reason that the presence of the Messiah constitutes the rule of God (not that this could be constituted in no other way). Where the Messiah, God's vicegerent, is, there is the Kingdom; and as the Messiah is, so is the Kingdom.

Accordingly, we find in the Gospels the clear statement that the Kingdom of God has come; and this statement appears always (except Mt. 3. 2) on the lips of Jesus and his disciples. The coming of the Kingdom is attested not only by particular words [2] but also by the repeated assumption that men who live in the company of Jesus are witnessing the fulfilment of the OT and the fruition of God's promise: "Blessed are your eyes for they see"—that which the prophets had only foreseen.

The Kingdom is here; but men do not recognize it. So blind are they that they petition Jesus for a sign, failing entirely to discern the evident signs of the times. The reason for this is that the Kingdom is a hidden Kingdom, not yet visible in uncontestable power, precisely as Jesus is a hidden and persecuted Messiah. This fact is most notably brought out by some of the parables. The Kingdom is like leaven, *hidden* in a lump of dough; it is like a seed which is *hidden* and rots when the dark and dirty earth is pressed about it. In this state it can be violently treated by its adversaries (Mt. 11. 11, 12; Lk. 16. 16), just as the Messiah not only lives an obscure life but has to die a death of suffering in persecution. (In the Fourth Gospel the metaphor of the seed is taken away from the Kingdom and applied to the Messiah; cf. Jn. 12. 24. See also 1 Cor. 15. 36 ff.) On the other hand, however, the Kingdom shares not only the obscurity of the Messiah but his vindication also. The disciples are bidden to pray, "Thy Kingdom come" (Mt. 6. 10; Lk. 11. 2), that is, to ask for the day when the Kingdom shall be present not obscurely as now, but in manifest power. This object of hope is expressed in the parabolic contrast between the small seed and the large plant, and is plainly stated in Mk. 9. 1:

Verily I say unto you, There be some here of them that stand by, which shall in no wise taste of death, till they see the Kingdom of God come with power.

It is implied that the Kingdom of God was, during the ministry of

---

[1] Cf. Mk. 9. 12, and the OT allusions in the passion narrative.
[2] Such as ἤγγικεν, ἔφθασεν; the interpretation of which is open to some dispute.

Jesus, not present *in power*. The vindication of the Messiah and the manifestation of the Kingdom in its proper majesty were no doubt thought of as one complex event.[1]

All the teaching of Jesus about himself as Messiah, and about the Kingdom of God, falls into two divisions—"Now" and "Then". "Now" means a proleptic realization of what appear elsewhere (so far as they appear at all) as hopes for the future, a hidden existence of the Messiah, stripped of his glory, and a manifestation of God's sovereignty subject to a similar concealment and limitation; "Then" means the complete divine vindication and revelation of the agent of God's rule among men, and of the rule itself. Again, we suggest that although Jesus may have disclaimed knowledge of when this vindication would take place, his disciples received the impression that it would immediately follow his suffering.

III. MESSIAH, KINGDOM AND SPIRIT[2]

Many of the facts we have noticed in our examination of the references to the Holy Spirit in the Synoptic Gospels can now be understood.

(*a*) To the Evangelists the beliefs which we have just examined (or their versions of those beliefs) were of the first importance. Their faith rested upon the Messiahship, the divine mission and status of Jesus of Nazareth. Hence, in comparison with the actual presence of the Lord's Anointed, and the operation of the powers of the Kingdom of God, the commonplace phenomena of prophetic and other inspiration were insignificant and irrelevant.[3] The writers of the NT are never content merely to align Jesus with the OT prophets, strongly as he resembled them in many respects, and they distinguish clearly between him and the other exorcists and miracle-workers of his day. The ancient world contained as many "spiritual" men as it wanted, and the Church had no motive in depicting Jesus as another of them; such a description of him would have attracted no attention and certainly could not have helped to create faith in him. On the other hand, it would certainly have been open to the danger of serious misunderstanding.

(*b*) At this point Jesus stands directly in the prophetic tradition. For, as we have seen, it was to avoid such misunderstanding, such confusion of themselves with ecstatic but non-moral n*e*bi'im, that many of the great prophets of the OT avoided both the title *nabi*' and the claim to be inspired by the Spirit. The prophets continually call their people to an obedience which has the radical nature of faith; that is, it is not based upon signs, nor upon a blind legalism, but upon a conscious and decisive commitment of the self to God.[4] The same attitude, was, at

---

[1] See above, pp. 154-156.   [2] See note on p. 121.   [3] See above, p. 68.
[4] The prophets do, of course, speak of "signs"; but they were generally not signs of the sort which were required of, and refused by, Jesus. Maher-shalal-hash-baz (Is. 8. 1-4, 18) was not an infallible demonstration of anything, nor was Ezekiel's portrayal of the siege of Jerusalem a proof of what was to take place.

least to some extent, preserved in later Judaism, as an interesting passage in *b. Baba Meẓia* 59b shows. "On a certain occasion R. Eliezer used all possible arguments to substantiate his opinion, but the Rabbis did not accept it. He said, 'If I am right, may this carob tree move a hundred yards from its place.' It did so. . . . They said, 'From a tree no proof can be brought.' Then he said, 'May the canal prove it.' The water of the canal flowed backwards. They said, 'Water cannot prove anything.' Then he said, 'May the walls of this House of Study prove it.' Then the walls of the house bent inwards, as if they were about to fall. R. Joshua rebuked the walls and said to them, 'If the learned dispute about the Halakah, what has that to do with you?' So, to honour R. Joshua, the walls did not fall down, but, to honour R. Eliezer, they did not become quite straight again. Then R. Eliezer said, 'If I am right, let the heavens prove it.' Then a heavenly voice said, 'What have you against R. Eliezer? The Halakah is always with him.' Then R. Joshua got up and said, 'It is not in heaven' (Deut. 30. 12). What did he mean by this? R. Jeremiah said, 'The law was given us from Sinai. We pay no attention to a heavenly voice. For already from Sinai the law said, "By a majority you are to decide"' (Exod. 23. 2)." [1] In comparison with the revealed will of God miracles have no authority, nor has even a heavenly voice, a *bath qol*, closely connected as it was with the Holy Spirit. [2] Neither portents nor religious feeling may be allowed to withdraw attention from God's action in history. It is to this that the prophets point, emptying themselves, as far as possible, of all personal significance. Accordingly, it is no more than should be expected that Jesus, who believed himself to be the divine deed to which the prophets had borne witness, should refuse to detract from the significance of that divine event by laying stress upon his own inspiration, whether for prophetic speech or miraculous acts. It is markedly indicative of this attitude that he refused to give an account of his "authority" when it was demanded.

(*c*) Direct emphasis upon the Spirit had to be avoided also because Jesus was keeping his Messiahship secret; to have claimed a pre-eminent measure of the Spirit would have been to make an open confession of Messiahship, if, as seems to have been the case, there was a general belief that the Messiah would be a bearer of God's Spirit. This point has already been made [3] and there is no need to repeat what has been said. But it was not merely that a secret had to be kept. Jesus acted under the necessity of a divine constraint. [4] Lack of glory and a cup of suffering were his Messianic vocation, and part of his poverty was the absence of all the signs of the Spirit of God. They would have been inconsistent with the office of a humiliated Messiah. The temptation narrative stands as a turning-point in the Gospel story. Immediately before it, the Spirit descends from heaven upon the Elect One, as was

---

[1] Translation from Montefiore and Loewe, *A Rabbinic Anthology*, 340 f.
[2] See pp. 39 f.   [3] Pp. 119 f.   [4] δεῖ, Mk. 8. 31 ; Lk. 24. 26.

proper (Is. 42. 1); it is the Spirit that drives Jesus out into the wilderness for the Temptation. There takes place the Temptation, a conflict whose theme is the meaning of Messiahship; Jesus returns from victory with the conviction that the way of God's Chosen is the way of humility and weakness, and from that time references to the Spirit are very few indeed. Even his miracles, though it is not hard to detect the marks of "pneumatic" thaumaturgy upon them, are not compelling signs, but are of significance and value only to the elect, and not to those who are without.[1]

(d) The Rule of God, if it means the fullness of the prophetic and apocalyptic hope of God's completed purpose for the world, involves the gift of the Spirit not to the Messiah only, but also to the whole Messianic community, the company of God's saved people. In fact, however, as we have seen, there is in the Synoptic Gospels little or no suggestion that anyone other than Jesus shared in the new gift of the Spirit. Jesus, the Kingdom and the Spirit are brought together in the saying of Mt. 12. 28 ("If I by the Spirit (probably correct interpretation of the earlier 'finger') of God cast out demons, then is the Kingdom of God come upon you"); but there is nothing to establish a similar relation between the disciples, the Kingdom and the Spirit, even though this might have been expected. This is, apparently, because the Kingdom, though present, was not present in the fullness of its power; it too, like Jesus the Messiah, was hidden, and under constraint. Therefore the Spirit was the possession of Jesus, as Messiah, alone, and in him it was veiled; and therefore, strictly speaking, there was no Church before the death of Jesus. The general gift of the Spirit belongs to the time of the vindication and manifestation of the Messiah and of the Messianic Kingdom.[2]

IV. The Spirit and Pentecost

(a) What, in the view of Jesus himself, was this vindication to be? No attempt to answer this question can be made without considerable uncertainty. We have already suggested that Jesus did not differentiate the events after his passion as they were in fact differentiated in history. The Church has left us an account of what took place, confused indeed in detail, but one in which certain events stand out as a framework. Jesus rose from the dead; his followers had no doubt at all that they had seen him alive. Where the appearances took place, and what was their nature, are questions to which the historian can give no confident answer; but he must confidently affirm that appearances there were. Not long afterwards (according to Jn. 20. 22 f. in the course of one of the appearances), the Church received the gift of the Spirit. We cannot be sure when this took place, or if it took place on one occasion only. There may be two

---

[1] Michaelis (op. cit.) gives a similar interpretation, which, however, differs significantly in that he thinks of Jesus only as *Messias designatus*, not as the hidden Messiah.

[2] Cf. Büchsel, *Geist Gottes*, Ch. IX.

accounts of "Pentecost" preserved in Acts itself.[1] But again we need not hesitate to affirm that some such event did happen. Two elements of the vindication were thus in the past; [2] the believing community awaited the third, the parousia of Jesus from heaven, the manifestation of his glory in the power of the Kingdom.

This framework of Church belief is quite clear; [3] but it was probably derived from the logic of events rather than from the teaching of Jesus, into which, however, the time-table seems to have been read back. Jesus himself foretold no more than a divine act of vindication.

(b) If this be true, it is easy to understand why Jesus did not foretell the gift of the Spirit to the Church. There was no occasion for him to do so. The period of the humiliation and obscurity of the Messiah and his people was to continue until its climax and the day of final glorification. In the former period, the general gift of the Spirit was inappropriate; it would have divulged the secret of Jesus' Messiahship and it was not yet within the range of the Kingdom, which was not yet ἐν δυνάμει. In the latter period it was not a sufficiently significant feature of the eschatological hope to be mentioned. If the Messiah was coming on the clouds of heaven, what point was there in saying that he had the gift of the Spirit? If his followers were "as the angels of God", what need was there to stress that they were not inferior to prophets?

Thus the eschatological thought of Jesus, so far as this may be known, accounts for his silence with regard to the Spirit. He could not in the time of his ministry speak of his own plenary inspiration, nor unmistakably reveal it, because that would have meant the betrayal of the Messianic secret. He did not bestow the Spirit upon his followers, because that gift was a mark of the fully realized Kingdom of God, and did not lie within the province of the germinal Kingdom which corresponded to his veiled Messiahship. He did not prophesy the existence of a Spirit-filled community, because he did not foresee an interval between the period of humiliation and that of complete and final glorification. He did not distinguish between his resurrection and parousia, and accordingly there was no room for the intermediate event, Pentecost.[4]

(c) Our primary question has now been answered. There is another which we have raised from time to time and to which we may turn again. What is the relationship between the religion of the Church, the experience, that is, of personal salvation, and the eschatological gospel of Jesus? It is obvious that we are not in a position to deal fully with this

---

[1] Acts 2. 1-4 ; 4. 31. Cf. Harnack, *Acts of the Apostles*, 175-189.
[2] We have omitted the ascension and heavenly session of the Lord, because these were essentially a matter of faith, not of experience ; they could not be apprehended in the same way as the phenomena of the resurrection appearances.
[3] See C. H. Dodd, *The Apostolic Preaching*.
[4] No doubt, if he had been questioned, Jesus would have said that, at the final manifestation of the glory of God, the Spirit would be given ; but there were other more important things that might be said about that time, and in any case Jesus was not in the habit of painting elaborate pictures of the last days.

problem, for it requires not only a full treatment of NT eschatology but also an examination of the faith and religious experience of the whole of the NT. Nevertheless, a few lines of thought may be suggested here.

The actual course of events inevitably created the belief that the Spirit was operative in the Ecclesia. The resurrection of Jesus made of the disciples a Messianic community, a phenomenon for which there was absolutely no precedent either in history or in speculation. Yet, though part of the promised salvation had been accomplished, its consummation was delayed. Before history could be brought to an end, the parousia must take place, and the Kingdom appear in power and glory. This position had to be thought out. It would, however, be entirely wrong to find the origin of the doctrine of the Spirit in a process of excogitation; the Church would have had no doctrine of the Spirit if it had not in the first place received an experience of the Spirit. But the experience once given could be, and apparently was, rationalized as follows. The Messianic community must be in possession of all the Messianic blessings except those which could not be separated from the final consummation, the divine glory of the parousia and the complete victory of the Messiah. Thus, death and sin had not yet been conquered; Christians still sinned and still died. But, on the other hand, it could be said, for example, that the Church enjoyed to the full the blessing of forgiveness, of reconciliation with God. This was a gift which could be received under the conditions of life in this world. Of course, what happened was not that the theologians thought this out and consequently supposed that they had been forgiven; but, on the contrary, that the believers, having been made aware that they had been forgiven and were living in fellowship with God, subsequently produced explanations of what they knew had taken place. Similarly, another of the Messianic blessings which could be given and received under the conditions of ordinary human life was the Holy Spirit. Here too the gift of the Spirit came first and the rationalization afterwards; but the place of the experience in the eschatological thought of the Church could only be determined in the way that has been suggested. It was (as Paul later expressed it) an earnest, a first instalment of ultimate beatitude.[1]

The Church's faith that it was the Spirit-inspired community, the New Israel created by the Messiah, was therefore based not directly upon specific words of Jesus, nor upon a possibly delusive religious excitement; it was based upon the fact of Jesus, upon his life, death and resurrection regarded as decisive events in the eschatological programme.[2] If it was indeed God's intention to bless his people with a new and unprecedented endowment of the Holy Spirit, the unexpected interval between the resurrection and the parousia was the time for this gift to take place. It was the answer to the question which, though no doubt at first not so clearly formulated, must soon have been asked, "What is come to pass that thou wilt manifest thyself unto us, and not unto the

[1] Cf. the "before" in Joel 2.

world?" (Jn. 14. 22). Paul and John bent the whole of their energy to the task of understanding and expounding who these people were who lived between the death and resurrection and the parousia of Jesus. It is a testimony to their insight that in doing so they used and developed freely the doctrine of the Spirit, although there was so little visible foundation in the tradition of Jesus' words to authorize such teaching.

(d) We are now in a position to understand the course of the Synoptic tradition so far as it uses the concept of the Spirit, and to explain it in a more satisfactory manner than Windisch. Jesus himself thought of his power to perform mighty works, and of his own status and divine mission, as an anticipation of the future; here and there his future glory as Messiah, and the power of the Kingdom, shone through the veil of their present humiliation and obscurity. The Church, however, as was natural, looked upon this same power and status as the fruit of the Spirit of God resting upon the Messiah.[1] Hence, inevitably, there arose a tendency to change the centre of gravity of Jesus' eschatological teaching, accommodating it to the standpoint of the post-resurrection community, and at the same time introducing into his words, either by the creation of new sayings or by the modification of already existing logia, teaching about the Spirit. The effect of this was to depict the Lord himself as a "spiritual" man. But this process was checked by the conviction, at once historical and theological, that "the Spirit was not yet; because Jesus was not yet glorified" (Jn. 7. 39); which is the last word that may be said about the Holy Spirit in the Synoptic Gospels. An account of his work in the Church which still lives "between the times" belongs to another study.

---

[1] Both these views preserve equally the fundamental faith that in Christ the transcendent Otherness of God was present in the world ; i.e., both lead ultimately, when theologically understood and expounded, to the doctrine of the Incarnation.

INDEX 1

REFERENCES AND CITATIONS

(a) OLD TESTAMENT

(Where necessary, Septuagint references are indicated by (S))

Genesis

1. 2	18 f., 21 ff., 38 f., 111
1. 3	85
1. 4	59
1. 6, 14	85
2. 4	17
2. 7	19 f., 22
5. 1	17
6. 1 ff.	11 f., 23
6. 3	111
6. 4	12
6. 17	19
7. 15, 22	19
15. 12	12
17. 15-22	8
18. 9-15	8
21. 1	9
21. 1 f.	11
21. 1-7	8
21. 6	24
22. 1	47 f., 51
25. 21	9
28. 11	12
29. 31	9, 11
30. 2, 22	11
38. 24, 25	10

Exodus

2. 22	9
4. 11 f., 16	132
8. 15	63
14. 31	73
15. 25	48
16. 4	48
17. 2	51
20. 20	48
23. 2	158
28. 3	132
31. 2 f.	22, 111
31. 3, 6	132
31. 18	63
34. 28	51
35. 31, 35	132
36. 1, 2	132
40. 29 (S), 35	12

Leviticus

26. 6	59

Numbers

5. 14, 30	7
11. 17	145
11. 25	123, 145
11. 26-29	145
11. 29	120 f., 123, 145, 153
14. 22	51
24. 2	123, 145
24. 4	145

Deuteronomy

5. 26	120
8. 2	48, 51
9. 9	51
9. 10	63
13. 2-4	151
13. 4	48
18. 15-18	94, 108
18. 22	151
30. 12	158
32. 11	18, 21
33. 8	51
33. 29	137

Judges

2. 22	48
3. 1, 4	48
6. 12	62
9. 38	132
13. 1 ff.	11
13. 2-25	8

1 Samuel

1	8
1. 5	11
1. 19 f.	8
9. 9	148
10. 1	42
10. 5-13	145
10. 6	42, 123, 145
10. 10	42, 123
16. 13	42, 145
16. 14-23	53
18. 10	98
19. 20-24	145

2 Samuel

7. 14	41
22. 31, 32, 33, 48	62
23. 2	145
23. 5	62

1 Kings

5. 9, 26	132
13. 21	132
18. 19	147, 149
19. 5	50
19. 8	51
19. 16	42
22. 1-28	150
22. 24	145

2 Kings

1. 8	28
2. 9	29, 76, 145
2. 15	29
2. 15 f.	145
5. 14 (S)	31

163

(b) NEW TESTAMENT

(c) JEWISH WRITERS

(d) GREEK AND LATIN WRITERS

(e) CHRISTIAN LITERATURE

INDEX 2
MODERN WRITERS AND PERIODICALS

SYNOPSIS OF CONTENTS

ARRANGED SO AS TO SERVE AS AN INDEX TO THE SUBJECT-MATTER